Interiors and Narrative

Bucknell University Press Latin American Studies Series
Series Editor: Aníbal González, Yale University

Dealing with far-reaching questions of history and modernity, language and selfhood, and power and ethics, Latin American literature sheds light on the many-faceted nature of Latin American life, as well as on the human condition as a whole. This series of books provides a forum for some of the best criticism on Latin American literature in a wide range of critical approaches, with an emphasis on works that productively combine scholarship with theory. Acknowledging the historical links and cultural affinities between Latin American and Iberian literatures, the series welcomes a consideration of Spanish and Portuguese texts and topics, while also providing a space of convergence for scholars working in Romance studies, comparative literature, cultural studies, and literary theory.

Titles in the Series

Interiors and Narrative

The Spatial Poetics of Machado de Assis, Eça de Queirós, and Leopoldo Alas

Estela Vieira

Published by Bucknell University Press
Co-published with The Rowman & Littlefield Publishing Group, Inc.
4501 Forbes Boulevard, Suite 200, Lanham, Maryland 20706
www.rowman.com

Unit A, Whitacre Mews, 26-34 Stannery Street, London SE11 4AB

British Library Cataloguing in Publication Information Available

Library of Congress Cataloging-in-Publication Data

The hardback edition of this book was previously cataloged by the Library of Congress as follows:

Vieira, Estela, 1975-
Interiors and narrative : the spatial poetics of Machado De Assis, Eça de Queirós, and Leopoldo Alas / Estela Vieira.
   pages cm.
 Includes bibliographic references and index.
 1. Machado de Assis, 1839-1908--Criticism and interpretation. 2. Queirós, Eça de, 1845-1900--Criticism and interpretation. 3. Alas, Leopoldo, 1852-1901--Criticism and interpretation. 4. Latin American fiction--19th century--History and criticism. 5. Spanish literature--Foreign countries--History and criticism. 6. Interior architecture in literature. 7. Architecture and literature. 8. Narration (Rhetoric)
PQ7082.N7 V53 2013
863/.50998

                    2012044903

ISBN 978-1-61148-432-8 (cloth : alk. paper)
ISBN 978-1-61148-622-3 (pbk. alk. paper)
ISBN 978-1-61148-433-5 (electronic)

For Johannes

Contents

Acknowledgements

I thank my mentors at the University of Virginia, Donald Shaw, David Haberly, and Fernando Operé, for their guidance and friendship and for supporting me in my wish to work in both Spanish and Portuguese. I owe my deepest gratitude to my professors at Yale University, K. David Jackson, Noël Valis, Roberto González Echevarría, and Rolena Adorno who read this manuscript in its earliest stages and who, along with my friends Ana María Mutis, Anke Birkenmaier, and Ana Valdez, fostered some the most intellectually stimulating years of my life. For helping me understand Heidegger I thank my colleagues in a theory reading group at Indiana University. I am grateful to Darlene Sadlier and Luciana Namorato for their support and for their devotion to a Portuguese program I am proud to be a part of. I thank my colleagues in Spanish and Portuguese for providing a stimulating environment to work in. I am especially indebted to Heitor Martins, Josep Sobrer, Consuelo López-Morillas, Catherine Larson, Edgar Illas, and Reyes Vila-Belda. I would also like to thank friends and colleagues, Eyal Peretz, Fritz Breithaupt, Michel Chaouli, Marie Deer, Herbert Marks, Perry Hodges, Krista Maglen, and Pedro Machado, for making Bloomington a delightful and thought-provoking place to live.

I thank my APSA colleagues for ongoing dialogues and their dedication to the field of Portuguese studies, especially Kathryn Sanchez, Anna Klobucka, Pedro Monteiro, Paulo de Medeiros, and Victor Mendes. My colleagues and friends at the University of Lisbon, Helena Buescu, Fernanda Gil Costa, Ângela Fernandes, Clara Rowland and Orlanda de Azevedo, for providing me with an intellectual home in Portugal. Lidia Santos invited me to New York to present on Machado de Assis. The Instituto Camões and FLAD contributed research support over the years and the opportunity to attend the seminar at the Foundation Eça de Queirós and work with Isabel Pires de

Lima. I thank the Biblioteca de Asturias, the Brazilian Academy of Letters, and the Yale University Art Gallery for their generous contributions of some of the images in the book. My parents have always been there to help me over the years. I dedicate this book to Johannes Türk and am indebted to him for making the manuscript and everything better.

Note on Translations

All quotations from the works of Machado de Assis, Eça de Queirós, and Leopoldo Alas are cited parenthetically in the text, along with citations to the published translations, where used. For all quotations not in English, if no translation is cited, then the translation provided is my own.

Introduction: Interiors and Narrative

There are many different theories that parents invent in order to explain the cause of thunder and lightning to their fearful children. My mother use to tell me that the terrible noise is nothing other than God moving his furniture around. If even God seems to be consumed with rearranging his interiors how should we not be preoccupied with them? The compulsion to transform and adjust the material world we inhabit is part of human nature. The frail human body needs a protected space to secure its survival. Our interiors are not only an expression of our identity, social status, and style, they also have their own language. They tell the story of the lives they shelter. But how and why do the arrangement, design, and components of the places we live in communicate meaning? This book is about this discourse of interiors and about how narrative privileges this language and in many ways gives form to it. The novel has a sense of interior space that is central to its composition. The connections between narrative and interior spaces are highly significant and as old as the literary genre itself, but these links become especially pronounced in the nineteenth century. When Honoré de Balzac claims in the preface to his *Human Comedy* to embark on a thus far ignored history of manners he calls the writer "an archaeologist of social furniture."[1] During this time, when an increased prominence of the novel parallels an intensification of society's interest in interiors, the link between interiors and literature becomes even more apparent. This is a period when narrative and stories emerge out of the experience of private dwelling. Thus it shouldn't surprise us that the sense of interior space informs the novelist's work. I would like to begin in this introduction by exploring this double sense of interior space, that of the novel and of the novelist.

THE NOVEL'S SENSE OF THE INTERIOR

One has only to recall Henry James's *The Spoils of Poynton* (1897) to be reminded of the ubiquitous trend of many nineteenth-century novels to turn not only homes into protagonists, but also the contents of houses into major characters of a story. Mrs. Gereth, who is introduced to us as a woman "who had been kept awake for hours by the wallpaper in her room,"[2] epitomizes the furniture- and object-crazed characters of this period who convince readers that there is indeed a lot at stake in their tables and chairs. In fact at this time it is as if characters that lose their furniture cease to exist. Maggie's mother, Mrs. Tulliver, for example, in George Eliot's *The Mill on the Floss* (1860) practically disappears from the narrative after the downfall of the family's fortunes implies the loss of all her furniture. At the end of Gustave Flaubert's *A Sentimental Education* (1869), Frédéric Moreau painstakingly witnesses as his lover's blue floral carpet, work-table, and a favorite wing-chair are auctioned away to covetous buyers. Madame Arnoux's household items not only bring back intimate memories for the protagonist, with every new object exhibited "he felt as if a piece of his own heart was being taken out."[3] In the late-nineteenth-century interiors are so central that it is hard to find a novel that is not fascinated with dwelling. Even novels that at a first look seem engaged with more abstract and theoretical concerns are in effect preoccupied above all with interior space. Take for example Adalbert Stifter's major work, *Indian Summer* (1857), a *Bildungsroman* and classic of German realism. Despite the fact that the protagonist is a natural scientist and spends most of the year exploring and studying the Alpine mountains and foothills, the novel primarily focuses on the aesthetics of rooms and the restoration of furnishings. Thus interiors are fundamental in Stifter's theoretical representation of an idealized world of art and nature.

Moreover, one only needs to take a cursory look at the literary studies on the American and northern-European novel of this period to see that domesticity and interior decoration were widespread topics in literature and culture. Most studies on interiors of dwellings in late-nineteenth-century fiction immediately focus on the rising exchange economy, the growing capitalist production of commodities, and the increasing fascination with material culture and fetishism, phenomena that undeniably characterize bourgeois culture and society at this time. This study goes beyond these preoccupations and takes a different approach to interiors and their literary role. In my reading of *Quincas Borba* (1891), *The Maias* (1888), and *La Regenta* (1884-1885), three masterpieces of the Brazilian, Portuguese, and Spanish literary traditions, I show that interiors reveal a lot more than just changing economic and social trends. There is no doubt that these three late-realist novels are biting critiques of their corrupt societies, inequitable economies, and stagnant political systems, but the intricate private settings in these works exceed satirizing social norms and political ideas. More than serving the novel thematically the interior space is one of its fundamental formal components. Inspired by Wayne Booth's reading of narrative, I argue that the interior space has a rhetorical function with significant consequences for the development of narrative and of ideas in general. These three authors collect, appraise, and include furnishings, objects d'art, windows, doors and other architectural features in their writing first and foremost for fictional purposes. Their novels invent and shape complex relations between an inner and an outer dimension of space that constitutes the core of their narrative world making. This rhetoric of interior space is telling not only of larger ontological and cultural changes that take place at the end of the nineteenth century, but also of how intertwined these philosophical and social transformations are with the development of fiction.

Why study these three novels and not any other three? These works represent the culminating moments of three literary traditions not often seen in conjunction, and which I hope to show have more in common than critics have acknowledged. Furthermore, too few readings of these classical books exist in English, and especially of *The Maias*, which is indisputably one of the greatest novels of the nineteenth century. These are three of the most important writers of the Luso-Hispanic nineteenth century, and the authors read and were greatly influenced by each other's work. Yet existing scholarship has tended to focus on one literary nationality or trend. Some work exists drawing comparisons between Leopoldo Alas and Eça de Queirós, a somewhat more common peninsular link. A number of these comparative studies point to the important and often ignored interaction between Spanish and Portuguese narrative at this time.[4] Eça de Queirós's *Cousin Bazilio* (1878) and *The Crime of Father Amaro* (1875) significantly inform Leopoldo Alas's *La Regenta*. Several critics have also emphasized the literary debates between Eça de Queirós and Machado de Assis. The two literary giants were very important intellectual figures of their time in Portuguese and Brazilian circles and they corresponded and wrote reviews of the other's writings. Still, the relatively extensive critical history that studies Machado de Assis and Eça de Queirós in conjunction has tended to focus on the authors' biographies and less on their work's common ground.[5] This study attempts to establish bridges beyond linguistic and national boundaries, enabling the reader to make trans-national comparisons and to think of the three authors as a contemporary group when it comes to their aesthetic concerns. By giving identical weight to each of the writers and engaging with their novels with equal attention and thoroughness, I aim to highlight their points in common and show the important parallels that exist in their approach to realist writing.

Moreover, Machado de Assis, Eça de Queirós, and Leopoldo Alas develop their rhetoric of interior space in a similar fashion. Their technique relies on a basic analogy between the novel and the interior space. In these novels

the representation, context, and content of the domestic settings have meta-
fictional qualities. In other words, for all three authors the furnishing and
experiencing of an interior was something akin to the writing of the novel. In
addition, the authors rely on the ambiguity of the threshold and on a dialectics of opposites, which in all three works formulates the narrative movement
that ties the representation of interiors to the construction of the fictional
story. The authors confront in the narrative representation of interiors a similar contradiction that Susan Bernstein studies in *Housing Problems: Writing
and Architecture in Goethe, Walpole, Freud, and Heidegger*. Bernstein looks
at the fundamental paradox of architecture: the inherent disjunction that exists within architecture considering that buildings both create a real space and
at the same time questions the nature of space. Her book attempts to open the
gap between architecture as concept and realization, and as she explains
nothing more emblematic than the threshold situates this rupture by pointing
"to the inevitable failures of finitude, the impossibility of conceiving and
carrying out a totalizing plan, and the painful failure to secure an interior."[6]
Machado, Eça, and Alas also understand the interior setting as both ideal and
real and rely on the different contradictions that arise from this disjunction as
the perfect metaphor for the challenges they face as they imagine a realist
novel.[7] The interior architecture of the novels tells us both about the writers'
notion of interior life and their conception of the novelistic project. Ultimately what this complex rhetoric of interior space shows is that through their
treatment of the interior these three late-nineteenth-century writers, which
are often classified as late-realists, or as latecomers to realism, and at the
same time are recognized by critics as having characteristics of modernist
writing, pave the way for major conceptual, ontological, and discursive
changes. These authors are transitional figures because one can see in their
work how the nineteenth-century obsession with interior spaces anticipates
and transforms into the fascination with interior life so prevalent in twentieth-century modernism.

The preoccupation with the interior in the nineteenth century is indicative
of much more than shifting cultural preferences and social and economic
changes. The growing importance of interior dwellings articulates a shift in
the ontological relation to the world. One could argue that it is around this
time that Aristotle's *oikos*, the household or place of reproduction, gains
prominence over the *polis*, or the city-state where the public work of citizen-
ship took place in classical Athens. In Book I of *Politics* Aristotle explains
that the *oikos*, which sustained the self, was a necessary part of the whole
political association, or the *polis*.[8] For the Greek philosopher the *polis* is by
nature prior to the individual and his household in the sense that it presup-
poses "the immanent impulse in all men" to live a true and full life.[9] But by
the end of the nineteenth century the home takes care of both body and mind,
and what appears to take place is a reversal of Aristotle's conceptualization.

Now the household, inhabiting one's domestic environment, becomes an existential need that precedes the individual's necessity to belong to political and social associations. The modern individual dwells and fashions his or her subjectivity in a designed space that wards off and opens the world at the same time. It is the protected center of his or her identity, which only contact with an outside world and past can maintain. In his introduction to Homer's *Odyssey* Peter Jones claims the foundational literary masterpiece makes "the household (Greek *oikos*), rather than the battlefield, the centre of its world."[10] It would seem then that in literature the home becomes the structural force from the very beginning of the narrative genre. The individual imagination gains its form in the private world of the household and of the interior. Thus the creative fictional process stands as a synecdoche for the way in which the modern world is inhabited. Tracing the thresholds and configurations of the novelistic abodes with their interstices is the same as reading and understanding our time. What gains visibility in the novels studied here is this existential shift of modern subjects towards the cultivation of the interior. In other words, inhabiting the world by creating an intricate, meaningful, and protected space has become the problematic mode of existence. These late-realist texts are especially important because they capture this process at its onset. By elaborating fictions of interiority, the novelists I read relate to the world in an exemplary way by placing in the same room the core of identity and of artistic composition.

Literary scholarship has by no means ignored the historical connection between interiors and the art of narrative, but its primary focus has been to study the social and psychological implications of literature's representation of interior space.[11] These critical readings have significantly contributed to our understanding of space, domestic space in particular, and to how private worlds relate to the development of social and gender identities. Critics have interpreted dwellings as settings that illustrate or comment on a specific historical moment or social circumstance, but they have rarely drawn connections between literary aesthetics and the interiors of rooms. As we will see, Machado, Eça, and Clarín use their interior settings to examine the workings of their societies' inherent contradictions, but they connect these to their primary engagement with inner life and with narrating as a mode of being. Without providing a comprehensive survey of the history of the domestic interior, or of the history and origins of interior design, it will be useful here to trace important developments in the culture of interior architecture in the nineteenth century. Not surprisingly transformations in the art of the interior have historically been related to changes in novelistic endeavors. It seems that both the novel and the novelist share a sense of interior space and raise similar aesthetic questions.

The nineteenth-century preoccupation with interiors and the growing sense that taste and practices in interior decoration were deteriorating parallels a rising desire in writers for new narrative forms. In his 1840 essay, "The Philosophy of Furniture," Edgar Allan Poe blames America's corruption of taste in interior design on the country's growing wealth. People are solely concerned with the monetary value of an object or furnishing and not its history, craftsmanship, and material. According to Poe, beyond drastic errors in the arrangement of their interiors, Americans offend artistic taste. Poe's attention to the composition of interiors influences his narrative technique. In his Exposés to *The Arcades Project* Walter Benjamin explains that with this essay and with his detective fiction, Poe "becomes the first physiognomist of the domestic interior."[12] Poe not only theorizes about how the interior becomes a reflection of the individual, but he is also one of the first to give furnishings and the enclosed setting a narrative life of their own. Poe's thoughts make the argument that the measure of aesthetic taste lies not with the person or the space, but in the form of narrating the relation between individual and interior. His experimentation with new narrative techniques coincides with a fresh and critical understanding of the arrangement of an interior.

By linking fiction and interiors, Poe prefigures Edith Wharton's 1897 manual *The Decoration of Houses*, which she co-wrote with her architect friend, Ogden Codman. For centuries, influential arbiters of style, collectors, and architects created catalogs on the art of the interior, and by the end of the nineteenth century an extensive literature on home furnishing already existed. Still, most historians of interior architecture and design agree that Wharton's successful and groundbreaking treatise is one of the more important works marking the beginning of interior decoration as we conceive of it today. Unlike histories that merely catalog furnishings and styles, Wharton's work deals with ordering and assembling. She not only denounces Victorian excesses and the dubious eclecticism that since the eighteenth and nineteenth centuries has combined different styles into one room, but calls for a reform in house-decoration, a return to proportion, symmetry, logic, and harmony between *décor* and architectural structure. It is no surprise that a creator of fiction should be so pivotal a player in the creation of spaces. Wharton's writing on interiors establishes an analogy between furnishing and writing and links the author's task to that of the decorator's. One can read *The Decoration of Houses* as Edith Wharton's early poetics because concerns, such as searching for an organic relationship between architecture and life and inquiring about how art reflects the quality of mind, informed her writing as well. Poe's and Wharton's writings on interiors, which begin to discuss how form affects the aesthetics of space, are also a dialogue on narrative art, suggesting that both in rooms as in fiction ornament is not independent of structure. Interior décor raises questions that lead writers to make time and space, and narrative and description, interdependent in their novelistic creations.

The shifts the late-nineteenth-century interior undergoes apparently stimulate writers to reassess the imaginative qualities of space, but only twentieth-century philosophical thought questions how interior dwelling enlightens our understanding of the workings of the imagination and how the ontological situation of the self relates to inhabiting space. Although Poe claims to be inspired by Hegel's idea that there is a philosophy in everything, his essay falls short of giving us the promised philosophy of furniture. Gaston Bachelard's *The Poetics of Space* fulfills this promise by presenting a phenomenology and methodology of the house and its contours. Wharton's writing on interiors is clearly a forerunner of Bachelard's, since both authors contend that a home is a text that can be read and written. According to Bachelard, a house is an oneiric shelter, "a house of dream-memory," that through the removal of exterior reality makes daydreaming possible and has the power of integrating thoughts, memories, and the imagination.[13] If, as Bachelard argues, poetry is a reflection of our daydreaming and imagination, then a philosophy, or phenomenology in his conceptualization, of the interior is necessarily a philosophy of literature, and hence a poetics of space. In his introduction to *The Poetics of Space* John R. Stilgoe writes that Bachelard's topophilia "reveals time after time that setting is more than scene in works of art, that it is often the armature around which the work revolves."[14] By taking "the house as a *tool for analysis* of the human soul,"[15] Bachelard discovers in the intimate places we inhabit what Stilgoe calls "a metaphor of humanness."[16] In *The Sense of an Interior: Four Writers and the Rooms That Shaped Them*, Diana Fuss observes how literature and architecture work in tandem to create one's sense of interior space and claims that, while Bachelard sees a house as a kind of poetry, Martin Heidegger, on the other hand, reads poetry as a special kind of building.[17] Yet Heidegger's and Bachelard's thinking go further in the sense that they are primarily interested in uncovering the nature of the poetic imagination and see the interior as being essential to its understanding.

In the essay "Building, Dwelling, Thinking," as in other of his writings, Heidegger reads human dwelling as the character of human existence: "Dwelling, however, is *the basic character* of Being in keeping with which mortals exist."[18] A building, or all the man-made objects inhabiting our immediate setting, is hence a consequence of the nature of dwelling. In other words we build and create interior spaces because of the primordial human need to dwell. The essence of the poetic, whose etymology Heidegger traces back to the Greek *poiesis*, to produce, is a form of building which lets us dwell. In a related essay, "Poetically Man Dwells," Heidegger writes "Poetic creation, which lets us dwell, is a kind of building."[19] Thus dwelling is not to be understood as being housed or to take shelter, but as a primeval condition of human nature that takes shape through poetry. For the German philosopher inhabiting is "in essence poetic" because poetry is the "authentic gauging of the dimension of dwelling."[20] Both Bachelard and Heidegger seem to conclude that in a fundamental sense to be is to dwell, and dwelling is an originary poetic act. While Bachelard claims that "Our soul is an abode"[21] and the self is in the houses and rooms of memory, Heidegger argues that authentic building can only take place in the poetic.[22] Both these philosophical approaches inform my own observations of how interiors tie into the author's sense of the poetic creation of the novel. While Bachelard and Heidegger rely primarily on poetry to corroborate their philosophical queries, I question how the novel, at one of its peak moments, explores what dwelling and interiors reveal about both existence and poetics.

Fiction's representation of interiors anticipates the philosophical idea that dwelling, existence, and poetics have more in common than we might imagine. Thus by looking at interiors from a theoretical perspective we see that the literary arts are intertwined with a sense of being and inhabiting. Observing interiors from a socio-historical perspective, and viewing them as indicators of social and economic changes, also allows one to discover parallels between interiors and narrative fiction. The social history of private space is curiously inseparable from the evolution of writing and reading. With the growth of modern cities and the industrialization of work, the bourgeois home undergoes an important transformation from communal living to the compartmentalization of specialized and private chambers. This shift fosters practices in the adornment of rooms and stimulates mass production of furnishings and decorative objects. In the nineteenth century, private life and domestic interiors begin to play an increasingly central and structuring role in social and literary history. This prevalence of interiors coincides with what could be called a domestication of the novel's main subject matter. Literary studies such as Ian Watt's *The Rise of the Novel* and Peter Brooks's *Body Work* argue that the rise of the novel, underway in the eighteenth century, parallels a growing sense of privacy and is characterized by the writing and reading of letters, an activity more common among women who begin to retreat to the privacy of their own closets or *boudoirs*. This implies that houses and their occupants become, along with the creative activity that takes place inside these interior realms, the focus of narrative. Through the creative work of embellishing and orchestrating the objects and dynamics of an interior a differentiated site of writing, reading, and reflection emerges. The imaginative act of writing seems no more than a continuation of what began as interior design.

The turn toward the domestic coincides with the novel's rising popularity and the undeniable leading role women play in these social and literary transformations. While women were increasingly confined to and associated with the domestic space, more women also become avid readers and writers of novels. Ann Romines's *The Home Plot: Women, Writing and Domestic Ritual* investigates the insistent presence in American culture and literature of an ideal female life centered in housekeeping. She looks at how American women writers began to depict the domestic ritual as a subject in itself, and argues that this interior competence ultimately dominates what she calls the home plot or the authors' "complex of domestic-literary concerns."[23] Even if not by their own choice, women became the pioneers of society's widely accepted devotion to interiors, but it would seem that this cultural practice was always inseparable from questions of writing and even, as *The Home Plot* shows, serves as a basis from which narrative techniques evolved. Home decorating is originally a feminine task and women become involved in the growing professionalization of interior design, which begins in cosmopolitan centers like New York and London at the turn of the century.[24] But the cultural and social shift toward the interior becomes a widespread phenomenon and it is not long before men begin to dominate the profession of interior decorating. Private dwelling becomes one's main form of existence and self-identity regardless of gender, although it is first and primarily governed by feminine traditions. In other words, the ontological shift that social and cultural history witness toward the end of the nineteenth century is highly informed by feminine experiences. Society and the narrative genre transition during this period toward a new theory for understanding reality and art, one that focuses on feelings, sensibility, the body, and an introverted exploration of interior worlds. The interior stands at the center of this endeavor both for society and narrative. The rising emphasis on the interior space implies a coexistence of emotion and intellect, and knowledge and creativity, creating an entryway for a possible synthesis that will ultimately change subjectivity and the sense of space.

If dwelling undergirds the workings of the imagination, the individual's illusions and desires seem to be both the cause and effect of the economic and social move indoors. More than any other work, Walter Benjamin's *The Arcades Project*, in its analysis of the bourgeois experience, best explores the process of interiorization and provides a social, if not anthropological, reading of what it means when rooms begin to express the personality of the individual. Benjamin evokes the interior as necessary not only to oppose the public place of work for the first time in history, but also to sustain the illusions of the private individual's universe. The interior, furthermore, acts as an asylum for art, whose dweller-collector is concerned with the transfiguration of things. From this experience arises what Benjamin calls "the phantasmagorias of the interior—which, for the private man, represents the universe."[25] In this universe, the private individual brings together "remote locales and memories of the past,"[26] and "the far away and the long ago. His living room is a box in the theater of the world."[27] Comparing the residence to a receptacle, Benjamin says that the individual is encased as "inside of a compass case, where the instrument with all its accessories lies embedded in deep, usually violet folds of velvet."[28] This image reinforces the importance of the figurative traveling that takes place in the interior setting. While a dwelling place is also an encasement or a receptacle, Benjamin speaks of the maternal womb as the first abode of the human being,[29] this doesn't mean that it is static. The interior allows one to bring the whole world inside, to represent the inner side of the individual but also the movement and transformations that constitute that interiority. As we will see, the authors of my study rely on their interior settings to represent their characters' imaginative, and at times subconscious travels and the historical contexts that inform their novels. Benjamin claims that the epoch of phantasmagoria is a condition of nineteenth-century existence, when dwelling reaches its most extreme form, and the illusory interior begins to define modernity.[30]

Art's ability to read intimacy and creativity in the representation of interiors is, however, already apparent in the early modern period, when Renaissance artists such as Miguel de Cervantes and Johannes Vermeer begin to show a preference for interiors and interiority. In a similar manner to Eça, Machado, and Alas, Cervantes and Vermeer are also transitional figures in the sense that their art reveals an evolution from abandoning and parodying conventions to adapting modern forms. The emphasis on interior settings in Cervantes's fully modern part two of *Don Quixote* (1615) or in the seventeenth-century paintings of Vermeer, whose main subject matter is the interior of a Dutch bourgeois chamber, seem to confirm the coinciding of art's shift toward modernity and its obsession with the interior space. What the work of these two artists also shows, another important point in common with the nineteenth-century writers, is that a favoring of interiors overlaps with a tendency to depict the world realistically. In *Art of the Everyday: Dutch Painting and the Realist Novel* Ruth Bernard Yeazell analyzes how Dutch painting informed realist writers and the implications this comparison has had for our understanding of literary realism. She explores how authors (Honoré de Balzac, Thomas Hardy, George Eliot, and Marcel Proust) reproduce in words some version of Dutch painting while also challenging the aesthetic debates and hierarchies of value that emerge around the genre. Yeazell reminds us of a centuries-old opposition between identifying the 'low' genres of the North with the absence of narrative and characterizing the historical or mythical scenes of the Italian Renaissance with an art that purportedly told more of a tale. As Yeazell explains the literary works identified with Dutch painting, those that depicted the everyday, the ordinary, and detailed domestic interiors, were considered to be the least plotted novels or those with less story than usual.

However a brief look at three quite different paintings will illustrate how the rendering of interiors is in fact also a representation of narrative. For Eça, Machado, and Clarín interior architecture gives shape to formal questions about the novelistic genre, and contrary to the paradigm described above, the authors, along with painters of interiors, reveal that there is room for high art and for the telling of stories inside the enclosed spaces of furnishings and things. Artists turn to houses and their interiors, and commonly to female figures, to mark a shift toward an artistic realism that is also modern, and to complicate the opposition between narrative and description.

In his celebrated painting of a young woman who is pregnant, *Woman in Blue Reading a Letter* (c. 1662-1663), Johannes Vermeer literally and metaphorically impregnates the room with its own ontology.

Furnishings and objects frame the universe that contains a self that encircles another. Interior objects and walls structure and contain human life. The hanging tapestry, which appears to represent a globe, is one of the powerful and suggestive details that inscribe the world into the space. The reading of the letter by the young woman reinforces the self-reflective aesthetic exercise. A more perfect rendering of Heidegger's philosophy that the self dwells and exists poetically can hardly be imagined. The proximity of the disguised life underneath the woman's heavy clothes to the written word, both to the letter and to the books that lie on the table, further reinforce the link between the story of art and the story of life. There is a narrative story being told in this "static" picture both of the continuity of life depicted, represented in the unborn child, and in the account being read in the letter and expressed in the painting. Vermeer's portrayal shows how artists and writers become increasingly aware of the significance of the interior and its décor, and of the ability of this intimate space to differentiate itself into a language and a narrative form.

The American artist Edward Lamson Henry was a painter primarily of what Amy Kurtz Lansing has called historical fictions. Curator and author of the accompanying catalogue, *Historical Fictions: Edward Lamson Henry's Paintings of Past and Present*, Lansing looks at how one of the most popular genre painters of late-nineteenth-century America used the past as a means of instilling cohesion and defining a new sense of national identity for the fractured society the country had become in the wake of the Civil War. As Lansing explains, Henry's more powerful paintings are not his representations of legendary historical events, but instead what she calls his furniture fictions, paintings with antiques and furnishings at their core. These pictures deal with memory, the passage of time, nostalgia, and obsolescence all within the context of a domestic interior crowded with carefully selected decorative objects and historic furniture.

Memories (1873) is contemporary to the time period represented in the three novels and recalls different settings in the texts, especially those depicting the female protagonists: Sofia's contemplative moments by windowsills, the different emblematic curtains and coverings of Ana Ozores's private quarters, and Maria Eduarda's red upholstered sitting-room. The disorder in the bedroom, with its clashing and multi-veiled patterns, implies that the thoughts of the woman are disturbed and chaotic. It is not certain whether she

Johannes Vermeer, *Woman Reading a Letter* (c. 1662-63). (The Rijksmuseum)

is packing or unpacking, coming or going, "the woman is caught in a transitional moment, her future, place, and identity as tenuous as her thoughts."[31] Lansing argues that in this painting Henry confronts the ambivalence of modern selfhood through the medium of memory by staging the sitter in a state of contemplation while holding a daguerreotype. Despite this and the title of the painting the woman could be as preoccupied with her future as she might be busy reminiscing about past events. While the heavy antique furniture, the tall canopy bed, stone fireplace, and large window anchor her sense

Edward Lamson Henry, *Memories* **(1873). (Permission, Yale University Art Gallery)**

of place, the trunk and hence the possibility of traveling also suggests she is questioning her dislocated self and place in the world. Along with the ambivalent plot that the room and its contents narrate, the daguerreotype that she holds in her hand represents yet another story that she is either trying to remember or forget. Henry's painting recalls Bachelard's search for memory in a space's poetics, especially with its emphasis on the many drawers and different containers, such as the hatbox, trunk, and basket. At the same time the painter's domestic interiors are also an interrogation of the importance of public history on defining the individual and national experience, a dilemma Machado's, Eça's, and Alas's novels also repeatedly confront.

Ramon Casas's influential work marks the beginning of modernism in Catalan painting, and his 1890 *Interior* literally includes the creative labor inside the room. The sketches, drawings, furnishings, and materials suggest that this is a bedroom that also serves as the working space of an artist. The painting gives us a narrow perspective of the room framed by the bed on one side and the drawing table on the other. These two incomplete furnishings, the half-hidden bed and drawing table, frame the interior of the room and the interiority of the woman, and suggest a narrative of the self where intimacy and art are interconnected. The solemnity of the female figure dressed all in black and with downcast eyes is at the center of this interior space and her position raises a number of questions. The ambivalent threshold is once again the key to the concept of the painting, since it is unclear whether the woman is preparing to face the world or retreating to her own thoughts and fears. The contrast between the black dress, the pastel colors of the room, and the bright light penetrating underneath the door point to the more enigmatic qualities interior spaces conjecture. Casas's representation tells an ambiguous, melancholic private story of existence, but a narrative that is also both inseparable from creativity, and from the public outside world threatening to penetrate inside the room. As the novelists, Vermeer, Henry, and Casas use the enclosed space to interrogate the sense of self and space, and analyze how both historical and private forces collide to influence character development. More importantly, as for all these painters, interiors serve the authors to structure and narrate the story as well. A number of transitions ensue in the late nineteenth century that provoke artists across geographical boundaries and forms of expression to convert the interior into a threshold that is illuminating both on the level of content and form. By literally furnishing the novel, authors and artists can create spaces where memory and history coincide with the modern search for an inner life, where emotions affect intellect, where fiction and reality, the public and the private, become indistinguishable, and where life greets death.

THE NOVELIST'S SENSE OF THE INTERIOR

The connection between interiors and Machado's, Eça's, and Alas's metafictional concerns surfaces not only in what I have tried to outline above as the aesthetic sense of interior space, but also in the novelist's own experience and relation to private life, rooms, and furnishings. Diana Fuss's unique research in *The Sense of an Interior*, quoted earlier, reveals how a space, animated with memory and significance, affects an author and his or her writing. Her interdisciplinary analysis convinces both literary and architectural critics that dwelling influences creativity and guides the inner self. Fuss closely reads, with both literary and architectural knowledge four modern

Ramón Casas, *Interior* (c. 1890). (Permission, Museu Nacional d'Art de Catalunya)

writers (Emily Dickinson, Sigmund Freud, Helen Keller, and Marcel Proust) and the rooms that shaped them. She discovers that the authors rely on sensual perception, using it to invent new ways of inhabiting space, and of having space inhabit their work. The exploration of inner life links these four authors and surfaces as their main subject of literary and cultural inquiry. Fuss's book focuses primarily on twentieth-century writers and the specific interior places that served as the workspaces for their writing in order to ultimately convey in her words "the way in which interiors shape imagination."[32] Although not twentieth-century writers, Machado, Eça, and Clarín also develop a discourse of settings and things in their work that reveals a rising preoccupation with interiority, a concern that later becomes so prevalent in the modernist literary imagination. The obsessive and exhaustive inventory and descriptions of rooms and houses so common in nineteenth-century realist authors like Balzac and Huysmans set the ground for modern writers to further develop their exploration of the self, but interiors are already in the nineteenth century tied to interiority. The difference is that Machado, Eça, and Clarín reflect on the interior as a site where the individual crisis of self-definition takes place inseparably from its unique historical and cultural constellations, which are present in the materials, furnishings, and architectural design of our interior spaces.

The sense that these authors derived from their personal surroundings helps us to better understand the role that interiors play in their fiction. Starting with the eighteenth-century rise of privacy in dwelling, the domestic interior becomes the typical working space for writers. None of the authors studied here made references to actively writing outdoors or even in the different public interior spaces they also inhabited. The Renaissance spirit, figured in the image of Luís de Camões saving his manuscript from a shipwreck in the middle of the Indian Ocean, has been dramatically transformed by the end of the nineteenth century. Now the creatively constructive theater is an enclosed, private, and refined setting. Biographical work and personal correspondence show that the writers cultivate throughout their lives important links with their own private spaces. These interior realms serve to transport them to their invented realities and to inspire their fiction in different ways. The writers adapt to the middle- and upper-class nineteenth-century move toward specialized spaces and create in their homes, as in their novels, designated places for their studies and libraries, whereby they assign meaning to different furnishings and objects. This sensitivity to space points to an interesting contradiction. On the one hand, the authors are living in increasingly industrialized societies, and their sense of privacy and attention to material comfort and its effect on one's mind and creative skills, is a result of this new modern existence. On the other hand, they use the representation of interior space to critique an evermore-interdependent market economy and fragmented society and the transfiguration and demoralization this produces on individuals. This is one of the many productive paradoxes that the authors work through in their fiction and throughout their lives. There are a number of important characteristics that defined the way the writers inhabited their own spaces that are relevant to explore in further detail.

Machado de Assis

Rio de Janeiro is the predominant setting for Joaquim Maria Machado de Assis's (1839-1908) fiction and life, although he moves a significant amount within the capital of the Brazilian empire.[33] Machado's father, a mulatto artisan, and his working-class Azorean-born mother were dependents or *agregados* of a wealthy family that owned most of Livramento Hill. The property's owner, Maria José de Mendonça Barroso Pereira, was also Machado's godmother, and between his family's poorer dwellings and the wealth and refinement of his protector's home, the writer probably experienced vastly contrasting interior settings as a young boy.[34] An early and successful career in the printing, publishing, and journalistic worlds, leads to constant relocating as his social status improves. In the 1860s, already a respected journalist, critic, and poet, Machado lives with his Portuguese colleague Francisco Ramos Paz, of whose extensive library he partakes.[35] In 1869 he marries the sister of a Portuguese friend and poet, and with his new bride, Carolina Augusta Xavier de Novais, lives in various middle-class homes in the center of town until finally settling in a chalet on Rua Cosme Velho 18.[36] Most critics and biographers consider Cosme Velho the main domestic space that encompasses Machado's private life, habits, and thoughts, and although the building itself has not survived, the house remains part of Brazil's cultural patrimony since many of its significant contents are today museum pieces. A 1997 protocol enlarges the Brazilian Academy of Letters' original collection of some of Machado's possessions, books, and a writing desk, with the furniture and objects that originally belonged to Machado and Carolina. The exhibition titled "Cosme Velho, 18" displays a large part of the interior contents of the couple's former home. The study *Rua Cosme Velho, 18: relato de restauro do mobiliário de Machado de Assis* provides historical background for the various furnishings and details the efforts involved in their restoration. This project, like the Foundation Eça de Queiroz, houses furniture, books, and decorative objects, and attempts to recreate the author's interior environment, drawing one closer to Machado's material surroundings. According to this study most of Machado's furniture adheres to the tendency at the time to reproduce French styles in national factories, to adopt what the authors call "uma conduta sobretudo imitativa, e não criadora" [above all an imitative conduct, and not a creative one].[37] Curiously Machado expresses a lot more confidence in the national production of furniture than do the authors of this study. They quote an August 16, 1895 editorial where Machado is clearly enthusiastic:

> As nossas grandes marcenarias estão cheias de móveis ricos, vários de gosto; não há só cadeiras, mesas, camas, mas toda sorte de trastes de adorno, fielmente copiados dos móveis franceses, alguns de nome original, o *bijou de salon*, por exemplo, outros em língua híbrida, como o porta-*bibelots*. Entra-se

nos grandes depósitos, fica-se deslumbrado pela perfeição da obra, pela rique-
za da matéria, pela beleza da forma.

[Our vast furniture workshops are full of rich furnishings, various of taste;
there are not only chairs, tables, beds, but all sorts of decorative pieces, faithfully copied from French furnishings, some with the original name, the *bijou
de salon*, for example, others in a hybrid language, such as the *bibelots*-carrier.
One enters these great warehouses, and is fascinated by the perfection of the
work, by the richness of the materials, by the beauty of the form]. [38]

Machado is impressed by the formal beauty of the national furniture production, and by its ability to inspire new linguistic modes. Another striking detail
in this study concerns the fact that the couple's matrimonial bed is an exception to the imitative norm since it is an original piece imported from England.
Choosing such a high-quality furnishing for their most intimate space seems
to reinforce the closeness between the couple and the interior design qualities
they valued most.

The way Machado relates to things and places explains how residences
become such dominant leitmotifs in his fiction, and why he calls the house a
symbol of his life experience and a kind of fictional theater.[39] Luciano Trigo
claims that Machado and his wife "iam mudando de casa à medida que
Machado avançava na carreira burocrática" [they would move to different
residences as Machado advanced in his bureaucratic career],[40] and on one
level, the frequent relocating suggests how social class is inevitably implied
in dwelling. But Machado always understood the association between interiors and social status ironically. One of his wry journalistic pieces begins,
"Fui ontem visitar um amigo velho, Fulano Público, e achei-o acabando de
almoçar...A casa em que mora, é um resumo de tôdas as habitações, desde o
palácio até o cortiço, para exprimir—creio eu—que êle é o complexo de
tôdas as classes sociais" [I went yesterday to visit an old friend, Public so-
and-so, and I found him just finishing his lunch...the house he inhabits is the
summary of all residences, from the palace to the humble abode, to express—I think—that he is the complexity of all social classes].[41] Despite the
sarcasm, it becomes clear that for Machado, the home reflects an individual's
values and contradictions, including his own. Although Francisca de Basto
Cordeiro's personal account of her experience with Machado and his wife
Carolina lacks accuracy and is at times biased, her testimonial does include
two important portraits of the couple's interiors. The first describes an apparently barren and modest home on the Rua do Catete and seems to contrast the
more luxurious setting at Cosme Velho. Despite Cordeiro's efforts to draw
distinctions, the details actually reveal that the furniture has mostly stayed
the same.[42] Lúcia Miguel Pereira gives a more modest description of Cosme
Velho: "A casa seria mais confortável do que a dos primeiros anos do casa-
mento, com duas criadas, móveis simples e cômodos, um ou outro quadro,

Machado de Assis's matrimonial bed. (Courtesy of the Academia Brasileira de Letras)

bons livros, algumas edições de luxo, mas o ambiente era o mesmo, de aconchego e de simplicidade digna. Tudo tranqüilo, decente e fino" [The house was more comfortable than those of the initial years of his marriage, with two servants, simple and comfortable furnishings, one painting or another, good books, some luxurious editions, but the atmosphere was unchanged, it was one of warmth and dignified simplicity. Everything was tranquil, decent, and refined].[43] Machado valued above all the emotional protection his home and wife provided, for the two were intertwined for him. And in fact Carolina devoted herself extensively to the enrichment of their interior. Cordeiro refers to Carolina's "personalidade artística" [artistic personality] and "espírito engenhoso" [ingenious spirit] in describing her commitment to interior décor, and from Cordeiro's descriptions and details, it is probable that Carolina would have designed her own patterns and some furniture pieces.[44] While Carolina develops a rising interest in the arts and crafts, Machado also becomes increasingly fond of acquiring and collecting meaningful objects and artworks. This combines with the couple's carefully meditated distribution of the floor plan to create a conscientious sense of their space, so that more than their social progression, consistent aesthetic concerns influence their interior improvements and alterations. Machado's study is purposely isolated from the rest of the house and from the exterior world. Cordeiro explains that in it, "A porta, para a varanda, fôra inutilizada por um armário envidraçado" [The door leading to the patio was made unusable by a glass cabinet].[45] The brightly lit and cheerfully adorned sleeping quarters, on the other hand, open up to the garden, and the fabrics and upholstery are full of representations of nature. Machado is exemplarily modern because of the way he dwells and fashions his subjectivity in a invented space that is able to bring the world inside, while at the same time keeping other forces out. He transforms his interior into the protected center of his identity and imagination.

With Carolina's death, Machado's sense of the space they inhabited together intensifies. Cordeiro tells us that toward the end of his life, Machado preferred to sleep in Carolina's sewing room, where he would have felt closer to her creative environment. The artistic or fictional process, which is present in both Carolina's crafts as in Machado's writing, thus stands for Machado as a synecdoche for the way in which the modern world is inhabited. Furthermore, Machado shared with his closest friends some of his melancholy and ideas about the connection between his interior and the memory of his wife. In a letter thanking Joaquim Nabuco for his condolences, Machado writes: "Aqui me fico, por ora na mesma casa, no mesmo aposento, com os mesmos adornos seus. Tudo me lembra a minha meiga Carolina" [Here I remain, for now in the very same house, in the same room, with her adornments. Everything reminds me of my tender Carolina, 3: 1071]. In a response to José Veríssimo's positive reviews of *Esaú e Jacó* (1904) he explains: "Cá vai o volume para o pequeno móvel onde guardo uma parte das lembranças dela" [Here goes the volume into the small furnishing where I have saved a part of her keepsakes, 3: 1073]. According to Pereira, this small piece of furniture, located by Machado's bedside, contained the couple's personal correspondence, later burned, and Carolina's jewelry and other personal items worn on her wedding day. Just as many of his characters showcased mementos, relics, and symbolic objects, Machado also collected and displayed certain meaningful pieces. The famous gift from Joaquim Nabuco, an oak-tree branch from Tasso, is clearly a prized possession. He writes to Nabuco: "O próprio galho, com a sua carta ao Graça, já os tenho na minha sala, em caixa, abaixo do retrato que V. me mandou de Londres o ano passado" [The branch itself, with your letter to Graça, is already in my drawing room, encased, underneath your photograph, which you sent to me last year from London, 3: 1075].

Machado's involvement with the Academy of Letters also demonstrates how significant the inhabiting of an interior is for the development of a meaningful ideal. The first president of the newly founded Brazilian Academy of Letters, Machado is assigned the difficult task of finding a house for the institution. He wanted to create an organization to advance a national literature, as well as build a meeting ground of minds for the Brazilian intelligentsia. Chapter one of Josué Montello's study of Machado's work in the Academy is very appropriately titled "A casa de Machado de Assis" [Machado de Assis's house]. Machado is evidently enthusiastic and good humored with respect to this undertaking. He writes to Joaquim Nabuco, "A Academia vai continuar os seus trabalhos, agora mais assídua, desde que tem casa e móveis" [The Academy will continue its work now more assiduously since it has a home and furnishings, 3: 1075]. The first temporary setting that Machado finds for the Academy is a shared space with the Academy of Medicine:

> Temos enfim uma sala no Pedagogium [...] Fui ver a sala, é vasta, tem mobília e serve bem aos nossos trabalhos. Naturalmente, os retratos e bustos que lá estão são de médicos, mas nós ainda os não temos de nossa gente, e aquêles, até porque são defuntos, não nos porão fora. Entendi-me também para obtermos um lugar em que possamos ter mesa e armário para guarda dos nossos papéis e livros.

> [Finally we have a room in the Pedagogium (...) I went to see the salon, it is vast, furnished and serves our work well. Naturally the portraits and busts that are there are of medical doctors, but we don't have any yet of our people, and those, especially since they are dead, won't kick us out. I also managed to obtain for us a place where we could have a table and cabinet to safeguard our papers and books, 3: 1050].

Like his own characters, Machado also reads and transforms the space around him bringing to life inanimate portraits and busts of dead illustrious men. The way Machado describes the influence of French novels on Brazilian writing in his infamous 1873 essay, which deals with national identity, shows how a home furnishes the upcoming native literary tradition with a space of its own as well: "As obras de que falo, foram aqui bem-vindas e festejadas, como hóspedes, mas não se aliaram à família nem tomaram o govêrno da casa" [The works I speak of were welcomed and celebrated here as guests, but they didn't become part of the family or take over the house's governance, 3: 805].[46]

These penetrating ideas about objects and spaces resurface in Machado's evolving concept of the narrative creation and its connection to national identity. What Machado called "certo sentimento íntimo" [a certain intimate sentiment] in the above-cited essay, is represented in his concept of interior space (3: 804). Anticipating Benjamin's thoughts, quoted earlier, on how the interior brings together remote locales and time periods, Machado claims that the author can speak of "assuntos remotos no tempo e no espaço" [remote subjects in time and space] and still feel Brazilian interiorly, this feeling he calls an "instinto de nacionalidade" [instinct of nationality, 3: 804]. Roberto Schwarz argues convincingly that Machado is able to observe and represent the complexities of Brazilian society once he has achieved a certain social status.[47] In other words, once he has his own private space, or his own fictional theater, he can more effectively in his writing compose, destroy, and rebuild different social spaces. Machado interiorizes a sense of nationality while developing an aesthetic sensibility of his private self. The interior world provides the intellectual freedom that motivates him to experiment technically and allows for his philosophical audacity. By enclosing himself in his study behind the glass armoire full of books, Machado ironically feels freer to reach his inner mind and sense of what to him defines his nation. This turning inward is already evident in his early writing. Many first-person-narrated journalistic pieces often begin by describing the comfort, silence, and particularities of a private salon or study, which then inspires philosophical reflection or debate with a similarly comfortably seated interlocutor. In his novels it becomes increasingly evident how Machado relies on the house, the drawing room, the private quarters as a rhetorical tool not only to explore the interior lives of his characters but also to frame many of the thematic concerns of his narratives. For Machado, the interior space acts as the point of departure for both the development of ideas and of the story.

Eça de Queirós

José Maria de Eça de Queirós (1845-1900) makes similar claims about how the ideal interior shelters, reflects, and inspires a mind's refinement. Eça's large collection of correspondence gives readers a significant perspective into the author's relationship to interiors and even to certain furnishings. The Portuguese author was fairly preoccupied with homes and attentive to the construction of comfortable interiors. This fascination is perhaps related to his vast experience with different settings.[48] Not only did his work as a diplomat take him to a variety of cities and countries but he also often moved from one residence to another due to financial burdens. The numerous settings where Eça lived throughout his life are fundamental icons of his existence as a writer, since scholars often turn to the geographical spaces associated with Eça for both biographical and critical purposes.[49] A late-nineteenth-century bourgeois family such as Eça's often rented a property for the summer season, so that after his marriage and while in France, Eça was constantly on the lookout for homes, both permanent and seasonal, a preoccupation that comes up often in his correspondence. According to José Calvet de Magalhães, the house-searching endeavor was a "tarefa que o cansava e aborrecia" [task that tired and bored him],[50] yet the financial frustration tied to finding the appropriate dwelling place seems more likely to be the cause of distress for Eça, and not the significant pursuit of the ideal domestic haven. He was not averse to exploring homes or to learning more about interior decoration. On the contrary, when he took charge of the inheritance negotiations between his siblings-in-law, he was quite enthusiastic especially about the property left to his wife, Vila Nova in Santa Cruz do Douro, which he visited with his sister-in-law, Benedita. The famous estate is today the picturesque home of the Foundation Eça de Queiroz and is well known for having inspired Jacinto's fictional Tormes in Eça's late novel, *The City and the Mountains* (1900). In a 1892 letter to Eça's wife, Emília de Castro, concerning the first of three visits to Santa Cruz, Benedita writes, "O José não lhe escreve, anda a tirar uma planta da casa" [José doesn't write to you, he's busy drawing a plan of the house].[51] When Eça writes to Emília three days later, his own words confirm his interest in the place, and his indulging in the possibility of turning the abandoned country estate into a comfortable retreat, as Jacinto will do in Eça's novel.

For Eça, the domestic interior is not only indicative of social class and taste, but also reflects the resident's intellectual pursuits and historical roots. Eça writes a number of compassionate letters from Havana, Cuba and North America to his lifetime friend and collaborator, Ramalho Ortigão, which echo these ideas.[52] The author is very critical of Cuban society, feels nostalgia for Europe, and his unhappiness seems primarily due to being "metido num hotel," [stuck in a hotel] and so he writes to Ramalho:

> Portanto, oh, querido amigo, Você alegre-se em poder continuar nesse *obscuro e velho armário* que se chama Portugal [...] Que há de melhor do que sentar-se o ser vivo a uma mesa—de ébano ou de pinho—e aparando a pena, compor às linhas e *à petites plumées*, alguma fina subtileza de arte ou de crítica?—Não há nada melhor.

> [So my dear friend, be happy that you remain in that *obscure and old armoire* that is called Portugal (...) What is better than for the living soul to sit at a table—of ebony or pine—and sharpening one's pen, compose line by line and *à petites plumées* some refined subtlety of art or criticism?—There is nothing better].[53]

Eça structures and imagines with different pieces of furniture not only what is absent, but also what he fictionalizes, combining a sense of national identity and history with the author's ideals. Ebony and pine are rare and more luxurious woods, typical of the more refined national craftsmanship, clearly pointing to Eça's continuous desire for sophistication. Eça's observations about North American culture reveal some mixed feelings; he says of New York, "é uma cidade que em parte amo e em parte detesto" [it is a city that I partly love and partly detest].[54] What he most admired of America he demonstrates in his praise of the society's indulgence in material comfort insofar

as it denotes social and artistic progress. In one of his letters to Ramalho, Eça
develops a highly significant paradigm of his poetics in an extended comparison between writing and the construction of an interior:

> Diz-se que os Americanos não têm arte: é verdade. Isto tem suas razões, que
> não são do género epistolar; mas têm sobretudo uma razão suprema: é que o
> seu génio artístico é inteiramente empregado na vida doméstica. Construir,
> estabelecer, ornar, criar um interior—é no fim de tudo matéria artística, tanto
> como desenhar a tomada de Constantinopla; e eu, por mim, julgar-me-ia mais
> profundamente artista por ter criado aos *meus* um interior sábio, colorido,
> doce, atraente, influente, inteligente—do que em ter contado aos outros a
> *História da Sibila* ou o que fez *Clemenceau*.

> [They say that the Americans don't have Art: it is true. This has its reasons,
> which are not for the epistolary genre; but above all they have one superior
> reason: this is that their artistic talent is entirely employed in their domestic
> life. To build, establish, decorate, create an interior—is in the end an artistic
> affair, as much as to plan the conquest of Constantinople; and as far as I am
> concerned, I would judge myself more profoundly artistic for having created
> for my *loved ones* a wise, colorful, sweet, attractive, influential, intelligent
> interior—than in having narrated to others the *History of Sibyl* or what Cle-
> menceau achieved]. [55]

Eça's point of view praises interior well-being so far as it symbolizes intellectual freedom and a devotion to art and reflection. He seems to anticipate
his later literary work, where the creation of an interior space and the actions
taking place inside it, substitute the narrative, and reveal a more reflective
and modern understanding of the world and of reality. In this respect, Eça
shares Virginia Woolf's opinion expressed in her prominent essay *A Room of
One's Own*, when she explains that wealth of experience and imagination is
tied to material things. During her walk through Oxford, she writes: "And
(pardon me the thought) I thought, too, of the admirable smoke and drink and
the deep armchairs and the pleasant carpets: of the urbanity, the geniality, the
dignity which are the offspring of luxury and privacy and space." [56]

Eça's relationships to colleagues are also telling of the importance he
placed on private settings. He often writes apologetic letters to friends can-
celing or postponing social events, as when he responds to Oliveira Martins's
invitation to come to Costa Nova: "Há lá decerto a brisa, a vaga, a duna, o
infinito e a sardinha—coisas essenciais para a inspiração—mas falta-me essa
outra condição suprema: um quarto isolado com uma mesa de pinho" [I am
sure the breeze, the billow, the dunes, infinity and the sardine will be there—
all essentials things for inspiration—but that other supreme condition will be
missing: an isolated room with a table made of pine wood]. [57] This also
brings to mind one of Ega's many requests of his friend Carlos in *The Maias*:
"Há cá um quarto para mim?...Basta-me uma alcova, com uma mesa de

pinho, larga bastante para se escrever uma obra sublime" [Have you got a room for me?...A little corner somewhere, with a good pine table, large enough for me to write some sublime literary work?, 381; 329]. An invitation for Christmas, from another close friend, Jaime Batalha Reis, focuses on the details of the guest room Batalha Reis has personally prepared for Eça, hoping to lure his friend to Newcastle in England:

> Tenho um quarto de trabalho tranquilo, isolado, confortável. Nele te instalarás, nele trabalharás só quando queiras, ao pé do fogo, defronte duma estante gótica, cheia de carácter, que aqui comprei num *old curiosity shop*, com os pés sobre uma pele que o Serpa Pinto me trouxe do Centro de África. A minha casa está num *terrace* isolado defronte de extensos campos que vão acabar num parque que fecha ao horizonte, à beira da estrada de Edimburgo. Em parte alguma terás mais tranquilidade para trabalhar.

> [I have a tranquil working room, isolated, comfortable. You will install your-self in it, work in it only when you want, by the lit fire, in front of a gothic bookcase, full of character, something I bought here in an *old curiosity shop*, with your feet over a fur that Serpa Pinto brought me from Central Africa. My house is in an isolated *terrace* in front of extensive fields that end in a park that closes the horizon, near the road to Edinburg. Nowhere else would you have more tranquility to work].[58]

Batalha Reis understands the importance and difference a perfect interior makes for Eça and his writing, and prepares a study furnished with exotic elements, such as the African rug. The Gothic bookcase bought in an old curiosity shop evokes Charles Dickens's work and merges the author's task with the interior space. The description of the workspace highlights the fu-sion of luxury with a peaceful natural exterior. Nature makes its way into this interior space. For Eça this symbiosis is crucial. The ideal interior spaces in his fiction are those that allow for an intercession with nature. In his own life, as his correspondence from the Douro valley reveals, he also prefers rooms that could interiorize the natural surroundings.

The friendship between Eça and Batalha Reis flourishes in the latter's Lisbon residence, where Eça often worked, and which would later serve as the stage for the intellectual reunions known as the Cenáculo, which brought together many of the members of the later named Generation of 70. This is also where Eça first admires a standing desk, a gift to Batalha Reis's father from Almeida Garrett (1799-1854), one of Portugal's most important roman-tic writers. Eça is so fascinated with this desk that he later has a copy of it handcrafted in Paris.

It is well known that on this desk he wrote many of his literary projects. This piece of furniture was a tremendous inspiration for his work. Recreating the desk attests to Eça's devotion to antiques and his enthusiasm for the improvement of interiors in general. But it also reveals that Eça associates

Eça de Queirós's desk. (Permission, Fundação Eça de Queiroz)

meaning and memory with furnishings and believes they can have historic and aesthetic auras that connect him to other moments in time. The repetition of the desk conveys the sense that the author desired to continue the work in this case of a most admired Portuguese writer and the literary tradition he represented.

Eça had some superstitions such as occur in writers, writing only on a specific type of paper for example, but others less conventional, like his famous fear of drafts. Still more curious, however, was Eça's insistence on entering a room always with his right foot. Jaime Batalha Reis, in his well-known introduction to *Prosas Bárbaras* (*Barbarous Texts*), describes Eça's habit: "Havia de sempre entrar no meu quarto com o pé direito, suspendendo-se por isso, no último momento, recuando o agourento pé esquerdo, quando já este inoportunamente se adiantasse e fazendo hesitante e confuso, ao passar enfim a soleira da porta, um ruído de inexplicável trepidação" [He would always enter my room with his right foot, stopping himself at the last minute in order to do so, drawing back the foreboding left foot when it would inopportunely get ahead of itself and making hesitant and confusing, while passing finally the door's threshold, a noise of inexplicable trepidation].[59] Eça's working place, the room he is about to enter, becomes a theater full of possibilities for the fictional creation, a mystical space that was already the fictional world occupying his mind; a clear transitional sphere whose threshold he is careful to mark. The writer's personal preoccupation with interiors reveals a concern with their symbolic, social, and creative power over individuals.

Leopoldo Alas

For the Spaniard, Leopoldo Enrique García-Alas Ureña (1852-1901), better known by his pseudonym, Clarín, a similar sense of intellectual and political liberalism plays a crucial role throughout his work and manifests itself in his devotion to inner integrity and private life. Like Machado, Leopoldo Alas is also mostly associated with one geographical setting, Oviedo, the capital of Asturias, and he seldom travels far from this northern Spanish region and its surroundings. Like both Machado and Eça, Alas was one of the most important intellectual and literary figures of his time, a prolific, outspoken, and controversial literary and cultural critic. In contrast to all the emotion he generated in his public and polemic dialogues, his private life was characterized by tranquility and a love of family life. Gonzalo Sobejano writes "parecen destacarse especialmente la ternura familiar (madre, esposa, hijos)" [what stands out the most is especially the family tenderness (mother, wife, children)],[60] and biographers such as Juan Antonio Cabezas and Adolfo Posada highlight Clarín's closeness to his family. Throughout the author's life, while Clarín's writing and ideas grow more comprehensive, complex, and wide-ranging, his devotion to a secluded personal life and attachment to a tranquil domestic space also gradually intensifies.

Born in Zamora in 1852, as a young boy Clarín moved among various Spanish cities because of his father's appointments as civil governor. He attended the Jesuit school of San Marcos in León, and later studied for a brief period in Guadalajara. But his life is spent largely in Oviedo, where he completes most of his secondary and university studies. Even when he doesn't live in Oviedo, Alas repeatedly returns home, both for personal and professional reasons, slowly converting Oviedo into the center of his life and work. His brief residence in Madrid, where he moves in 1871 to do his doctoral studies, is marked by feelings of estrangement. Although he lives with other friends and students from Asturias, he still seems to feel alienated. In "Rafael Calvo y el teatro español" Clarín admits his "*horror* de la posada madrileña" [*horror* of the Madrid inn, 4: 2 1407]. He claims that only poetry provided him with a sense of refuge for his melancholic soul. As he searches different abodes throughout the capital city for an ideal and poetic dwelling place, Clarín makes it clear that home is a mystical place, where he can find moral thoughts and feelings, and a devotion to the arts. He writes: "En aquel Madrid que me parecía tan grande y tan enemigo en su indiferencia para mis sueños y mis ternuras y mis creencias, encontraba algo parecido al calor del hogar...en el teatro y en el templo" [in that Madrid that seemed to me so large and an enemy in its indifference toward my dreams and my affections and my beliefs, I found something similar to a home's warm...in the theater and in the church, 4: 2 1408]. The Ateneo en Madrid, calle de la Montera, is another place where Clarín spends a significant amount of time. Martínez Cachero calls the Ateneo the author's "hogar madrileño" [Madrid home],[61] and this is where Clarín writes his dissertation, *El Derecho y la moralidad* (*Law and Morality*) under Francisco Giner de los Ríos's direction.

Like Machado and Eça, Alas's successful early and prolific publishing career undeniably results in ongoing work, which along with repeated illnesses confine him to his domestic space that increases in importance especially once he marries and establishes his household. After holding different professorships, first at the University of Salamanca, and later at the University of Zaragoza, he finally returns permanently to the University of Oviedo in 1883 and is appointed professor of "Historia y Elementos de Derecho Romano" (history and Roman law). He marries Onofre García Argüelles y García Bernardo in 1882 and settles at Calle Uría 34 with the couple's first-born. A number of letters to and from his wife make his dedication and attachment to his family home evident. During one of Clarín's trips to Madrid, Onofre writes to him claiming that the house is just not the same without him, reinforcing the positive and strong presence the author seems to have over his domestic space. This is also the point at which he confesses to the leading Spanish realist and his lifelong and highly esteemed friend and colleague Benito Pérez Galdós, how his domestic environment provides him with aesthetic fulfillment:

> De Oviedo no pienso salir (a no ser por temporada) en algunos años. Hago una vida de hombre bueno que me sienta muy bien. Mi mujer y mi hijo (seis meses) mi casita con luz, aire, techos altos y vistas a la nieve de Morcín; por café la casa de mis padres, que ambos viven; en el casino billar, en cátedra algún discípulo listo, y libros de Vds. Y trabajo mió. No es mal lote.

> [I don't intend to leave Oviedo (other than temporarily) for some years. I lead the life of a good man that suits me very well. My wife and son (six months) my little house with good lighting, air, tall ceilings and views over snow-covered Morcín; my parent's house for coffee, both are still alive; the casino for billiards, at the university some bright pupil, and your books. And my own work. It is not a bad lot].[62]

Like Machado and Eça, Clarín also appreciates his interiors for bringing in the natural world, the light, fresh air, and views of snow-covered mountains. His letters suggest that it is in this type of sheltered environment that the author feels best to work on his literary pursuits.

The University of Oviedo organized and hosted an important bibliographic exhibition in 2001 to commemorate the centenary of Clarín's death. This exhibit integrated a recreation of Alas's study and personal library including furnishings, books, photographs and various other personal objects, all holdings of the Library of Asturias. The replica gives us a sense of what Clarín's personal study might have looked like. The organizers of the exposition's catalog, *Un siglo con Clarín: Exposición bibliográfica en el centenario de su muerte* (*A century with Clarín: Bibliographic exhibition on the centenary of his death*), describe the furnishings as "muebles de líneas sobrias y diseño funcional, con una decoración mínima" [furniture of sober lines and functional design, with minimal decoration].[63] The most original pieces are Clarín's fretworked bookshelves with collapsible wings and shelves.

As the authors explain, these smaller, more transportable furnishings often came from Spanish America: "Los muebles de este tipo, pequeños y manejables, solían llegar de las antiguas colonias y constituían un elemento exótico en la decoración austera de las estancias del norte de España" [Furnishings of this type, small and manageable, would often arrive from the former colonies and constituted an exotic element in the austere decoration of bookshelves from northern Spain].[64] The restrained and solid furnishings give a sense of permanence and intransience, but the room is in fact anything but static. The allusion the traveling bookshelves make to the colonial empire and its varied forms of commerce, economic, social, and historical, reinforce the complex systems of exchange that also influence the interiors in *La Regenta*. Although not pictured in the figure "Leopoldo Alas's study" there

Leopoldo Alas's study. (Courtesy of the Biblioteca de Asturias Ramón Pérez de Ayala)

was a small globe that Clarín kept on his desk that reinforces this allusion to travel.

Besides home in Oviedo, Alas will also spend time in his family's country estate, in Guimarán. Gómez-Santos's biography includes a chapter titled

"Clarín enfermo" [the sick Clarín], where he narrates some of Alas's habits during his illnesses from intestinal tuberculosis, which aged and saddened him with time. These and other spiritual and physical ailments repeatedly afflict Clarín throughout his life, and as his health declines he turns more and more inward and devotes himself to his private space, family, and self. Gómez-Santos writes: "Trabajaba Clarín cerca de la chimenea, que encendía hasta bien entrado el mes de Julio" [Clarín worked by the fire which he lit even as late July].[65] With age, Alas becomes increasingly preoccupied with death, religion, his children's future, and his diminishing sight and hearing. Gómez-Santos's biographical work quotes Clarín's daughter, Elisa, who remembers that when her father was too ill to go the university, his students would come and hear his lecture in his study at home:

> El día que no lograba librarse de la pesadez intestinal, los alumnos recibían las clases en el despacho. Todavía recuerdo que Adolfín y yo nos divertíamos en mirar por la cerradura a los veinte jóvenes atentísimos a la palabra de nuestro padre, ya más apagada, pero con más alma y más emotividad.

> [On the days he could not free himself from the intestinal burden, the students would hear lecture in his study. I still remember that Adolfín and I would have so much fun looking in through the keyhole at the twenty students extremely attentive to our father's word, now more subdued, but with more soul and emotion].[66]

This recalls the actions of some of the characters in *La Regenta*, who peak through keyholes to expose the privacy of others, but who at the same time discover and uncover their true selves with the constant penetration of interior spaces, which is a crucial leitmotif in Alas's novel.

Clarín's biographers constantly point to his reclusive nature, and Adolfo Posada, for example, emphasizes the author's increasing withdrawal from public life and describes his private self as "sereno, recatado" [serene, reserved],[67] someone who prefers "la vida de relativo aislamiento" [a life of relative isolation].[68] Posada claims that Alas's avowal to a secluded lifestyle begins already during his adolescence: "Alas vivía ya entonces, volcado, digámoslo así, hacia adentro: un vivir recatado, íntimo, espiritual, constituía su supremo goce, goce a veces amargo con dejos de anhelos insatisfechos" [Alas lived already at this time, turned over, shall we say, turned inward: a reserved, intimate, spiritual life constituted his supreme pleasure, a pleasure at times bitter with accents of unsatisfied desires].[69] The cultivation of a retreated and ethical existence is something Clarín strives for his whole life. Shortly before his death in 1901, Alas moves with his family to a cheerful, spacious house with a large vegetable garden in Fuente del Prado 3. This new home marks the end of a long search for a poetic reality, domestic peace, and an escape from a life constantly plagued with melancholy and disillusion. It is fitting that another writer's interior experience should bring us closer to Alas's ghostly domestic dwelling. Azorín visits Clarín's last home and private library and writes:

> Estoy en la biblioteca de *Clarín*; reina un silencio denso, profundo, en toda la casa. No hay nadie en ella; todos sus moradores habituales veranean en lejanas aldeas. Y yo voy respirando aquí, a mis solas, esta paz inquietadora, este sosiego misterioso, inexpresable, que se escapa de las salas, de los corredores, de las alcobas, de los patios, que han sido animados por el espíritu de seres queridos y cuyas puertas y cuyos muebles ahora callan, inmóviles, resignados, llenos de sensaciones muertas y de recuerdos...

> [I am in Clarín's library; a dense, profound silence reigns over the entire house. There is no one in it; all its usual inhabitants vacation their summers in far away towns. And I am here, all alone, breathing in this disquieting peace, this mysterious, inexpressible stillness that escapes from the drawing-rooms, from the hallways, from the bedrooms, from the patios, all of which have been animated by the spirits of dear beings and whose doors and furniture now keep quiet, immovable, resigned, full of dead sensations and memories...][70]

The house's most impressive architectural feature appears to be a long corridor lined with windows, where according to Azorín, Clarín spent his last days. Azorín describes the "ancha solana de cristales...un espacioso corredor que se aleja, en recto ángulo, a la derecha y a la izquierda; claras y altas vidrieras lo cierran; una cenefa de cristales rojos, azules y morados, encuadra los blancos cristales" [the wide glass balcony...a spacious corridor that continues in a right angle to the right and to the left; clear and tall windows are used to close it; a border of red, blue, and purple stained glass encases the clear glass].[71] Azorín's account of Clarín's intellectual resonance relies on interior details that give form to the memory of Alas, while at the same time evoking the author's own fiction. This window-lined corridor visibly recalls the circular balcony of the Vegallana country home in *La Regenta* where climactic encounters with the heroine take place.

Machado, Eça, and Clarín cultivate a sense of interior space throughout their lives that affects their philosophical views of the world and on writing. Their working spaces are inseparable from the progress and evolution of their own narratives and from the literary interior spaces that emerge in their fiction. These real-life interior realms inspire the development of their fictional worlds by serving them as points of departure to their imaginative spaces. Interiors connect the writers to important historical and literary contexts, and are intimately related to fundamental aesthetic and ethical questions that they raise. The domestic space is essential for each of the authors because it draws them closer to their inner selves, and inspires the critical inquiries that governed their view of reality and their sense of history and cultural identity.

I have attempted in this introduction to examine the growing fascination with interior dwelling widespread in literature and culture in the late nineteenth century, and trace its effect on the development of the narrative genre, ontological theories of the imagination, as well as on the authors themselves. In order to show the historical connection between dwelling and the art of narrative I looked first at how interiors become meaningful topics of inquiry for certain writers and philosophers who use interiors to question the nature of narrative, our sense of being, and the workings of the imagination. Secondly, I analyzed three paintings whose content and formal features emphasize art's ability to read intimacy and creativity in the representation of interiors. Lastly, by using biographical information and the personal correspondence of the writers, I assessed Machado's, Eça's, and Alas's own experience and relation to private life, rooms, and furnishings. In the chapters that follow, while reading three powerful novels in particular, I examine how the rhetorical function of interior architecture in narrative has important consequences for our theoretical understanding of the development of fiction more broadly. On the one hand, this book analyzes how the interior dwelling, a fundamental leitmotif for the three Luso-Hispanic writers, connects to the historical, political, and cultural critiques the novels write. On the other hand, *Interiors and Narrative* also examines how private dwelling and its contents underline and are an essential component of our understanding of a novel's formal structure, while contributing to our comprehension of how interiors relate to imagination and our sense of being.

Part One is titled "Furnishing the Novel" and explores the analogies between the architectural and decorative design of the novels' interior settings and the way the authors prepare and equip their narratives. In other words, how do the authors furnish their novels? Namely, how do rooms, furnishings, and homes function as metaphors for the writing of the texts? In all three novels there are important parallels between the narrative's larger aesthetic objectives and the makeup and layout of dwelling spaces. Part Two, "Interiors and Interiority," investigates the complex relation between interiors and human interiority by focusing on how the authors deploy interior space in relation to character development. It looks at how the novels underscore the shift toward interiority and the workings of consciousness by examining how characters and narrators interact with and contradict their private spaces. The third and final part, "The Discourse of Interiors," argues that the interior design of rooms both by the narrators who describe the interior settings and more importantly by characters that renovate and decorate their dwellings becomes a discourse that gives furnishings and decorative objects a narrative life of their own. I explore how the language of things is expressed through the frame of interior design. As I hope to show, the story of homes and furnishings in these novels creates a semiotic language of objects and objectified things that both readers and characters rely on in order to make sense of fiction and reality.

Notes

1. Honoré de Balzac, *The Human Comedy: Introductions and Appendix* (Hazleton, PA: Pennsylvania State University *Electronics Classics Series*, 2002), 47.

2. Henry James, *Novels 1881-1886: Washington Square, The Portrait of a Lady, The Bostonians* (New York: Literary Classics of the US, 1997), 2.

3. Gustave Flaubert, *A Sentimental Education*, trans. Douglas Parmée (Oxford: Oxford University Press, 1989), 450.

4. See Carlos Reis's *Estudos Queirosianos: Ensaios Sobre Eça de Queirós e a Sua Obra* (Lisboa: Presença, 1999), Roger L. Utt's *Textos y con-textos de Clarín* (Madrid: Istmo, 1988), and Alan Freeland's "Evolution and Dissolution: Imagery and Social Darwinism in Eça de Queirós and Leopoldo Alas" *Journal of the Institute of Romance Studies* 2 (1993): 323-36.

5. See Alberto Machado da Rosa's *Eça, Discípulo de Machado? Formação de Eça de Queirós* (Lisboa: Presença, 1965), and Constantino Paleólogo's *Eça de Queirós e Machado de Assis* (Rio de Janeiro: Tempo Brasileiro, 1979).

6. Susan Bernstein, *Housing Problems: Writing and Architecture in Goethe, Walpole, Freud, and Heidegger* (Stanford: Stanford University Press, 2008), 2.

7. I will mainly use Machado, Eça, and Clarín (or Alas) to refer to the three authors. These are the names customarily used by literary historians in the field.

8. Aristotle, *The Politics of Aristotle*, trans. Ernest Barker (London: Oxford University Press, 1958), 37.

9. Ibid., 7.

10. Peter Jones, "Introduction," *The Odyssey* (London: Penguin, 1991), xi.

11. The majority of the critical work on the topic of interiors and homes in nineteenth-century literature treats mainly American and northern-European narrative fiction, focusing primarily on gender roles and on the structural changes in the private and public realms. See for example, Liana F. Piehler's *Spatial Dynamics and Female Development in Victorian Art and Novels: Creating a Woman's Space* (New York: Peter Lang, 2003), Marilyn Chandler's *Dwelling in the Text: House in American Fiction* (Berkeley: University of California Press, 1991), Kirsten Belgum's study, *Interior Meaning: Design of the Bourgeois Home in the Realist Novel* (New York: Peter Lang, 1991), which focuses on the German realist novel, Katharina Hansen Löve's *The Evolution of Space in Russian Literature: A Spatial Reading of 19th and 20th Century Narrative Literature* (Amsterdam: Rodopi, 1994), and María Teresa Zubiaurre's *El espacio en la novela realista: Paisajes, miniaturas, perspectivas* (México: Fondo de cultura económica, 2000).

12. Walter Benjamin, *The Arcades Project*, trans. Howard Eiland and Kevin McLaughlin (Cambridge, MA: Belknap Press of Harvard University Press, 1999), 20.

13. Gaston Bachelard, *The Poetics of Space*, trans. Maria Jolas (Boston: Beacon Press, 1994), 15.

14. John R. Stilgoe, "Foreword," *The Poetics of Space*, trans. Maria Jolas (Boston: Beacon Press, 1969), x.

15. Bachelard, *Poetics of Space*, xxxvii.

16. Stilgoe, "Foreword," vii.

17. Diana Fuss, *The Sense of an Interior: Four Writers and the Rooms That Shaped Them* (New York: Routledge, 2004), 4.

18. Martin Heidegger, *Poetry, Language, Thought*, trans. Albert Hofstadter (New York: Harper Collins, 1971), 158.

19. Ibid., 213.

20. Ibid., 225.

21. Bachelard, *Poetics of Space*, xxxvii.

22. Heidegger, *Poetry, Language, Thought*, 225.

23. Ann Romines, *The Home Plot: Women, Writing, and Domestic Ritual* (Massachusetts: University of Massachusetts Press, 1992), 9.

24. See the entry "Interior Design, History and Development" in Joanna Banham, *Encyclopedia of Interior Design* (London: Fitzroy Dearborn, 1997).

25. Benjamin, *Arcades Project*, 9.

26. Ibid., 19.

27. Ibid., 9.

28. Ibid., 220.

29. Ibid.

30. Ibid.

31. Amy Kurtz Lansing, *Historical Fictions: Edward Lamson Henry's Paintings of Past and Present* (New Haven: Yale University Art Gallery, 2005), 39.

32. Fuss, *Sense of an Interior*, 215.

33. Machado claims frequently in his correspondence and writings that he was destined to live, die, and not travel far from Rio de Janeiro. In 1897 he writes to José Veríssimo: "Eu sou um pêco fruto da capital, onde nasci, vivo e creio que hei de morrer, não indo ao interior senão por acaso e de relâmpago" [I am a withered fruit of the capital where I was born, live, and I believe shall die, not going into the interior other than by chance and for very brief periods]. (Machado de Assis, *Obras Completas*. 3 vols. [Rio de Janeiro: Aguilar, 1962], 3: 1042).

34. See Jean-Michel Massa's biography, *A Juventude de Machado de Assis (1839-1870)*, trans. Marco Aurélio de Moura Matos (Rio de Janeiro: Civilização Brasileira, 1971) for Machado's early years.

35. According to Lúcia Miguel Pereira's biographical study, *Machado de Assis: Estudo Crítico e Biográfico* (Rio de Janeiro: José Olympio, 1955), Machado most likely lives with Ramos Paz between 1860 and 1869.

36. The couple first lives in Rua dos Andradas 119 in the center of town until 1873. Then for shorter periods from 1873 to 1874 on Rua Santa Luzia 54, on a second floor of Rua da Lapa 96 from 1874 to 1875, and from 1875 to 1878 at the Rua das Laranjeiras 4. They move to Rua do Catete 206 in 1878, the year during which they spend three months in Nova Friburgo, and live there until 1883 before moving to Cosme Velho.

37. The authors write: "O mobiliário machadiano reflete a tendência geral de 'importação do estilo francês.' Era construído no país, com madeira brasileira, por artífices nacionais ou estrangeiros aqui residentes, mas seguindo a influência dos estilos europeus, com inserção apenas de sutis interpretações à maneira brasileira" [Machado's furniture reflects the general tendency at the time of "importing the French style." It was made in Brazil with Brazilian wood, by native craftsmen or foreigners residing here, but following European styles, with but a few subtle insertions in the Brazilian fashion] (*Rua Cosme Velho, 18: Relato de restauro do mobiliário de Machado de Assis* [Rio de Janeiro: Academia Brasileira de Letras, 1998], 40).

38. *Rua Cosme Velho*, 39.

39. See Beatriz Berrini's "A Casa: Uma em Machado, Outra em Eça," *Recortes Machadianos*, eds. Ana Salles Mariano and Maria Rosa Duarte de Oliveira (São Paulo: EDUC, 2003), 277-295.

40. Luciano Trigo, *Viajante Imóvel: Machado de Assis e o Rio de Janeiro de Seu Tempo* (Rio de Janeiro: Record, 2001), 21.

41. Machado de Assis, *Obras Completas*, 3: 449. Subsequent quotations from the works of Machado, Eça, and Alas are cited parenthetically in the text, along with citations to published translations, where used. Where no translation is cited, the translation provided is my own.

42. Francisca de Basto Cordeiro's brief description begins: "Na sala da frente, havia apenas uma modesta mobília de palhinha (sofá, 2 cadeiras de braço e outras comuns), estantes de ferro com livros e uma escrivaninha onde papéis e jornais se amontoavam. As paredes, nuas. Nada embelezava o modesto ambiente onde a instável felicidade elegera domicílio" [In the front drawing-room there was only a modest set of wicker furniture (a couch, two armchairs and others), some iron bookcases with books and a desk on which papers and newspapers piled up. The walls were naked. Nothing embellished the modest environment in which the unstable happiness chose to reside. (Francisca de Basto Cordeiro, *Machado de Assis na Intimidade* [Rio de Janeiro: Pongetti, 1965], 20). It is important to note that when the couple moved to the

Catete they were already married nine years, which would seem to contradict Cordeiro's reference to the "instável felicidade" [unstable happiness]. Cordeiro also provides a lengthy description of the interior of Cosme Velho (31-33).

43. Lúcia Miguel Pereira, *Estudo Crítico*, 183.
44. Cordeiro, *Machado de Assis*, 31.
45. Ibid., 33.
46. The essay is titled, "Notícia da atual literatura brasileira: Instinto de nacionalidade."
47. Roberto Schwarz develops these ideas in his essay "Duas notas sobre Machado de Assis." *Que horas são? Ensaios* (São Paulo: Companhia das Letras, 1987).
48. Born in Póvoa de Varzim, Eça spent his first childhood years (1845-1855) at the home of his paternal grandparents in Verdemilho, Aveiro. He completed his preparatory studies in Porto at the Real Colégio da Lapa (1855-1866), and in Coimbra, where he studied law, he first lived at Rua do Loureiro 12, and two years later at Rua do Salvador 16. Upon graduating from Coimbra University, Eça settled in his parents' home in central downtown Lisbon, the Rossio 26, 4th floor, today an important landmark in the capital. He moved temporarily during the first half of 1867 to Évora to direct a newspaper, *Districto de Évora*, where he lived at the Travessa dos Grilos. Upon his return from a months-long trip to Egypt and the Middle East, during which he witnesses the inauguration of the Suez Canal in 1869, he is appointed administrator from July 1870 to July 1871 of the town of Leiria: the setting of his first novel *The Crime of Father Amaro* (1st edition 1876). Eça was later nominated consulate in Havana where he lived between 1872 and 1874, during which time he traveled throughout North America. In 1874 he was transferred to Newcastle-on-Tyne where he remained until 1878, when he was moved to Bristol. He married on February 10, 1886, and moved with his wife Emília de Castro into Vashni Lodge, 38 Stoke Hill, and after a vacation in Torquay, the family moved to 23 Ladbroke Gardens, Nothing Hill, London. In 1888, with two children, Eça was nominated consulate in Paris where he remained for the last 12 years of his life (1888-1900). There, the family lived first in Passy (rue Crevaux 5, summer 1889 to 1891), then in Neuilly, rue de Charles Laffitte 32 (1891-1893), and finally on avenue du Roule 38, where Eça died in 1900. When he returned to Portugal, Eça divided his time between his parents in the Rossio and his wife's family in Porto at either of his in-laws' properties: A Granja or A Quinta de Santo Ovídio.
49. The titles alone of some of the biographical and critical work on Eça reveal the focus on settings: Beatriz Berrini's *Portugal de Eça de Queiroz* (Lisboa: Imprensa Nacional-Casa da Moeda, 1984); A. Campos Matos's *Imagens do Portugal Queirosiano* (Lisboa: Imprensa Nacional-Casa da Moeda, 1987) and *Viagem no Portugal de Eça de Queiroz: Roteiro* (Amarante: Fundação Eça de Queiroz, 2000); and Marina Tavares Dias's *A Lisboa de Eça de Queiroz* (Lisboa: Quimera, 2001) focuses on Portugal's capital, one of the most significant settings in Eça's fiction.
50. José Calvet de Magalhães, *Eça de Queirós: A Vida Privada* (Lisboa: Bizâncio, 2000), 207.
51. A. Campos Matos, *Eça de Queiroz-Emília de Castro: Correspondência Epistolar* (Porto: Lello & Irmão, 1995), 735.
52. Ramalho Ortigão (1836-1915), Eça's friend since his years at the Cólegio da Lapa in Porto, is one of the author's closest companions and collaborators. They write *O Mistério da Estrada de Sintra* (1870) together, and the satirical journal *As Farpas* (1871-72), which Ramalho continues on his own until 1888.
53. Guilherme de Castilho, *Eça de Queirós: Correspondência*. 2 vols. (Lisboa: Imprensa Nacional-Casa da Moeda, 1983), 1: 71-72; orig. emphasis.
54. Ibid., 1: 81.
55. Ibid., 1: 80.
56. Virginia Woolf, *A Room of One's Own* (San Diego: Harvest, 1981), 23.
57. Castilho, *Eça de Queirós: Correspondência*, 1: 217.
58. Beatriz Cinatti Batalha Reis, *Eça de Queiroz e Jaime Batalha Reis: Cartas e Recordações do Seu Convívio* (Porto: Lello & Irmão, 1966), 43-44.
59. Ibid., 13.
60. Gonzalo Sobejano, "Introduction," *La Regenta* (Madrid: Castalia, 1981), 8.

61. José María Martínez Cachero, ed., *La Regenta. Obras completas* (Oviedo: Nobel, 2003), 14.

62. Soledad Ortega, *Cartas a Galdós* (Madrid: Revista de Occidente, 1964), 215.

63. *Un siglo con Clarín: Exposición bibliográfica en el centenario de su muerte* (Oviedo: Universidad de Oviedo, 2001), 135.

64. Ibid.

65. Marino Gómez-Santos, *Leopoldo Alas "Clarín," ensayo bio-bibliográfico* (Oviedo: C. S. I. C., 1952), 50.

66. Ibid., 67.

67. Adolfo Posada, *Leopoldo Alas: Clarín* (Oviedo: La Cruz, 1946), 16.

68. Ibid., 18.

69. Ibid., 70.

70. Azorín, "Oviedo. En la biblioteca de "Clarín," *Leopoldo Alas "Clarín,"* ed. José María Martínez Cachero (Madrid: Taurus, 1978), 60.

71. Ibid.

Part One: Furnishing the Novel

The authors of *Quincas Borba*, *The Maias*, and *La Regenta* place a tremendous weight on domestic environments, furniture, and decorative objects. Some of their characters consume themselves with experiencing, creating, and renovating different houses and rooms. Interior spaces clearly play a major role in the plot development and thematic content of these classic works. Because these novels fall within the realist and naturalist traditions, one could simply argue that the obsession with dwelling is typical of this period, and that giving detailed descriptions of settings is characteristic of literary realism. But the rooms and furnishings in these novels far exceed their traditional functions of representing a symbolic background or an important extension of a character's persona, and in fact participate in the narrative discourse. Hence the title of this first part is also to be understood literally. I mean to explore the analogies between the architectural and decorative design of the novels' domestic settings and the way the authors prepare and equip their narratives. Still, I don't claim that the meta-literary questions at stake in the private settings dismiss the narrative function that rooms and furnishings have traditionally had in literature and continue to have in these texts. Clearly the novels also intend to convey through their representation of interiors the contradictions and complexities of their historical contexts and characters. The interior space emerges as the ideal stage for the authors' tragic-comic rendering of their late-nineteenth-century bourgeois societies. The novels, however, also use interiors to experiment with innovative narrative forms and pose philosophical questions that take these novels beyond their recognized place in literary history and articulate new narrative functions for interior spaces. René Wellek claims that Erich Auerbach develops in his classic work *Mimesis* two contradictory conceptions of realism: historicism and existentialism.[1] But perhaps this is in fact not contradictory but a

characteristic phenomenon of literary realism. The authors in my study find
in their interiors a place to conflate history with metaphysical concerns. The
concept of interiors in these novels allows the authors to inquire about the
development of historical time and also question the individual's anguish in
the face of reality's enigmas. Hence they use interior architecture to develop
these two apparently opposing perceptions of realism.

The ideas and intentions that mostly concern the novels are intertwined
with the representation of interior space. Despite a number of significant
differences between the novels, there is no denying that these are all stories
of decline. Noël Valis identifies the descent from the heights as a dominant
movement in *La Regenta* and as representative of the heroine's fall.[2] The
leitmotif of degeneration is also apparent in the mental disintegration of
Machado's protagonist, Rubião, and in the collapse of the aristocratic Maia
family in Eça's story. Furthermore, all three plots are circular, opening and
closing with the same setting, and the endings, although ambiguous, are all
intentionally disturbing. The novels follow a pattern of dissolution by developing a parallel between private and public existences. Although products of
diverse cultural backgrounds, all three authors seem to find in the interior a
useful metaphor to express their societies' malaise. The novels breakdown
character identity, social order, and meaning into pieces, which are then
dispersed inside the interior settings. Hence one can read the interior space as
a frame for the major themes and driving forces in the novels. How do
interiors plot and imagine the sense of decadence, fragmentation, and stagnation so prevalent throughout these stories?

As I hope my analysis will show, the authors hold their countries' complex transatlantic history of greed and betrayal as largely responsible for the
collapse of their societies and for stripping individuals of their sense of self
and community. Like Walter Benjamin's image of the compass in its purple
velvet case, which as he explains emerges as a precious object that produces
the world, the interiors in these novels similarly bring forth a specific past
experience.[3] They become historical metaphors that transport characters and
readers to Brazil, Portugal, and Spain's colonial past, its reliance on slavery
and on a political culture of dominance. The dynamics developed between
the inside and outside of an interior space, and the dialectics of the movement
that takes place inside enclosed settings, imply that the individual and social
reality are interconnected. This indicates that the authors are interested not
only in how collective corrupt histories resonate on private identities, but
also in how a philosophical and artistic self comes into being in light of a
harsh historical and social reality. The novels suggest then that it is not only
the socio-political context but also the experiencing of the interior as such
that changes ontological conceptualizations of the inner self. It is only when
left alone in an interior space of his or her own that individuals become
conscious of their interior world. Thus without the interior setting the con-

cept of interiority would hardly be possible. One cannot be indifferent to one's interior surroundings and still question the meaning of being. In their treatment of interiors the authors begin then to develop a Heideggerean philosophy of existence. Furthermore, because they locate their literary concerns inside these same spaces they are also suggesting that existence is inseparable from narrative. This is why interiors function both in terms of form and content and participate in a parallel development of the novels' structure and themes. Enclosed settings contribute to the unity of the text and prove to be significant metaphors for the writing of the novel. Rooms, objects, decorative styles, and changing senses of private space all furnish the authors with material with which they can articulate their meta-literary inquiries. The writers transform the interior into the site where fiction and reality interact and into a literary space that introduces readers to a troubled milieu.

While similar historical and existential questions preoccupy all three authors, each expresses these with a specific narrative world and technique. Machado de Assis's *Quincas Borba* creates a threshold and opposing tension between interiors and exteriors, which explores how the self and the mind struggle with an existence marked by enslavement. Eça de Queirós's *The Maias* figures into its language of real estate and furnishings important colonial ties, namely the slave trade, while juxtaposing modernity to a sense of stagnation. Leopoldo Alas's *La Regenta* too makes for a powerful commentary on modernity, colonialism, and morality, while its interiors formally duplicate the central narrative project of the search for an inner life. Interiors ultimately contribute to the authors' disturbing reading of their respective societies, in which the moral dissolution and intellectual stagnation seem complete. But these highly pessimistic masterpieces could never have been written without a true love both for the real and fictional worlds that constitute the texts. Thus the critique reinforces the political and social consciousness of the authors. The interiors serve as a crossroads for the meeting of antithetical forces, some disillusioning and others creative. Inside these spaces the progressive and stagnating tendencies and the pessimistic and optimistic possibilities seem to collide. They are the places where fiction meets reality and life greets death.

THE THRESHOLD: THE INS AND OUTS OF *QUINCAS BORBA*

The second of Machado's "modern quintet," a term coined by critic Jorge de Sena to refer to the Brazilian's five late novels, *Quincas Borba* (1891) is undoubtedly one of the author's more powerful works.[4] The exceptional dramatization, the highly unreliable narrator, and the allegorical implications alone make *Quincas Borba* an invaluable modern tragedy, or comedy, and a foundational fiction of the Latin American literary tradition. The novel deals with a wealth of subject matter; it is about the nature and writing of fiction, the imagination, the inner mind, mental illness, social mobility, the nineteenth-century Brazilian bourgeoisie, servitude, nationhood, love, greed, narcissism, and violence. This thematic variety has provoked a number of readings and interpretations from a wide range of theoretical perspectives. The formal challenges, even if these give the false impression to be more subdued than in some of Machado's other work, further make it impossible to settle on one reading of the novel as a whole. António Cândido's classic essay "Esquema de Machado de Assis" (Scheme of Machado de Assis) traces the predominant critical approaches that have tried to unravel Machado's work and identifies the problems that most preoccupied Machado in his fiction. Many of these "obsessões fundamentais de Machado de Assis" [fundamental obsessions of Machado de Assis] materialize in *Quincas Borba*.[5] Enylton de Sá Rego calls *Quincas Borba* a tragic re-writing of the classical comedy because of the many intertextual references to the Lucianic tradition,[6] while Helen Caldwell sees the tragedy in the novel, insisting Rubião is presented from the beginning as a tragic hero. Like all of Machado's great novels, *Quincas Borba* incorporates classical motifs, anticipates modernist techniques, while still retaining important points in common with nineteenth-century Brazilian realist and urban literature. Earl Fitz argues that Machado's *The Posthumous Memoirs of Brás Cubas* should be considered a modernist work written before modernism. The characteristics he defines which make Machado's 1880 novel modern, however, also describe to a large degree *Quincas Borba*.[7] Celso Favaretto claims that *Quincas Borba* reveals the "falsity of modernity and the illusory nature of the new bourgeois ideal of private life."[8] This is clearly an important part of the complex and open project of *Quincas Borba*.

Despite the variety and wealth of subject matter and the complex challenges the novel poses, I would like to argue that indeed a consistent objective emerges: which is to create spaces and forms that reflect on different paradoxes. In *The Posthumous Memoirs* (1880), Brás Cubas claims that the "puxar e empuxar de coisas opostas" [pushing and shoving of opposite things, 1: 608] unsettles his spirits. This movement appears to also disconcert Machado de Assis and his narrative project in *Quincas Borba*. In much of his work, the Brazilian writer is attentive to unresolved forces affecting both individuals and societies, but in *Quincas Borba* he uses the interior setting and its components specifically in order to address the problem of defining lines between antithetical events and emotions. The author relies profoundly on an engagement with the threshold, a place between the inside and the outside, in order to give shape to these paradoxes. The novel develops an important spatial metaphor and dynamic to act out different opposing pressures. Surprisingly, however, little critical work has focused on the crucial motif of interior space in *Quincas Borba*. Cassiana Lacerda Carollo's short essay is one exception. In it she notes that space and objects in the novel act as signs for the disconcerting effects of the newly industrialized Brazilian society. My reading of the novel will focus on these interior spaces and material objects as much more than symbols. The interior architecture in the novel, which proves to be central to any possible interpretation of the text, does not simply function as an allegory of Brazilian modernization and its bourgeoisie's pursuit of a "so-called inner life,"[9] but in fact frames the novel's fundamental questions. Critics emphasize how Machado articulates characters and situations through antithesis and duality. I believe that the juxtaposition of opposites and contradictions in *Quincas Borba* is spatially structured. Machado relies on a dialectics of space between interiors and its margins, or thresholds, to discern some of his characters most intimate experiences and explore a number of his society's most pressing contradictions. The thresholds serve as a crossroads for the encounter of conflicting forces. As we will see the fundamental topics that come up repeatedly throughout Machado's work are closely tied to the interior settings and to the intimate encounters his characters experience in this decisive in-between place.

More often than not *Quincas Borba* is interpreted as the story of Rubião's rise in society. Since a long flashback following the opening scene relates how he becomes the sole heir of the late philosopher Quincas Borba, the tendency is to emphasize the protagonist's desire to advance in class status. The first pages of the novel do indeed introduce Rubião at his social peak, but the time of the story is the brief period he spends in Rio de Janeiro, from 1867 to 1871, during which he quickly descends into abandonment and oblivion. The novel is therefore much more an account of his fall. Like *The Maias* and *La Regenta*, *Quincas Borba* is a novel of decline, dissolution, and fragmentation. The narrative of social advancement is found in Palha and Sofia's disguised story, thus reinforcing Quincas Borba's philosophy of *Humanitism* already developed in *The Posthumous Memoirs of Brás Cubas* where only some get the spoils or the potatoes.[10] It is one's dwelling, or the interior domestic space, that plays out this comic-tragic game and structures this opposition in the novel. The crossing over from one private space to another symbolizes the disillusion in the novel. If at the beginning of the story Rubião has recently moved into his Botafogo mansion, at the end Palha and Sofia find themselves preoccupied with the construction of a new "palacete em Botafogo" [mansion in Botafogo, 1: 797; 258], the fruits of usurping Rubião's position in society. In a short time the couple manages to move down from Santa Teresa to Praia do Flamengo and finally to a new house in Botafogo. Curiously then the couple's rise in social status is figured in a downward geographic move within the Brazilian capital city. Descending Rio's hills toward the seaside neighborhoods paradoxically denotes a rise in class. This doesn't surprise us since this demographic contradiction remains true today. Machado's representation of social climbing is intentionally ironic. Hence a downward movement is most appropriate. He aims to stress what was unfounded and inconsistent in social mobility in Brazil at this time. As historian Emilia Viotti da Costa explains in *The Brazilian Empire*, social progress was possible in the second half of the nineteenth century due to the expansion of the export-import economy, but Brazil's social structure and infamous system of clientele and patronage remained largely intact and dominated social relations. [11] In Machado's stories characters often become wealthy by pure chance, inheriting fortunes, or by profiting from the misfortune of others as in the case of Palha, who not only "adivinhou as falências bancárias," [guessed that there would be bank failures, 1: 667; 47], but also has connections to the coffee trade which we know relied primarily on slave labor. [12] Patterns of domestic relocating are not only an ironic reflection on some of the contradictions inherent in nineteenth-century Brazilian society, but also reinforce a particular movement that relies on reaching a certain threshold that then tips characters over the top or bottom. Major Siqueira and his daughter Dona Tonica also switch homes throughout the narrative, first to "Rua Dous de Dezembro" [Second of December Street] then to a house "na dos Barbonos" [on Bourbon Street], and finally to "Cajueiros, Rua da Princesa" [Cajueiros, Princess Street]. Critics like David Haberly and Helen Caldwell have pointed to how character names in Machado act as ironic subtexts, but in *Quincas Borba* street names tell stories as well. [13] Major Siqueira's streets allude to France's trials in the nineteenth century, Napoleon's victory in Austerlitz and to the Bourbon Restoration (1815-1830). The father and daughter's moves, therefore, connect to Rubião's madness and imagination, since believing himself to be Napoleon III he integrates, as does the city of Rio de Janeiro, French culture into his sense of self. Rubião and Dona Tonica are ultimately joined together in their defeat, since toward the end of the novel, the two characters are utterly vanquished and ironically end up princely. Rubião on "Rua do Príncipe" [Prince Street] and Dona Tonica on "Rua da Princesa" [Princess Street].

This ironic upward-downward movement tied to the characters' residences and symbolizing a turning point for better or for worse in the characters' lives is further characterized by a repeated reference in Machado's writing to climbing and descending the city's hills. This is something Machado's characters often do and not only in *Quincas Borba*. In Santa Teresa the rolling surroundings encourage Rubião to declare himself to Sofia: "No morro, entre o céu e a planície, a alma menos audaciosa era capaz de ir contra um exército inimigo, e destroçá-lo" [Up there on the heights, between the sky and the flatland below, even the least audacious soul was capable of going against an enemy army and destroying it, 1: 669; 51]. Dona Fernanda believes that out in the countryside and on a hilltop she would have a stronger impact on Maria Benedita and says to her: "se você tem ânimo de trepar comigo um pedaço de morro, então é que ficaremos bem" [if you feel like

climbing, come up the hill a bit with me, then it'll be just right, 1: 744; 172].
Clearly the image of climbing up and down the Rio landscape suggests the
possibility of reaching a specific threshold, one that could provide individuals an existential experience. The metaphor is especially important in *Quincas Borba*, where characters not only trek the mountainous landscape but
also cautiously go up and down steps and slanting streets. One could even
attempt to climb the skies. The encounter between a beggar and the heavens
in Chapter XLVI epitomizes this upward and downward game that governs
the tensions in the novel:

> Olhavam-se numa espécie de jôgo do siso, com certo ar de majestades rivais e
> tranqüilas, sem arrogância, nem baixeza, como se o mendigo dissesse ao céu:
> —Afinal, não me hás de cair em cima.
> E o céu:
> —Nem tu me hás de escalar.
>
> [They looked at each other in a kind of judgment game, with a certain air of
> rival and tranquil majesties, without haughtiness or wretchedness, as if the
> beggar were saying to the sky:
> —Well, you won't be falling on me.
> And the sky:
> —And you won't be climbing up me, 1: 676; 62.]

The vast distance between the celestial skies and the proud beggar would
seem to suggest an impossibility of finding a threshold or place in between.
But the irony lies in the fact that theoretically one should be able to climb his
or her way up to heaven. The up and down movement is Machado's way of
representing how social mobility and stagnation are intertwined because
what is done can easily be undone. As we will see this metaphor takes a
spatial shape in the threshold to an interior space and reinforces the contradictions that mattered to the author: those found in Brazilian society, in the
passage of time, in personal ambition, and in the conflict between Europe
and America.

The motif, as represented in Palha and Sofia's residential moves, suggests
a paradoxical social progression since descending the *morros* toward the
seaside neighborhoods denotes a rise in class status. If *Humanitism* parodies
the positivist world view, then this ironic twist points to the highly intricate
and unjust social changes that take place in Imperial Brazil. The movement
also appears to signal the passage of time. Critics often observe that time
comes full circle in Machado's narratives. But perhaps more than circling,
time is in fact measured by this continuous up and down shift that pulls and
tugs away at life. At the beginning of the story, in Barbacena, Rubião learns
that he has been declared heir to Quincas Borba's fortune and with the
excitement "Ia assim, descendo e subindo as ruas da cidade" [He went along

like that, up and down the streets of the town, 1: 653; 24]. Back in his native city at the end of the novel and approaching his death, Rubião wanders disoriented on the streets of Barbacena: "levantava-se e punha-se outra vez a descer e subir ladeiras" [he would wake up immediately and start going up and down the hill again, 1: 803; 268]. Existence seems measured by the intensity of this tug of rope, and as Rubião draws near the end of his life he climbs up and down evermore anxiously.

This important trope played out in the exterior or natural world finds a counterpart in the interior settings in the novel. Inside their homes and rooms, characters switch continuously from a sitting or horizontal position to a standing one. The changes between standing and horizontal positions occur during crucial dialogues and encounters between characters. The opening flashback is set mostly in the philosopher's bedchamber, where throughout the whole dialogue between Quincas Borba, the philosopher, and his pupil, Rubião, while one is standing the other is lying or sitting down. If one changes to a standing position, the other sits down. After the Santa Teresa dinner party Sofia and Palha discuss their impressions of their guests and constantly switch places. In both these scenes the movement stresses the tension between the characters. A similar interaction occurs during the private conversation between Dona Fernanda and Teófilo. But here, when the husband sits or stands the wife does the same. Teófilo "estava sentado em um canapé" [was on a settee] and "Ao pé dele, sentada também" [Next to him, also sitting] is Dona Fernanda (1: 786; 241). In this case the movement underlines a sense of harmony in the relationship. This dynamic takes place in exterior and interior settings, suggesting that there are paradoxes inherent both in Brazil's social structures that parallel those found in human relations. In other words, Brazil's system of clientele and patronage, which underscores the problematic of social mobility, materializes in a struggle for power between characters. Once again both mobility and stagnation regulate this image. In this way, Machado rewrites the myth of Sisyphus and creates a form with which to reach a deeper understanding of the self and of the social. This is clearly one of the *"relações* e *formas"* [relations and forms] that Roberto Schwarz claims Machado searches for in order to explore Brazilian reality.[14] Furthermore, the idea of making and unmaking progress foreshadows Tancredi's famous line in Giuseppe Tomasi di Lampedusa's *The Leopard* (1958), in which he tells his uncle: "If we want things to stay as they are, things will have to change."[15] These emblematic words epitomize a quintessential nineteenth-century historical problem and Machado's worldview, but what is unique is that the author chooses to structure this dilemma with the interior space.

The metaphor exists on an interior and exterior level, refers to tensions governing human and social relations, and embodies the encounter between subjective and objective perspectives on reality. In other words, this threshold mediates the contradictions that surface when an individual's interiority encounters the physical surroundings. To govern these different tensions Machado places his characters on the frontier between the interior and the exterior of private spaces. There are numerous scenes where characters and narrators stand at the door and look in, hesitate, turn back or venture inside. Sofia, the novel's female protagonist, often roams about these in-between places, and it is important to observe her wanderings more carefully, but first I would like to draw a connection between Machado's threshold and the one that surfaces in Homer's *Odyssey*. Not only did classical texts have a great influence on Machado's writing but also in depicting Sofia the author makes a number of allusions to Penelope, albeit ironically, which readily make this analogy noteworthy for my analysis. In fact one could argue that the threshold of Homeric houses constitutes both the foundation of an architectural structure and the beginning of a tradition of a metaphor. E. V. Rieu, translator of Homer's epic, explains in a footnote that between "rooms in Homeric houses there was a wooden or stone 'threshold,' a raised structure into which the door jambs were fixed."[16] The original threshold was tangible and material, a sill of wood or stone forming the bottom of a doorway, which was crossed when entering a house or room. Today the threshold is a spatial detail that connotes a number of abstract ideas; it is the limit, the beginning, the end, an obstacle, and a turning point. The threshold opens and encloses, protects and makes vulnerable, and while it confines the individual to a space it also marks the point of a possible transgression. Certain scenes in the *Odyssey* of emotional pressure and ambivalence bring this architectural trait into focus and clarify some of these ideas. When Medon tells Penelope about her Suitors' ensuing plan to assassinate Telemachus, she is left speechless and in tears:

> Penelope was overwhelmed by the anguish that racked her. She could not even bear to sit on one of the many chairs in her apartments, but sank down on the threshold of her lovely room, weeping bitterly, while all the maids of her household, young and old, stood round her sobbing.[17]

Penelope expresses indecision and anxiety while positioned in this strategic place. On the one hand the threshold gives urgency to the problems she is facing by centering her in this in-between place, but on the other hand it is also an advantageous position allowing her irresolution to continue. This scene takes place quite early in the epic, yet the significant return home of Odysseus toward the concluding events also makes use of this building feature. Disguised as a beggar, Odysseus enters his own house where Telemachus and the Suitors share food with him. Odysseus transforms the threshold of his home into a beneficial but ambiguous place that will also serve as the catalyst for his final attack on the Suitors. Odysseus sits on the threshold of his house before entering and taking the final step of his return home. He first "sat down on the ash-wood threshold just inside the door, with his back against a pillar of cypress smoothed by some carpenter long ago and expertly trued to the line."[18] Later Odysseus regains "his seat on the threshold without having to pay for his experiment with the Suitors."[19] Finally, he "went back to the threshold, where he sat down, dropped his bulging bag, and addressed the Suitors."[20] The threshold allows Odysseus entry and return, it both opens and closes worlds and past experiences for him, and yet it is also what pushes him over the edge; it is clearly a place of reflection, uncertainty, and action. It is the transition from past to future.

Like Penelope and Odysseus, Sofia depends on the threshold to interrogate her deeper feelings without necessarily having to act upon them. On several occasions Sofia wanders between her garden and the inside of her house feeling "Tédio por dentro e por fora" [Tedium inside and out, 1: 774; 222]. The day after Rubião declares his love to her in Santa Teresa, Sofia, alone and lost in thought "foi sentar-se à porta de casa, no jardim...Não estava bem em si nem fora de si, nem com Deus nem com o diabo" [went to sit in the garden by the door of the house...She didn't feel right or wrong, either with God or with the devil, 1: 684; 74]. She then goes back and forth between the outside, where she sees Carlos Maria pass, and the inside of her home. Sofia's emotions are disturbed: "Tudo a aborrecia, plantas, móveis, uma cigarra que cantava, um rumor de vozes, na rua, outro de pratos, em casa, o andar das escravas, e até um pobre preto velho que, em frente à casa dela, trepava com dificuldade um pedaço de morro" [Everything was bothering her: plants, furniture, a cicada that was singing, the sound of voices in the street, another of dishes in the house, the coming and going of the slave girls, and even a poor old black man across from her house who was having trouble climbing up a section of the hill, 1: 684; 75]. Sofia's extremely important reflections here switch very precisely between an exterior and an interior element. Sitting between worlds or possible life choices, and while apparently contemplating adultery [implied by the fact that Carlos Maria walks by], Sofia faces irreconcilable pressures. In her troubled mind it is impossible to separate the interior from the exterior. Furthermore, with the "escravas" [slave girls] and the "pobre preto" [poor black man], slavery is present both in the interior and exterior worlds. Not surprisingly we find the old man futilely trying to climb up a hill. This all suggests that the Brazilian social condition is inseparable from the construction of the self and her desire, Carlos Maria, emerges together with these other individuals that occupy her space. The threshold allows slavery and adultery to simultaneously penetrate Sofia's mind. On a different occasion Sofia is again lost in her romantic thoughts, and in her bed about to fall asleep, she is caught in that intermediate state when one is neither conscious nor unconscious. At this very moment, a slave woman comes into her bedroom with some soup. The servant penetrates Sofia's interiority by entering the room exactly at this point as if becoming part of her subconscious. Sofia's dilemmas concern not only her adulterous desires but are also intertwined with society's contradictions, slavery being the foremost of these. Besides telling us that the individual is inseparable from the social reality, the author suggests that adultery is also tied to slavery.

The threshold serves then to interrupt the narrative and bring forth what critic John Gledson has called significant "uncomfortable truths."[21] The scenes involving Sofia's inner spaces and thoughts suggest that a form of interdependence exists between adultery and slavery. It is possible to trace such a relation throughout the novel both on the level of imagery and on the level of plot. Interestingly this connection between national histories and adulterated love affairs not only emerges in *Quincas Borba*, but also in *La Regenta* and *The Maias*. Hence the well-known trope of adultery, so characteristic of the literary period, takes on a unique role in these Spanish and Portuguese novelistic traditions. Unlike in Brazil where slavery is part of the quotidian, in Spain and Portugal slavery is nonetheless tied to the fabric of society because of the interaction between these countries and their colonies. Still, all three texts refer to slavery in a similar fashion: rarely and indirectly. These allusions, however, are powerful in their discreetness and haunting force. The brief but significant references carefully associate slavery and the slave trade to important events in the plot that build on the romantic affairs so central to the stories. All three novels link the private adulterous thoughts of the characters to certain lingering remnants of their nation's past. The adultery plot in the narratives suggests that the new private self is unconsciously tied to a history of greed and violence. The inner desires of these bourgeois characters involuntarily repeat patterns of human and social interaction that a history of slavery has set in place.

Tony Tanner's classic study *Adultery in the Novel: Contract and Transgression* argues that the infidelity motif serves to challenge the social order and to represent the disintegration of bourgeois society. Elizabeth Amann takes this dominant line of thought of the adultery novel in a different direction in *Importing* Madame Bovary: *The Politics of Adultery*. Her comparative study claims that the complex and allusive Iberian rewritings of Flaubert's novel, Eça de Queirós's *Cousin Bazilio* and Clarín's *La Regenta*, in fact turn to adultery in order to consolidate the conventional middle-class order. Perhaps opposite interpretations of the trope are possible and even compatible. But what becomes clear is that by connecting colonial history with the adultery motif, Clarín's, Machado's, and both of Eça's novels, *Cousin Bazilio* and *The Maias*, are also suggesting that adultery alone can neither reinforce nor break down a social or political order. Instead, the new interior search for self-understanding, which tends to involve adulterous private desires, proves to be dependent on external and historical forces that pull characters in multiple directions. But ultimately the trope functions both as a self-reflection and as a meta-reflexive tool, since the authors, conscious of the trope's archetypical status, borrow it to think about how social and political specificity influences the making of narrative. The connection between adultery and slavery in *Quincas Borba* does not imply that the two are the same or that they are equally consequential, but instead shows that the contradictions at the core of each are analogous. Moreover, the narrative is more interested in framing possibilities to reflect on these and other inconsistencies, which is why characters in the novel spend a lot more time thinking about adultery than consummating it. The space for reflection is the in-between realm that Machado ingeniously furnishes in his narrative.

In Machado's fiction the mediation between a character's interior emotions and his or her exterior reality usually involves a garden, another of the author's architectural thresholds. Machado's characters are often near or looking out at the garden, as if to suggest that their thoughts, subconscious, and inner worlds, are composed of both intellectual insights and sensory perceptions. The exterior or natural world represents in this case a unique New World landscape while the interior world is characterized by sitting-rooms populated with imported furnishings and decorative objects. With nineteenth-century urbanization in Brazil, the upper class and rising middle class begin to replace colonial style pieces with European furniture, wallpaper, lamps, and other objects, imported primarily from France and England. In *Quincas Borba* these interiors appear in constant and close contact to their gardens outside. Therefore, Machado is also commenting on the interaction between Europe and America, pointing to the irreconcilable contradiction that exists in nineteenth-century Brazilian society between being both a European Empire and a New World colony. If exterior and interior worlds stage the conflict between New World and Europe, then the garden is a territory in the middle, and it is not by chance that the garden serves as the setting for important climactic events in the novel. During the brief but significant Dutch occupation of northeastern Brazil (1624-1654), Europeans first established gardens there with the objective of containing all the originality of Brazil's flora, defining and classifying the unknown. A sort of microcosm that encloses all the parts of the New World, the garden becomes thus American in content and European in form. Machado's gardens are not interested in drawing boundaries around the autochthonous, but in creating a path that leads characters and readers from a known to an unknown cultural setting, and from one level of understanding or feeling to another. This is why when we find Sofia and Rubião in these threshold areas undergoing perception-changing experiences they are often roaming about. They hardly ever stand still. This back and forth is not merely symbolic of a character's fickleness, but is indicative of a search for alternative ontological ways of escape. We have seen that the movement of Machado's characters, be it outside or inside their homes and rooms, is not arbitrary. Places such as gardens, porches, and windowsills are openings and closings which act as vehicles to different social or psychological realities. By giving both form and content to this threshold Machado is also confronting his own narrative work, which one could argue also reveals a struggle between an American content and a European form. Silviano Santiago coins the theoretical term the "space in-between" to define the complex place of Latin American culture: a realm of tension between originality and dependency where the Brazilian critic claims "se realiza o ritual antropófago da literatura latino-americana" [the anthropophagous ritual of Latin American discourse is constructed]. [22] Machado's threshold already prefigures this difficult abstract location where creativity takes place.

The encounter between the exterior and the interior is therefore also a debate Machado maintains between the European and the Brazilian experiences and traditions and their influence in defining the self and the nation. Machado often writes about how a person is divided between his or her interior and exterior self. [23] One of Machado's most famous essays, "O instinto de nacionalidade" [An instinct of nationality] suggests that a more profound interpretation of the self or of the national or local elements requires looking deep inside oneself. [24] In *Quincas Borba*, characters, the narrator, and the story of the novel itself look inward and outward to reflect on their possible identities. As we will see later in *La Regenta*, a similar movement inward is also part of the development of the plot and of the narrative perspective. In Machado's novel, this penetration is symbolized in the act of seeing, which is important in much of the author's writing. Vision is one of the keys to understanding *Quincas Borba* although it is also framed ironically. Characters continually close their eyes to look inside themselves or stand by windows and look outward onto nature in order to attain a deeper understanding of their inner selves. The novel draws on these various ironic interactions between interior and exterior creating the important threshold where contradictions can play themselves out, and as we shall see, where Machado himself can contemplate the making of his novel.

If the windowsill represents something like the self or the society out on a limb, the point of reflection, instability but also possibility, then the inside of the room attempts to center the individual and give meaning and order to the narrative. This is why the middle of a space is as important in Machado's interiors as are the openings and closings. At key moments, characters stand in the center of a room in an attempt to grasp their reality. At the beginning of the story, Rubião "foi sentar-se no *pouf*, ao centro da sala" [went over to sit down on the ottoman in the center of the room, 1: 642; 7], and later "deixou-se estar na sala, no *pouf* central, olhando" [he sat there on the couch in the parlor watching, 1: 694; 90-91]. When Teófilo says goodbye to his books he is "Parado no centro" [Standing in the middle] of the room (1: 791;

247). In Sofia's frustration with Carlos Maria she considers that he has left her all alone "no meio do salão" [in the middle of the ballroom, 1: 775; 222]. Holding Sofia's letter to Carlos Maria in his hands Rubião "pára no meio da sala" [stands in the center of the room, 1: 724; 139]. In all of these examples the centrality comments significantly on the imbalance of a character's feelings or thoughts. The inner setting stands for the totality of their fragile reality. If at the edge of the room one encounters incompatibilities and points of contention then this interior focal point ought to ground characters and readers alike. Instead it leaves them feeling uncertain. This irony is present on the meta-fictional level as well. As we have seen Machado's architectural features function not only to bring up important themes but also to furnish the narrative. The interior space also attempts to give centrality to the narrative as a whole by framing the complexity of time and place in the novel. Machado, like Johannes Vermeer in *Woman in Blue*, uses a room to question the meaning of existence and the sense of narrative creativity.

The opening Botafogo sitting-room sets the stage for most of the initial third of the novel, or the first twenty hours of the story. The salon leads us inside Rubião's thoughts and into another text, a long flashback. The rest of the novel traces a period of a couple of years during which the narrator abandons Rubião at times and focuses on other characters and events. The narrative thus starts with a personal view of Rubião's intimate space, past, and mind, and moves toward other characters' perspectives on the protagonist. During the first third of the novel the reader explores Rubião's interiority from within, while in the latter part of the narrative the reader feels more as a guest coming in from the outside. Since the novel studies both a mind and a society, it needs an internal and external point of view. The form of the novel then places the reader on a similar threshold as its characters. Readers also juggle internal and external perspectives and possibilities. Furthermore, the one long day that opens the novel is not any more or less intense than the three to four years that follow. Both the moment of reflection, symbolized in this frozen-in-time endless day which both brings back memories and envisions the future, and the unperceived passage of time, Rubião's years in Rio, are equally necessary to make sense of reality and of one's inner spirit. The novel begins with the flashback and with Rubião, who in his sitting-room "Cotejava o passado com o presente" [was comparing the past to the present, 1: 641; 5]. The narrative blends in this way the sense of place with the sense of time. In fact many of Machado's characters typically confound time periods, and equally important to their reflections on time, the past or the future, is the room where they are situated. The literary interior fuses the past, present, and future and becomes a concept, or in other words, an understanding of time, which for Machado the narrative genre makes possible.

The idea that an interior can raise questions about narrative time and space is one Machado already contemplated in his first novel and developed throughout his writing. The introduction of Rubião and the Botafogo salon recalls Machado's first novel, *Ressurreição* (*Resurrection* 1872). The novels have parallel beginnings that show how the setting of a story conveys both a real space and time period together with a more abstract time and place: the textual place of the narrative project. To a certain degree, *Quincas Borba* rewrites some of the problems set up originally in *Ressurreição*. Like *Quincas Borba*, Machado's first novel is also about impossibility and incompatibility, and both Félix and Rubião are incapable of happiness, albeit for different reasons. There are interesting similarities and points of comparison between the introductions of the two main characters. Both novels begin with the protagonist contemplating the exterior world, specifically the sky and the sea, from an interior space, in the two cases an upper-class domestic environment. As many of Machado's characters, Félix and Rubião can devote themselves exclusively to contemplation thanks to unexpected inheritances. While in *Ressurreição* the narrator's point of view is from the future and the narration begins with a flashback, which only ends with the last chapter of the novel, in *Quincas Borba* a flashback follows the opening scene. Therefore, while Félix "entregue à contemplação interior" [given in to interior contemplation] was "como se interrogasse o futuro ou revolvesse o passado" [as if he interrogated the future or turned the past over in his mind, 1: 115], Rubião, as I pointed out earlier, was contemplating the past with the present. These different perspectives on time have the similar effect of confounding the past, present, and future in the salon where the reader meets the characters. The interior space thus articulates the complexity of real and narrative time. On the meta-fictional level then interiors function to create a simultaneous inhabiting of time and space. By suggesting that the narrative experience is also a form of dwelling, Machado understands being in relation to the poetic experience, a philosophical perspective he shares with Bachelard and Heidegger.

Although Machado's characters are centered in their rooms they find themselves insecure. The author seems to say that a center of existence and a balance of mind are in fact nonexistent. This is reinforced by Machado's recurring thematic interest in madness. After his best-known short-story, "O alienista" (The psychiatrist), *Quincas Borba* is probably the narrative that more directly deals with the madness leitmotif. Machado's fiction, while studying the various degrees and depths of a character's intellect, often suggests that all minds are on the brink of madness. Ultimately characters (and authors and readers) are unsuccessful at finding a center in their interiors, and it slowly becomes clear that the margins of an interior space have more at stake. These margins are another threshold that the author uses as a form of interrogation and discovery. In *Quincas Borba*, although Rubião is the official character to go mad, many others tread the fine line between sanity and madness. Sofia also talks to inanimate objects and listens attentively to a long conversation between two of her garden's roses. It seems Carlos Maria would be far less surprised than Rubião if someone decided to crown him emperor: "Se um dia acordasse imperador, só se admiraria da demora do ministério em vir cumprimentá-lo" [If he woke up emperor one day he would only be surprised at how long it had taken for the position to have come his way, 1: 702; 103]. Furthermore, Machado's characters jump in and out of sanity and in and out of being conscious of their mental state. Brás explains that "Quincas Borba não só estava louco, mas sabia que estava louco" [Quincas Borba was not only mad, but he knew that he was mad, 1: 636; 202]. All characters are somewhat mad at some point or another, and they wander, either back and forth or up and down, between these different states of mind. Again the interior is central for Machado's exploration of this existential experience. The author connects madness to interiors by figuratively situating on the periphery of a room the brink of madness.

The coming into a specific interior territory clearly articulates the problem of defining and locating madness. In chapter CLXXI, Rubião surprises Carlos Maria and Maria Benedita with an unexpected visit. This is an important incident that once again demonstrates how Machado's spatial configurations give shape to his thematic concerns. In this scene the narrator focuses a lot of attention on the characters' movements in and out of the salon, and especially on Rubião's. The protagonist first peeks into the newlyweds' sitting-room: "A varanda, que comunicava para a sala, por três portas, tinha uma destas aberta. Dali viera a voz; dali espiava e ria a cabeça de Rubião" [The veranda, which was accessible from the living room by three doors, had one of them open, 1: 784; 237]. Rubião is not warmly welcomed by the couple and is apparently the mad one in the scene, yet he interrupts the couple at a decisive moment. His madness invades an interior space that is in fact saturated with the couple's own absurd, if not mad relationship. Rubião clearly disturbs their peace, reminding them not only of the fragility of their own mental state but also of their indifference towards others. Unsurprisingly then Carlos Maria tries to banish him quickly from the room, but Rubião attempts to stay inside as long as possible, and even when exiled to the veranda "não foi tão pronto" [he wasn't all that ready, 1: 785; 238]. Carlos Maria eventually closes the door on his guest's face and stands with Maria Benedita: "Da vidraça miravam o nosso amigo" [They were watching our friend from the window, 1: 785; 238]. While they try hard to keep out the mad forces, they actually lock themselves up inside their own delusional reading of love and understanding of one another. With these spatial dynamics the author not only gives aesthetic form to different variants of madness but also asks how we define or locate illogical and unjust actions.

The veranda acts as the stepping ground onto the interior space where madness resides. The open windows and doors extend out to the balcony and garden, which serves once again as a frontier area. In relation to madness then the garden represents a gray realm where characters are only half mad. This is clear in the scene where Sofia and Rubião sit together by the window looking out onto her garden. Sofia's roses outside her window inspire her and Rubião's imagination to the point of delusion. Here the characters are almost mad, and only once they move inside their minds and inside her house, or the enclosed interior space, does their delusion seem total. The architectural representation in the novel suggests that mad spirits inhabit interiors surrounded by walls. The narrator often makes comparisons between Sofia and Rubião's thoughts and closed spaces. As noted earlier Sofia's imagination consistently traps her inside different rooms. Rubião's servant claims that his master often converses with the walls during his mad crises. In fact Rubião's imagination is frequently full of a wide variety of walls, halls, corridors, and rooms. Hence interiors serve likewise to include and stage the scenario of madness.

If on the one hand interiors give a sense of structure to madness, mental illness on the other hand frames the narrative project. As we have seen Machado not only uses the representation of interior space in connection with his thematic concerns but he is also interested in linking interiors to the genesis of his narratives. Quincas Borba, the philosopher, dies mad twice; first at the end of Machado's *The Posthumous Memoirs of Brás Cubas* and a second time at the beginning of *Quincas Borba*. Madness links one aesthetic project to another and synchronizes the latter, since Rubião returns at the end of the novel to Barbacena to follow in his master's footsteps. Madness ironically emerges as a rational and cyclical experience that can give continuity to art. For Machado madness is tied to artistic form because, like art, madness is something in between fiction and reality. The enclosed space is this threshold that functions to explore both the genesis of art and the transformations of the mind. Machado does not put forth a philosophical or scientific explanation for the mysteries of thought and of our imagination, but instead creates an aesthetic and architectural solution to explore its many facets.

Furthermore, the scene in Carlos Maria's house also points to another important question in the novel that concerns the dividing line between the private and public involvement with illogical forces: whether these are present in individuals or in a society. If in chapter CLXXI Rubião invades the privacy of the young couple, he also reminds them of their own private delicate affairs and their indifference toward the suffering of others or toward the public good. It becomes clear throughout the novel that Rubião's troubles are also to a certain degree the problems of his fellow characters, of a society, and even of a nation. This is why Dona Fernanda feels personally responsible to help Rubião. Her kindness is an act of public service. But Dona Fernanda is an exception in the world of Machado's characters. As in *La Regenta* and *The Maias*, there are no defining lines between public and private in *Quincas Borba*; the individual is not capable of escaping the public pressures of contemporary society and in turn society has no respect or room for one's private self. The structural transformation of the public space, expertly traced by Jürgen Habermas, results in the bourgeois institutionalization of a sense of privacy turned outward toward an audience, which explains why the private salon begins to serve society.[25] These dynamics are played out on an ironic level in Machado's novel most clearly in how Rubião hosts in his salon an increasing number of dinner guests. These parasites slowly begin to invade and plunder his home in Botafogo as they grow in number and the meals in frequency. They gradually start to penetrate the more private parts of the house and they become increasingly comfortable and at ease. When Palha moves Rubião to a new home, his regular household friends "receberam a notícia da mudança como um decreto de exílio" [received the news of the move as a decree of exile] because everything in the old dwelling "fazia parte deles" [had been part of them, 1: 779; 229]. Rubião's private interiors are transformed into a public stage where the circus of society meets and performs. To further complicate and ironize these scenes, the narrator describes how often even when the host is not present the show goes on. Rubião is absent from many of these meetings, busy with other affairs, and his guests still gather nonetheless to eat, drink, and smoke away his inheritance. The visitors not only invade Rubião's privacy but his absence during their debacles further implies that they rob him of the possibility and of a room for his private self to be in this world. These inconsistencies suggest that the public structures in place are unfit to cope with people's intricate private experiences. And at the same time, as Carlos Maria and other self-centered characters make clear, most individuals are too selfish to care about public concerns.

Quincas Borba is a novel then that anticipates modern day sociological ideas of private and public space. According to Richard Sennett in *The Fall of Public Man* (1974), the nineteenth-century witnesses a new sense of privacy tied to the nuclear family that attempts to create a morally superior space separate from the corrupt public dominion. In the twentieth century, on the other hand, Sennett claims people begin to view interiority as an end in itself. He writes: "We have tried to make the act of being in private, alone with ourselves and with family and intimate friends, an end in itself."[26] In Machado's novel, as in *La Regenta* and *The Maias*, interiors and homes tend to mirror the decadent world outside. The interiors in these novels are made public not only by a variety of invasions of privacy but also by reflecting the immorality of both the public and private realms. Although privacy sometimes provides a place for escape, these interiors are unable to separate themselves from the larger corrupt society and hence are not capable of affording a true sense of independence to the individual from the outside world. The novelistic spaces fail at providing the moral retreat desired in the nineteenth century and begin to display the contradictions that develop in the twentieth century in our sense of privacy and interiority. In the novels there is a clear incompatibility between the private feelings of the characters and the public way of life. In the Brazilian, Spanish, and Portuguese societies of this time, the borders between public and private are unclear both in the exterior world and in the characters' inner selves. The modernity of these narratives is evident not only in the turn toward the individual's search for interiority, but also in their contemporary sociological reading of the impossibility of separating the private from the public. That is, they purposely want to make their readers and societies uneasy with their protagonists' private crises. These novels go beyond the realist talent of invading and making public the mundane private world of bourgeois characters. The objective of these late-realist texts in exposing the private thoughts, fears, and feelings of their vulnerable characters is also to reveal how these are incompatible with the public structure. The concern for interior life clashes and is at the same time inseparably connected to the anachronistic public forms in place in society. Thus the novels already begin to argue that private stories should be of public concern, a very contemporary, twentieth-century problematic discussed widely in theoretical studies on social relations in urban environments.

The same way that no dividing line exists between the private and the public, interior spaces and narrative are also inexorably tied together. The authors of *Quincas Borba*, *The Maias*, and *La Regenta* reveal an understanding of the parallel historical development in narrative and privacy because they use the interior domestic space to comment on the development of their novels. Drawing on Ian Watt's thesis in *The Rise of the Novel* Peter Brooks explains in *Body Work* that the "rise of the novel is closely tied to the rise of the idea of privacy" and he asks an important question.[27] Was it because privacy characterized the reading and writing of novels that private life is from the beginning the novel's subject matter as well? Or was it the other way around: "the need to explore the relatively new concept of private experience entailed the invention of the novel."[28] Machado, Eça, and Clarín suggest no clear answer exists to Brooks's inquiry, and that the turn toward privacy is in fact a condition inseparable both from art and the social make-up. The intimate atmosphere where the interior search takes place is full of significant exterior pressures, contemporary and historical, human and material. The interior space in these novels emerges as a place that acts out the contradictions challenging the development of the self and of society. Many social paradoxes seem to tie into one's interiority, so that while traditional realist narrative focuses on interiors to highlight the new bourgeois material interests, these novels use the intimate dwelling space to underscore modern concerns about the self's growing alienation, drawing attention to the need of a public and moral response to the decay of the social order. As we have seen Machado's portrayal of thresholds is a narrative technique that allows him to illustrate how one's interiority is not an isolated concept, but a complex and

fragile phenomenon oscillating between the different understandings we
have of our mind, imagination, and social community. The domestic interior
in *Quincas Borba* frames the key image of the threshold as a place for
reflection and interruptions. This leitmotif engages with formal concerns and
with questions of plot. The ups and downs and ins and outs that I have
highlighted above allow the novel to confront a number of unresolved tensions and connect national histories to individual identities. This spatial form
generates specific disturbances on the verge of manifesting themselves and
gives readers access to the intricacies of Machado's characters and narrative
worlds.

MOVABLES AND IMMOVABLES: THE LEGEND OF *THE MAIAS*

Eça de Queirós's verbose descriptions of interior settings have more in common with Clarín's long expressive digressions than with Machado's minimalist style in portraying interior spaces. Still, the interior in all three novels
is not, as I have mentioned earlier, merely a semantically rich background
setting, but a central technique framing the novelistic project. Eça draws on
an abundance of furnishings and lavish interior spaces to give form to specific socio-political preoccupations. A prolific furnisher of his fiction, Eça
makes interior spaces central to his most ambitious depiction of nineteenth-
century Portugal, *The Maias* (1888). As *Quincas Borba* and *La Regenta*,
Eça's classic family narrative is also simultaneously comic and tragic. *The
Maias* paints a portrait of an utterly stagnated society filled with mostly
failed characters, but the masterpiece is much more than a powerful realist-
naturalist rendering of this time period. Although many critics have focused
on the plot's decadent and tragic turn, pessimism is not at the core of the
narrative.[29] More important in the novel than what Alexander Coleman calls
Eça's "historical pessimism with regard to Portugal's irredeemable decadence" is the opposition set up between immobility and dynamism.[30] Isabel
Pires de Lima argues in her invaluable work *As Máscaras do Desengano*
(Deceitful Masks) that this central opposition structures the process of disillusionment in the novel.[31] In another study, Pires de Lima adds that "Pensar
Portugal é, pois, em *Os Maias*, tomar consciência de um tempo português
presa do imobilismo" [To think Portugal in *The Mais* is therefore to be
conscious of a Portuguese time prisoner to immobility].[32] My thesis elaborates on this insight by further demonstrating how Eça frames the complexities of this dialectic with homes and furnishings.

Eça's novel, satiated with elaborate interior settings and furnishings, has
unsurprisingly received more critical attention than Machado's with regard to
the topic of domestic interiors, but by no means enough. Odete R. G. de
Barros Martins's study is one of the few to focus on the significance of the

arrangement of interiors and their relation to the characters. Carlos's consulting rooms and Ega's Vila Balzac, to borrow the critic's examples, reveal much more, however, than the protagonists' failed and false projects and their unconscious search for love. Interiors serve as the foundation for both the construction and collapse of the self and of the novel. What is *The Maias* if not the story of homes and interior decorating? Elaborate architectural and interior descriptions make up a large part of the narrative content, and the characters are constantly preoccupied with touching, touring, experiencing, and remodeling their interior space. Narrators and characters consume themselves and the narrative with the details and intricacies of spaces and things. The profusion of interiors in *The Maias* does not, however, reduce the subtle and multifaceted role that rooms and furnishings play in the novel. Eça's rich descriptions of settings have not only important symbolic functions but also significant formal purposes.

I believe that homes and interiors are the most fundamental structuring dynamic in the novel. The decadent city residence of the Maia family, Ramalhete, opens and closes the circular plot. The exposition introduces the artistic project of remodeling and re-inhabiting the mansion and establishes from the onset two narrative lines: one follows the destinies of homes, while the other tracks the characters' lives. Redecorating Ramalhete is tantamount to the writing of *The Maias*. The narrative project can thus be read as an attempt at renovation. Once again the link between writing and the adorning of one's surroundings is reinforced. In other words Portuguese society, history, and characters can best be read and written via the art of a space: its fixtures, tones, and design. Ramalhete contains the story's main time line as well, the years 1875 to 1877 when old Afonso da Maia returns with his grandson, Carlos da Maia, to live in Lisbon. The novel is the story of the two years Ramalhete is inhabited. Carlos is correct on various levels to say at the end of the novel: "É curioso! Só vivi dois anos nesta casa, e é nela que me parece estar metida a minha vida inteira!" [It's odd, you know, I only spent two years in this house, and yet it seems to contain my whole life, 714; 622]. Eça's character Carlos da Maia is wholly contained inside Ramalhete, namely his life as a fictional character does not exceed the fictional life of the house. Hence, in the creation of fiction, spatial configurations are as important as character portrayal. If the Lisbon mansion houses the main storyline, additional homes take the reader down other narrative paths. The Toca, Ega's Vila Balzac, the Santa Olávia estate in the Douro valley, Maria Eduarda's first floor on the Rua de São Francisco all stage the different acts of the comic-tragic play that is the novel. Dwellings enclose important episodes in the narrative and in a character's life. Yet their role is not restricted to that of a passive background; they also become anthropomorphous agents. Homes and furnishings have histories, fates, feelings, and undergo transformations just as the human characters.

Residences are closely tied to the development of the characters. For example, Carlos's crucial intellectual formation is entirely enclosed in his house in Coimbra. This "linda casa em Celas, isolada, com graças de *cottage inglês*" [lovely, secluded little house in Celas, as pretty as an English cottage] reflects an important chapter of the protagonist's life (89; 75). Carlos, unlike his cousin Eusebiozinho, who receives "uma educação à portuguesa" [a Portuguese upbringing], is taught from a young age by an English tutor to be physically active and interact with the natural world (78; 65). Afonso opts for this imported style of education, known by its opponents as "a aberração inglesa" [the English aberration, 206; 179], in hopes his grandson will grow up and be "útil ao seu país" [useful to his country, 88; 74]. In Coimbra, Carlos chooses the medical profession exactly because as Afonso explains: "Num país em que a ocupação geral é estar doente, o maior serviço patriótico é incontestavelmente saber curar" [In a nation whose main occupation is being ill, the most patriotic work one could possibly engage in is that of healing people, 89; 74]. Carlos is the first to recognize the limitations of the English upbringing and its social utility, however, and already in Coimbra he begins to succumb to the literary arts that will make him, according to Ega, one of those "médicos literários" [literary doctors, 90; 76]. This transformation from the obsession with the natural world and physical activity, which is furthermore what characterizes Carlos as a young boy, to a devotion to the fictional and artistic fields begins in the house in Celas. Carlos's house is a space of transition that confounds nature and civilization, aristocrats and bohemians, and the natural and the human sciences. Carlos and his friends occupy different rooms of the house with a variety of activities ranging from scientific experimentations to poetry recitals and fencing. The abundant action deliberately contrasts with the house's "aparência preguiçosa e campestre" [appearance of rural indolence, 90; 75]. The divisions in the house mirror the different parts of Carlos's thinking, a mind at odds with various metaphysical, scientific, and aesthetic debates, ideas, and experiments. The commotion hidden underneath the house's impression of laziness also parallels the protagonist's active and thinking mind concealed behind his idle lifestyle.

If on the one hand dwellings, such as Celas, affect a character's existence and development, individuals can also determine how a place changes throughout the narrative. The Santa Olávia estate in the Douro, for example, accompanies Afonso's emotional state over the years. Following his son Pedro's suicide, Afonso has Santa Olávia covered in tones of black and its windows closed. But, as years pass and Carlos grows up, Afonso's happiness increases and Santa Olávia is improved and made more cheerful, and the old man becomes engaged in redecorating: "As salas tinham agora soberbos panos de Arrás, paisagens de Rousseau e Daubigny, alguns móveis de luxo e de arte" [The rooms were hung with superb Arras tapestries and landscapes by Rousseau and Daubigny, and furnished with a few very select pieces, 91; 76]. Similarly, the excitement of Ega and his friends has a strong impact on a dining-room in the Hotel Central. During Ega's dinner party for Cohen, the heated debate turns violent and "a correcta sala, com os seus divãs de marroquim, os seus ramos de camélias, tomava um ar de taverna, numa bulha de faias, entre a fumaraça de cigarros" [the very neat room, with its morocco leather sofas and its camellias was taking on the appearance of a tavern, in which some good-for-nothings were brawling in a cloud of cigarette smoke, 174; 150]. The settings are inseparable from the action or non-action of the scenes that take place inside them. That is, the plot or the movement of the narrative relies on the immovable spaces.

The tension between movement and the immovable is the central thematic and formal device in the novel. *The Maias*'s main preoccupation deals with the struggle between the stagnating and progressive forces that influence both individuals and societies. The juxtaposition of fixity and mobility echoes the divergences between fiction and reality, Portugal's decline and Europe's industrial progress, difference and tradition, and historical experience and modernity. The *móveis* and *imóveis* (which means in Portuguese "furnishings" and "real estate" besides movables and immovables) serve as metaphors to reflect on the possibilities and impossibilities of self and collective reform. Words for furniture and real estate in Spanish, Portuguese, and a number of other languages come from the Latin *mobilis*, that which can be moved, and *imobilis*, that which is fixed. In Latin, only the latter referred to personal property, and, as Benjamin notes in the *Arcades Project*, Adolf Behne writes that "Movables [furniture] quite clearly developed out of immovables [real estate]."[33] Today *imóveis*, real estate property or residences, are fixed spaces, while for the original nomadic cultures home consisted of a flexible and movable structure that could be changed from place to place. The original concept of real estate was to some degree a movable entity. On the other hand, the eighteenth-century excavations in Mesopotamia and Egypt that led to the post 1750 classical revival period revealed that the earliest artifacts that served as tables, beds, and chairs were platforms made of stone, and other heavy and inflexible and immovable materials. Ironically the original notion of furnishings was not movable but one characterized by permanence. At the same time, the eighteenth-century transition in domestic dwelling from communal living to the privatization of rooms also shows that movables once again create immovables. In his contribution to the multivolume work *A History of Private Life* Orest Ranum notes that what were originally pieces of furniture—bibliothèque, cabinet, étude—later become separate rooms.[34] Property, whether movable or immovable, has not always been faithful to its Latin root, but what becomes clear is that there is a historical significance in the interconnectedness of furniture and the interior space it occupies.

The inseparability of what is permanent and what changes holds *The Maias* together. The interdependence of these two models is reflected in the distribution of settings and action in the novel. Criticism often emphasizes the portrayal of Lisbon in *The Maias*, yet most of the novel takes place inside elaborately represented interior settings. The depictions of the city focus on views, noises, and sensations dealing with natural phenomena: sunlight, rain, ambiances, and the blowing of leaves and wind. Otherwise, when characters are outside they are constantly on the road and on the go. The novel focuses on the interiors where little happens, and interrupts this with the sudden action of the characters in constant movement from one place to another. Lisbon is the locus of the characters' relentless traveling that seems to lead them nowhere. This would explain the text's exceptionally rich vocabulary referring to different carriages and other forms of transportation available in late-nineteenth-century Portugal. This might even explain why Eça found the satirical scene of the horse races fitting for the novel's larger narrative objective. The Lisbon that is made part of the history, memory, and imagination of the novel is a dialectical one, reinforcing the interdependence between movement and stagnation.

Residential properties or *imóveis* are the true settings and arrange the action by making room for the furnishings or *móveis* that give the narrative its development. The furnishings animate a fixed and empty space with movement and meaning and therefore give progress to the narration. Eça fills the rooms and salons of his novel, as he does Portugal and the blank page, with significant objects, experiences, and events. The *móveis* or furnishings represent a form of imagination that provides the reality and society portrayed with a sense of development. The English translation of *imóveis*—real estate—reinforces this dialectic, since it is literally the real, the reality that is thus complemented with the fiction or the furnishings or *móveis*. Eça sets up the opposition between movables and immovables to reflect on the classical opposition between fiction and reality, which increasingly preoccupies him both in his day to day and in his mediations on the workings of the imagination. Carlos hopes to turn Ramalhete into "um interior confortável, de luxo inteligente e sóbrio" [an interior that would combine comfort with intelligent, sober luxury, 8; 3]. In Eça's correspondence we find that these are the characteristics the author himself considered most significant when it came to creating an ideal sense of place in the world. For Eça, inhabiting a comfortable home of one's own is an artistic project, and this idea surfaces repeatedly throughout the novel.

The writing of *The Maias* reinforces the artistry of interiors by implying that the author's task resembles the work of an interior designer. Authors and decorators invent a narrative when they create a space that tells a story to both the dwellers and observers. Both artists fashion new individual and collective ways of being in the world. By connecting the novelistic creation to interior design, Eça comments on literature's role at the end of the nineteenth century as well. The author suggests that a writer should be an independent artist whose social and political action is implied in the more important work of imagining, reflecting, and creating meaning. Given his experience abroad, Eça is quite aware of the growing professionalization of the decorator. Of course, societies have always been interested in shaping the appearance of their surroundings, and in order to do so architects have historically worked in conjunction with a variety of craftsmen, upholsterers, painters, and cabinet and furniture makers in order to decorate the interior of rooms. But at the turn of the century interior decorating begins first in England and the United States to branch out and become an independent artistic practice and industry. While Vilaça hires the Portuguese Esteves "arquitecto, político" [an architect, a politician] to renovate Ramalhete, Carlos "apareceu em Lisboa com um arquitecto-decorador de Londres" [arrived unexpectedly in Lisbon accompanied by an architect-cum-decorator from London, 7-8; 3]. Eça is mocking the fact that the Portuguese architect is also a politician, and a friend of Vilaça's, suggesting that a faithful artist ought to concentrate on his or her work and not on his petty politics. Similarly a writer should be fully engaged with his fiction and writing, devoted to his craft, and not attempt to simultaneously be a writer and hold other professions. Eça's contribution to Portugal's cultural, social, and political progress is precisely his uninterrupted dedication to his artistic work. Biographies and a significant portion of Eça's correspondence reveal that the author is chiefly committed to his writing. He spearheads a number of different creative and journalistic projects often in conjunction with other intellectuals, whose idleness he often must combat, and he always sets very high quality and accountability standards for his endeavors. It is in the devotion to their expertise, in the furnishing of novels and spaces that both the modern writer and the new interior architect ought to express their commitment to progress.

At the same time, Eça's political and social engagement with Portugal's state of affairs throughout his writing, beginning with the first appearance in 1871 of his political caricatures, *As Farpas*, which he coauthors with Ramalho Ortigão, points to the struggle he faces in separating politics from his fiction. Eça is undoubtedly one of the foremost politically committed and ethically engaged writers of his time, but his fiction reveals a certain sense of uncertainty about the relationship between aesthetics and politics. His many intellectuals and dandies such as Carlos, Ega, and the notorious Fradique help the author develop a critical analysis of the idea of art for art's sake. This difficulty also surfaces in the ambiguity created in *The Maias* with respect to the role that modernization both of the country's infrastructure and of aesthetic production ultimately plays. Behind the framework of movable and immovable property at the core of the novel lies a fundamental irony since the obsession with interiors or with the movables, in turn immobilizes characters and authors. Eça's portrait of building and renovating new interior spaces in *The Maias* shows how the moveable or innovative forces face dormant contradictions. Critics often set the author's interest in progress against his critique of a stagnant Portugal. But the inseparability of *imóveis* and *móveis* in the novel is more concerned with deconstructing and articulating the irresolvable contradiction of these dichotomies than privileging one state against another.

The scene involving Sr. Vicente, the "mestre-de-obras" [foreman] responsible for the renovation work done on a warehouse near Necessidades that Carlos hopes to turn into a scientific laboratory, is a perfect example that illustrates this important paradox (100; 2007, 84). "Obras" in Portuguese, as in Spanish, refers both to construction and artistic works. Vicente, as Esteves, is a master builder that is also apparently too involved in politics, and therefore falls short of his artistic creation. In other words, the repairs are progressing awfully slowly and Carlos is growing increasingly aggravated. Vicente preoccupies himself instead with what he considers to be his country's most needed political changes. While he wishes "homens de saber e de progresso" [knowledgeable, progressive men] to take over Portugal's politics, Carlos hopes to advance scientific inquiry with the completion of his laboratory (101; 85). This is another of Carlos's frustrated plans that illustrates how the furnishing of places could theoretically serve to promote Portugal's modernization, but appears ultimately to be inseparable from a continuity of tradition. Carlos follows the restoration work on the building that "arrastavam-se sem fim" [dragged on endlessly]:

> Sempre um vago martelar preguiçoso numa poeira alvadia; sempre as mesmas coifas de ferramentas jazendo nas mesmas camadas de aparas! Um carpinteiro esgrouviado e triste parecia estar ali desde séculos, aplainando uma tábua eterna com uma fadiga langorosa; e no telhado os trabalhadores, que andavam alargando a clarabóia, não cessavam de assobiar, no sol de Inverno, alguma lamuria de fado. (100)

> [There was always a vague sound of indolent hammering and a cloud of whitish dust; always the same baskets of tools lying on the same layers of shavings! A sad, gawky carpenter seemed to have been there for centuries, planing the same eternal plank with weary languor; and on the roof, in the winter sunshine, the workers, who were supposed to be enlarging the skylight, were constantly whistling some mournful *fado*, Costa 2007, 84.]

While building something new and modern, the workers also prolong the past. The repetition of words such as "always" and "same" emphasizes both the passage of time and a sense of continuity of the status quo. The selection of analogies and vocabulary seems more appropriate to describe a project of the Baroque than a scientific or enlightened plan that might materialize as is suggested with the enlarging of the "skylight." The construction work is intended to further Carlos's and Portugal's future plans. But, instead, these "obras" seem to repeat a type of sacred eternal form. Furthermore, this is a case where, as Benjamin notes, "Construction plays the role of the subconscious."[35] Apparently the forced attempt to modernize contradicts the wishes and needs of the collective. The ultimate irony of this passage is of course its ability to show the immobility of a constant movement, because the workers are constantly laboring away for what seems like centuries and yet the project is not advancing fast enough for Carlos's needs. This irony is what I argue structures Eça's novelistic project, and he uses the architectural interior as a grand metaphor to explore the impossibility of separating the future from the past and the unmovable from the movable.

The passage above shows that it is unclear whether Portugal needs to catch up to the rest of Europe or whether it needs, in Afonso's words, "menos progresso e mais moral" [less progress and more morality, 566; 491]. A call for more morality from one of the strongest opponents of the church is yet another irony that governs the ideas of progress in the novel. In fact, Afonso devotes himself religiously to secular values. His morning prayers take the form of "um grande mergulho na água fria" [a bracing cold water bath, 11; 7]. Similarly, Carlos hopes to create with his new lab a "santuário de ciência" [scientific sanctuary, 100; 84] and begs Vicente to swiftly move the work along: "Não lhe peço como proprietário, é como correligionário" [I'm not asking you as a man of property, but as a fellow counter-religionist, 101; 85]. Both a politically engaged member of the working class, Vicente, and a progressive aristocrat, Carlos, believe faithfully in the possibility of improvement and in art, but they doubt about how to balance the two, and while one is responsible for the *imóvel* and the other mostly concerned with the *móveis*, it is uncertain whose ideas will move society forward. The complex ambiguity reinforced by the interplay of real estate and furnishings forces the reader to ask whether modernity or progress would ultimately on a social and subjective level create new ways of understanding reality. The novel is interested in setting up oppositions in order to show that a conflict is not a matter of option; it is not about choosing between old and new ideas, English or Portuguese values, Catholic or Protestant beliefs, liberal or conservative politics, or romantic or realistic artistic forms, but about identifying incompatibilities and unknowns. The interdependence of contradictory forces and views seems to be the ultimate arbiter of a society and time period. Just as we have seen Machado disconcerted by the push and pull of opposing views, Eça is primarily interested in exploring the logic and possible truths that different inconsistencies reveal.

This opposition further functions to frame the complex historical developments plaguing late-nineteenth-century Portugal. As in *Quincas Borba*, the interior spaces in *The Maias* hide allusions to the contradictions that constitute and directly influence a society's decay. Critics have generally and correctly read the incest motif in the novel as symptomatic of Portugal's decadence and of the author's disillusionment with the parameters of naturalism.[36] Maria Manuel Lisboa's two revealing Freudian interpretations of the theme of incest are especially ground breaking in their ability to connect theoretical cultural readings with history.[37] I also propose that a specific historical context is critical in Eça's work and that the experiences of colonialism and slavery, as in Machado's writing, are what ultimately bring about the characters' final ruin and the tragic conclusion of the novel. Family chronicle novels repeatedly take up the classic motif of incest to rewrite the tragic fate of their characters and societies. *Cecilia Valdés* (1882), by the nineteenth-century Cuban writer Cirilio Villaverde (1812-1894), and Gabriel García Márquez's well-known twentieth-century family saga *A Hundred Years of Solitude* (1967) are two seminal classics of the Latin American literary tradition that also tie bleak social and historical events to a family's end. In *The Maias*, as in a number of literary masterpieces, social injustices and unsuspected historical occurrences eventually result in a tragic decomposition of a society. But Eça explores this decadence through his play with domestic spaces, suggesting that the past has consequences on our subconscious and emerges in our most intimate world. In the novel, the incest connects to colonialism and slavery through a series of colors that penetrate the characters' interiors: their private spaces and their inner thoughts. A constellation of red, blue, and black emerges to furnish important interiors and interiorities. These colors become identified with what I would like to call a narrative of blood that underlines the significant connection in the novel to the colonial past.

Therefore, before exploring and analyzing these tinted and multicolored interior spaces it is important to highlight the way the novel tells this story or legend of blood. *The Maias* is an account of the love between a brother and sister. Their incestuous blood is connected to their father's blood, Pedro's, and his, as we will see, is in turn bonded to the blood shed by the African slaves in the Americas. The incestuous blood is also the "poça de sangue" [pool of blood] that Pedro lies in after committing suicide (52; 42).[38] This bloodshot blemish resembles his lover Maria's scarlet parasol that fully covers Pedro "como uma larga mancha de sangue" [like a large bloodstain, 30; 23]. But as the narrator explains earlier, the "sangue das facadas que dera o papàzinho!" [blood from the knife-thrusts inflicted by her Papa!] is what brings wealth to Monforte, known as a murderer and slave-trader, and eventually transports Monforte and his daughter to Lisbon (25; 19). This makes the union between Pedro and Maria Monforte possible; a union that "estragara o sangue da raça" [had tainted the blood of the family, 45; 36]. This marriage leads to Pedro's death, and also to the separation of son and daughter, which results in the subsequent tragic incestuous relation between Maria

Eduarda and her brother Carlos when they meet years later. After his son's suicide, Afonso initially attempts to take his granddaughter from Maria Monforte, because in his words "a pequena é do meu sangue" [the child is of my blood, 82; 69]. From the moment he saw her, Carlos's love for Maria Eduarda had been "como o próprio sangue das suas veias;" [like the very blood in his veins, 484; 418]. There are continuous references and significant preoccupations to the family's aristocratic blood and other forms of blood throughout the story. In fact, the novel draws so much attention to blood that one is motivated to ask, Whose blood is the story really concerned with?

It is not an inferior match that is at stake in the staining of the blue blood of the Maia family, but instead the Monforte "legenda de sangue e negros" [tale of blood and negro slaves, 24; 19]. The aristocratic blood, which is what bonds the lovers together, is also linked to the blood shed by slaves associated with Monforte's illicit trafficking. The blue of the aristocratic blood is an illusion, which can be invented and bought, and the corruption of the family's blood emerges in the novel in Maria Monforte's interiors. She always has her *boudoir* decorated in blue in every new house she occupies. Her Lisbon nest, or private closet, is all "azul-ferrete" [dark blue silk, 24; 18] and in Paris it is all "veludo azul" [blue velvet-upholstered, 33; 25]. In a portrait hanging in the family's library, Pedro is also dressed "todo de veludo azul" [all in blue velvet, 47; 38]. Vilaça senior, while visiting Santa Olávia, stays in the blue room, whose furnishings he himself chose and bought in Porto. The room's rug is "semeado de florzinhas azuis" [scattered with small blue flowers] while the curtains "repetiam as mesmas folhagens azuladas sobre fundo claro" [were printed with the same bluish flowers and leaves against a light background, 56; 47]. The blue of Maria Monforte's dressing rooms are not meant merely to embody Maria Monforte's desires to climb in society, nor is Vilaça senior's careful attention to this guest room just a comical remark about how a stewart is responsible for creating the illusory nature of his master's superior social class. Instead the blue symbolizes how intertwined the aristocracy is not only to other social classes, but also to other cultures, races, and their historical experiences. Connecting Vilaça's interior to the Maias' blue blood, for example, reinforces the fact that the bourgeois Vilaça family is the backbone of the aristocratic character of the Maia family. It will become clear that Afonso and Carlos and Vilaça senior and junior are intertwined to such a degree that one pair could not exist without the other. The deception and perversion of the aristocratic blood is represented in the bluish of these interior worlds.

The red and blue colors, which refer directly or indirectly to different concepts of blood, are also faintly but significantly connected to the color black. This aura of black alludes to the Portuguese role in the slave trade and the country's historical heritage of the Arabic culture. The expression *blue blood* comes from the Spanish "sangre azul," which came to define individuals and families not racially mixed with Arabs. Although the Maias are an old aristocratic family from the north of Portugal, which would presumably make them less likely to have Arabic forefathers, the author chooses as their defining physical feature their black Arabic eyes. Pedro is like "um belo árabe" [a handsome Arab, 20; 14]. Both Maria Eduarda and Carlos Eduardo have "olhos muito negros" [very dark eyes, 46; 37]. Carlos has the Maia eyes, "aqueles irresistíveis olhos do pai, de um negro líquido" [the same irresistible eyes as his father, as liquid-black, 96; 81]. When Carlos sees Maria Eduarda on the Aterro all he could focus on was "o negro profundo de dois olhos que se fixaram nos seus" [two intensely dark eyes fixed on his, 203; 176]. The black of the Maia eyes seems to tragically connect the family the same way the different blood stains of red and blue do. It is not the breakdown of class difference or the impurity of Christian blood that contaminates Portuguese society, but the violence of a historical past. The novel suggests that the expelled or re-conquered Arabic cultural tradition and the conquered worlds of Africa and the Americas have left their mark on Portuguese society. The narrative makes very significant references to the blackness of specific African servants that populate the novel. These black characters become a sort of synecdoche for the entire history of slavery. Their blackness brings together in a type of darkness the family with the historical past, as black becomes the symbolic color of the tragedy connecting the domestics to the family's black eyes and the dark final events of the novel. Once Ega discovers that Maria Eduarda is Carlos's sister he continuously refers to this tragic piece of news he must now reveal to his best friend as that "negra desgraça" [black misfortune, 638; 555], "aquele negrume que desde a véspera lhe pesava na alma" [the gloom that had been oppressing his soul since the previous night, 630; 548], and "os negros cuidados da véspera" [the black anxieties of the previous night, 626; 545]. When Maria Eduarda departs in the penultimate chapter to Paris, she is all covered in black and melancholy. The vision of her "toda negra na claridade" [black figure against the glaring station lights] and "envolta numa grande peliça escura" [wrapped in her dark fur coat] functions not purely to contrast with Maria Eduarda's first appearance in white, but more importantly to mark the tragedy with the color black (686-687; 598). The first time she walks down the acacia path in Olivais, Maria Eduarda is already "vestida de preto" [dressed in black, 430; 370].

These repeated images of blackness also emerge in the description of another important character, Guimarães, who serves as a type of intermediary. This mysterious figure comes from abroad bringing the truth to Lisbon about Maria Monforte and her daughter, Maria Eduarda, which results in the tragic turn of events. He too is usually spotted all dressed in black, and the narrator focuses specifically on his black gloves. When he tells Ega that Maria is Carlos's sister, Guimarães "passava os dedos calçados de pelica

preta pelos longos fios da barba, fitando o Ega, num esforço de penetração"
[was stroking his long beard with his black-gloved hands and gazing at Ega,
as if trying to penetrate his mind, 615; 535]. Guimarães's attempt to penetrate Ega's deepest thoughts parallels the novel's wish to communicate to the
readers the more profound meaning of these details. Characters often refer to
this enigmatic man as the famous or legendary Guimarães, alluding to the
malevolent reputation that a person such as himself, a "brasileiro," tended to
have. The "brasileiros" were Portuguese emigrants sometimes newly and
quickly enriched in the Americas, primarily in Brazil, whose fortune was
often made illegally and through connections to the slave trade. The legendary Guimarães is the one that announces the incestuous relationship, but it is
of course also Monforte's legend as a slaver that already determined Afonso's rejection of Maria Monforte and brought on Pedro's doom. Vilaça
makes a very interesting comment about a certain legend affecting the Maia
family. He refers to "uma lenda, segundo a qual eram sempre fatais aos
Maias as paredes do Ramalhete" [the legend, according to which the walls of
Ramalhete had always proved fatal to the Maias, 7; 3]. But, since the key
legend that pervades the entire novel is predominantly the dark tale associated with Maria Monforte's father, his legend of blood and negro slaves, and
this is what brings misfortune to the family, then the novel is suggesting that
it is Portugal's past that is hidden in the Ramalhete and fatal to the family.
Hence the Lisbon mansion is both the womb and catacomb of the story, a
kind of mausoleum of the Maia family and of the novel itself. Eça brings
inside the interiors the different pieces of the story line, connecting the dots
and the colors in order to hide in the interior space these historical allusions.
Eça as a writer is also an artist of the interior and hence a reader of his time
and of how a past of violence and injustice penetrates the characters, society,
our intimate spaces, and the imagination.

Finally, the only other seemingly minor legend in the novel, that is in fact
highly significant, also refers to interior decorating. Ultimately it will be
through the interior details that the author reveals the implied narrative of
Portugal's deep-rooted genealogy of slavery. When Carlos asks Craft about
the superb collection of antiques and furnishings his friend has gathered in
the famous Olivais house,

> Craft sorriu daquela legenda. A verdade era que só em 1872 ele começara a
> interessar-se pelo bricabraque; chegava então da América do Sul; e o que fora
> comprando, descobrindo aqui e além, acumulara-o nessa casa dos Olivais,
> alugada então por fantasia, uma manhã que aquele pardieiro, com o seu boca-
> do de quintal em redor, lhe parecera pitoresco, sob o sol de Abril. Mas agora,
> se pudesse desfazer-se do que tinha, ia dedicar-se então a formar uma colecção
> homogénea e compacta de arte do século XVIII.

[Craft smiled at this legend. The truth was that he had only become interested in collecting in 1872, when he returned from South America; and he had gradually bought various objects here and there and collected them all together in the house in Olivais, which he had rented on a whim, one sunny April morning when that old ruin of a place, with its little garden, had seemed to him picturesque. Now, however, if he could get rid of what he had, he would devote himself to creating a small, homogeneous collection of eighteenth-century art, 156; 133]

Craft reminisces about the origins of his fondness for collecting antique furnishings and decorative items. Like the other legends that pervade the novel his story of objects and things also comes from America. Craft is one of the novel's more important interior decorators and his thoughts here summarize the connection between the colonial experience and the novel's obsession with interior renovating. If the writer is himself to some degree an interior designer then it is also significant that it was in 1872 that Eça publishes his Farpa "O Brasileiro" (The Brazilian). Eça was quite interested in this enigmatic cultural figure and in theorizing about his historical and social significance. In Eça's essay the person designated as the "brasileiro" serves as a mirror image of the Portuguese, suggesting that what has happened abroad is intertwined with what has taken place at home. Craft's tale of interior decorating is also the narrative story of furnishing interiors, which is what composes *The Maias* and links the fall of the family to the tragic consequences of colonization and slavery.

The Maias does not necessarily adhere to the classifications of the anti-slavery genre of the nineteenth century, but it structures into its spatial form a very strong critique of societies dependent on slavery. The narrative places the violent human actions that sustain colonization at the root of the family's downfall and the nation's disintegration. The figure of the "brasileiro" links Portugal with its colonies and the tragic destinies of the African slaves with that of the Maias. Different "brasileiros" or characters returning from Brazil or the Americas intervene in the plot's development and in the family's affairs, especially in their domestic and decorative affairs.[39] A "comendador brasileiro" [Brazilian *comendador*] buys the historic family mansion in Benfica (6; 2). When the "brasileiro" Castro Gomes notices the splendid "tela de Constable" [Constable portrait] in Ramalhete, he boasts of having his own small landscape by the English painter in his Paris collection (478; 412). Carlos cures the daughter of a "brasileiro" who pays him for his medical services: "Salvara de um garrotilho a filha de um brasileiro, ao Aterro—e ganhara aí a sua primeira libra, a primeira que pelo seu trabalho ganhava um homem da sua família" [He had saved from diphtheria the daughter of a Brazilian who lived on the Aterro and had thus earned his first *libra*, the first that any man in his family had ever earned from his own work, 129; 110]. Nothing belongs wholly to the Maia family. A series of economic interac-

tions link the Portuguese aristocracy to the corruption that brings these figures their wealth. The most important transatlantic figure in the novel is
Monforte, one of the most ambiguous characters in the narrative, and one of
Eça's best readings of the complex role that the "brasileiro" plays within the
social and historical context. It is unclear whether Maria Monforte is really
his daughter. There is no doubt, however, that Monforte's wealth resulted
from his work as a slave trader and that his timid personality is marked by
paranoia and violence. As Machado does throughout his work, Eça attempts
to write in the character of Monforte, and especially in Monforte's peculiar
bond to his daughter, some of the intricacies involved in the relationship
between a master and a slave. Monforte acts as a slave-servant consistently
hiding in the shadows and in the corners of a room: "escondido como sempre
no canto negro" [hidden, as always, in the darkest corner of the box, 26; 20]
and "rondando pelos cantos, refugiado pelos vãos das janelas" [skulking in
corners, loitering by windows, 36; 28]. He is almost always found taking
refuge in a corner of a removed, dark, and black nook or corner of an interior
space. The narrator uses words such as "entalado" [entrapped],
"embarcadiço" [seafarer], "encolhido" [shrunken], "apavorado" [terrified],
"encostado" [leaning], "enterrado" [buried], "taciturno" [taciturn], and "escondido" [hidden] in order to describe Monforte's attitude in society, with
himself and towards his daughter. He always walks behind her and carries
Maria's purchases and personal things: "No assento defronte, quase todo
tomado por cartões de modista, encolhia-se o Monforte" [The seat opposite
was almost entirely filled with packages from the dressmaker, and next to
them sat the shrunken figure of Monforte, 29; 22].

One of Eça's "Farpas" might help us decipher some of Monforte's more
enigmatic qualities. Eça recognized the significance of the cultural type and
contributed to the caricature of the "brasileiro" quite early on in his career.
He writes with Ramalho Ortigão "O Brasileiro" a typically excessive and
highly ironic "Farpa." Many of the critics who repeatedly accuse Eça of
racism toward Brazil and Brazilians base their criticism on the author's portrayal of "brasileiros." Alexandre Coleman calls Eça's 1872 version of "O
Brasileiro" "um insulto dirigido por junto à nação brasileira" [an insult di-
rected at the entire Brazilian nation] and a "grosseira caracterização...do
povo brasileiro" [a gross characterization...of the Brazilian people] and
claims it fueled the silent and latent hate that Machado de Assis felt toward
Eça de Queirós.[40] Certainly one can condemn Eça's ideas for being too
inconsistent and Eurocentric, but Coleman's interpretation, as others, clearly
misses the point of what the "brasileiro" signified for Eça and his work. The
"brasileiro" is not a Brazilian national. The sarcastic piece he writes begins
by clearly pointing out that the "brasileiro" is one of us; in other words, a
Portuguese. In addition, at this time the conceptualizations of these national
identities are not independent of one another. According to Eça's essay,

every Portuguese has the seed of the "brasileiro" planted inside him. The "brasileiro" is the Portuguese "dilatado" [dilated] and "desabrochado" [blooming].[41] Therefore, while the "brasileiro" is fully developed and hence authentic, the Portuguese is incomplete, embryonic, and in turn hypocritical. Furthermore, the essay's form is particularly fascinating, resembling in many of its rhetorical tropes a typical avant-garde manifesto. From this description Monforte would seem to resemble both the Portuguese and the "brasileiro," because he is already both the rich slaver and at the same time his timid "encolhido" [shrunken] self seems to represent a not yet fully developed identity. This interdependence is exactly what Eça argues when he claims that the other is inside the self. He sees in the "brasileiro" a double consciousness similar to the recognition between the dependent and independent consciousness in Hegel's master-slave dialectic. Thus if the master can not exist without the slave, the Portuguese is also nothing without the "brasileiro." The author is hence implying that the civilized self carries inside himself a violent and uncivilized other. Monforte brings with him an experience that is both Brazil's and Portugal's.

Monforte's arrival in Lisbon with his beautiful young daughter is a clear foreshadowing of when Maria Eduarda comes to the capital city with the "brasileiro" Castro Gomes. The repetition of one appearance with the other serves not only to show that little has changed between the Portugal of Pedro da Maia and Carlos's time, but more importantly to tie Monforte's and Castro Gomes's overseas experience with the family's fatal destiny. Both Maria Monforte and her father and Maria Eduarda and Castro Gomes cause a sensation in Lisbon while both pairs are also associated with a sense of secrecy and mystery that underscores their historical background. The muffled history that connects them to America and slavery is exactly what the novel attempts to draw attention to. Monforte embodies some of the complexities of slavery through his characterization, but with the arrival of Castro Gomes slavery is less figurative since the couple are accompanied from abroad with their African servants. These figures strongly impress Carlos and Maria Eduarda and her servants penetrate his consciousness simultaneously. One rainy evening Carlos sees for the first time two black youths, ostensibly servants, in the São Carlos Theater. Carlos is at once mesmerized and puzzled by their presence: "Quem seriam, porque estavam ali, aqueles africanos de perfil trombudo?" [Who were they, these sullen Africans, why were they here?, 137; 117].[42] If Maria Eduarda pierces Carlos with her black eyes that are also his, he cannot take his eyes off these young servants: "aquele preto de que os seus olhos se não podiam despegar" [unable to take his eyes off that small black boy, 136; 116]. The blackness of the lover's eyes reflects the blackness of these young Africans and the dark tragedy that repeatedly penetrates interiors and interiorities. The second time Carlos sees Maria Eduarda she is accompanied by "um esplêndido preto" [a splendid black servant, 157; 134].

The vision of this "preto grisalho" [grizzled black manservant] keeps returning to Carlos's thoughts: "o escudeiro preto voltava" [the black manservant
was there again, 184-185; 159]. When Carlos deliberates about whom the
sick member of the family might be that he has been called upon to see, he
immediately guesses that perhaps it is the "esplêndido preto de carapinha
grisalha" [the splendid negro servant with the grizzled hair, 343-344; 297].
Carlos is first fascinated and haunted by these African servants prior to
realizing that he has fallen in love with Maria Eduarda. These figures recon-
nect brother and sister, and it is not surprising that Carlos considers the black
servant part of Maria Eduarda's family, which is of course also his.

This legend of colors that Eça uses to paint his tragic story of the Maia
family penetrates the characters' domestic interiors and their interiorities. We
find Carlos toward the end of the story in his cherry-velvet upholstered
sleeping quarters as if, like his father, he was lying in a pool of blood: "a luz
sobre o veludo espalhava um tom de sangue" [the light falling on the velvet
stained it the colour of blood, 668; 581]. Similarly to the way these colors
make their subtle penetration of the interior, a specific wind also enters
different rooms and houses. This strong southwest wind, which points geographically to the South American continent, appears together with the black
servants.[43] The wind, comparable to the blood imagery, blows throughout the
narrative. It is a recurring image that turns up at important scenes in the
novel. The night Carlos sees the two African boys at the São Carlos theater,
which is incidentally covered with "velho papel vermelho" [faded red wall-
paper] there are repeated references to the evening's strong southwest wind:
"um bafo de sudoeste, parecia penetrar ali, derramando o seu pesadume, a
morna sensação da sua humidade" [with a southwest wind blowing, seemed
to have seeped into the theatre, infecting it with melancholy and a kind of
tepid dampness, 136; 116]. The wind mitigates the effect and meaning that
the figures of the African boys have on the protagonist. It is most appropriate, thus, that the evening he returns from the theater the narrator pays special
attention to Baptista, Carlos's *valet de chambre*. Baptista is analyzed and he
in turn discusses Pimenta, Count Gouvarinho's butler. The conversation between Carlos and Baptista becomes an evaluation of the relationship between
butlers and their masters that strategically mirrors the role of the young
African servants and their owners. Their presence forces the narrative, characters, and readers to reflect on the nature of servitude and connects the
master-slave relationship to the romantic bond between Maria Eduarda and
Carlos. Like the young Africans, the southwest wind also announces the
couple's future union and serves as a kind of murmuring throughout the text,
evoking past and upcoming tragedies. Inside Castro Gomes's hotel rooms
Carlos compares the alluring perfumes in the air to a "bafo suave de carícia"
[soft caressing breeze, 261; 225], which alludes to the "bafo de sudoeste"
[southwest wind blowing] the night at São Carlos (136; 116). This reminds

us again of the breath of warm southwest wind that Carlos observes as he
woke up on the day of the Cohens' *soirée* when he goes to Maria Eduarda's
hotel for the first time. Not long after this first meeting between the future
lovers, Carlos is asked to return to the Hotel Central on a night when "fora
uivava o sudoeste" [the southwest wind moaned outside, 290; 251]. When he
begins to go on a regular basis to see Maria Eduarda in the house on the Rua
de S. Francisco where she is temporarily living, the days are rainy and sad
"cheios de sudoeste e de chuva" [full of rain and a constant south-west wind,
365; 316]. This gust also attacks during the stormy night Pedro commits
suicide, when Afonso sits, worried about his son, "escutando o sudoeste
contra as vidraças" [listening to the southwest wind battering the window
panes, 49; 40]. The stormy scene of the night of Pedro's tragic death foreshadows the subsequent incestuous love affair that begins in the rainy and
windy days in the Rua de S. Francisco. The function of this emblematic
natural element, although the characters hear it coming from the outside, is to
penetrate the interior spaces in the novel and the inner thoughts of the characters.

The southwest wind points to the Americas and to the individuals, the
slaver and the "brasileiro," that bring first Maria Monforte and later Maria
Eduarda to Lisbon to link their transatlantic voyages to the story of the Maia
family. This leitmotif comes inside the interior spaces just as the symbolic
colors of red, blue, and black taint the intimate rooms and inner feelings of
the characters to tell their narrative of violence. The novel connects the slave
trade to the tragedy, suggesting there is a link between the historical bloodshed and the breakdown of society. The Maia family name seems to further
emphasize the interdependence between Portugal and its overseas empire,
even if only ironically. There are many possible meanings for the name
Maia. Critics have linked it to the important language of flowers in the novel
and to a real historic and illustrious Portuguese family.[44] Nonetheless, Maia
might also sarcastically evoke the pre-Columbian Mayan empire. The author
would thus be implying that the colonial experience, which would ultimately
vanquish the famous Mesoamerican civilization, is the same that destroyed
the homogeneity and stability of the old European aristocracy. This possibility creates an ironic and subtle inversion, where the novel is also a narration
of how colonization destroys both the colonizer and the colonized (to use
Albert Memmi's seminal title of his foundational theoretical work of post-
colonial studies).[45] As we saw earlier the author creates a similar ironic
inversion with the juxtaposition of movables and what is fixed, or furnishings
and real estate. The ambiguity created in the novel around the juxtaposition
of interior decoration and homes is used to question the dichotomic conceptualization of modernity. The interiors house contradictions and ironic constructions that at the same time serve as interrogations of historical developments. Thus, just as Machado does, Eça also makes the interior space the

decisive literary trope fundamental for his novel's themes and formal structure.

THE CORNERS OF THE WORLD: INSIDE *LA REGENTA*

If *The Maias* includes a subtext connecting the family's story to Portugal's overseas empire, Leopoldo Alas's novel also links the interior of rooms with Spain's colonial history of exploitation and its effects on late-nineteenth-century Spanish Restoration society. The sense of conquest and feeling of enslavement play an important role in *La Regenta* (1884-1885), whose selfish characters are obsessed with dominating inner territories while others, such as Ana Ozores who struggles for a kind of impossible freedom, battle to escape being imprisoned within different interiors. All three novels include in their interiors important references to the consequences of their countries' colonial pasts, yet the hidden historical critique is inseparable from the authors' meditation on how to narrate the novel. At the same time, the design and décor of the interior is also a form of reflecting on the wider dilemmas of modernity. Jo Labanyi argues in *Gender and Modernization in the Spanish Realist Novel* that Vetusta internalizes modern capitalism but experiences it simultaneously with frustration and stagnation.[46] And indeed one can read the opening scene as an exposé of this conflict, since the movement of the flowing pieces of debris contrasts with the immobility of the cathedral's gothic tower. While *The Maias*'s language of real estate and furnishings figures the dual experiences of modernization and tradition, and *Quincas Borba* spatially explores the contradictions that arise from juxtaposing modern and pre-modern forms of existence, Clarín's work is likewise preoccupied with what emerges and with what remains inert. If Eça uses homes and interior décor to extend his metaphorical and ironic constructions, and Machado turns a room's threshold into an intricate symbol for the possibilities and impossibilities of being and the imagination, Alas makes penetrating the interior space and an individual's private inner experience one of his governing narrative techniques. *La Regenta* insists on piercing and penetrating rooms and enclosed spaces. Specific movements and components related to interior spaces in the novel reveal an intense, sometimes violent, process of interiorization, which at the same time acts as a meditation on the function of the novel.

Many narratives and literary traditions influence *La Regenta*. The novel overflows with inter-textual references, and characters and narrators devour books as they write and read their life stories. But Eça's own fiction was especially significant for Clarín. In his much quoted introduction to *La Regenta*, Gonzalo Sobejano notes that Eça's *Cousin Bazilio* has a stronger impact on Alas's novel than *The Crime of Father Amaro*.[47] One would expect the latter to be more important because of its strong critique of the clergy. Like the two Portuguese stories of adultery, the content of Clarín's masterpiece and its strong anti-clericalism made *La Regenta* at the time scandalous and even pornographic. But the public reacted to the relatively equally scandalous works very differently. Beatriz Berrini investigates the polemical response to Eça's work in her essay "A Polémica Recepção" (The Controversial Reception), especially the reactions to *Cousin Bazilio*. She discovers that the apparently indecent material ultimately intensifies the popularity of the novel. Although criticized for their excessive immorality, even by such close people as his own father and his friend Ramalho Ortigão, Eça's novels commonly enjoyed a positive reception. *La Regenta*, on the other hand, was never well received by the public nor widely read. Today *La Regenta* is indisputably one of Spain's most important classic novels, perhaps the country's best nineteenth-century narrative, if not its greatest novelistic creation since *Don Quixote*. Still, it was never a popular novel and it was especially disregarded under Franco's dictatorship. Only in the 1960s do critics begin to give long-overdue and well-deserved critical consideration to *La Regenta* and to Clarín's vast corpus of non-fictional writing. Nonetheless, a brief introduction to his life and works published as late as 2005 still refers to Leopoldo Alas as "un clásico desconocido" [an unknown classic].[48] This is because *La Regenta* continues to challenge and perplex readers even today. Like *Quincas Borba* and *The Maias*, Clarín's open and provocative novel still generates new meanings and interpretations.

A number of critical readings have focused on topography in *La Regenta*. As in the case with Eça's writing, and to a lesser degree with Machado's fiction, critics have primarily focused their attention on the rich settings that divide Vetusta and the novel's territories into different areas, starting with María del Carmen Bobes Naves's studies on *La Regenta*'s novelistic spaces to Sergio Beser's elaboration of "Espacio y objetos en *La Regenta*" (Space and objects in *La Regenta*). The work of Elizabeth Doremus Sánchez on Clarín's writing as spatial-form narrative makes a strong case for the modernity of Alas's style, but focuses primarily on relations between characters, while María Teresa Zubiaurre privileges the novel's panoramas as a metaphor for patriarchal power. In an attempt to elucidate realist poetics in general, Dale J. Pratt in "Mapping, Realist Narrative and Cartographic Imagination in *La Regenta*" explains how mapping characterizes narrative in the novel,[49] while Jacqueline C. Nanfito's "Topographies of the Self" explores how the novel breaks the boundaries between physical and psychological space. Different notions of space, visual metaphors, the contrast between the natural and civilized worlds, and the interaction between public and private spheres, all occupy an important role in the overall conception of the novel, but it seems to me that one particular spatial movement is privileged. The interior realm underscores the governing project in the novel, as *La Regenta* is primarily concerned with interiors, interiority, and the act of penetrating interiors both physical and abstract. Interior spaces play a dominant role in the novel's structure less for what they represent, symbolize, or render ironic, and more so for the way they function in relation to characters and plot. This narrative technique, which relies on the interior setting, resembles the function Eça and Machado attribute to intimate spaces. With its complex representation of interiors, the novel explores the diverse levels of the interiority of the self and the different inner meanings of life and art.

In a critical essay analyzing Pérez Galdós's *Tormento*, Clarín shows his enthusiasm for interiors in literature. Adopting Marcelino Menéndez y Pelayo's term *"interiores ahumados"* [smoky interiors] Alas writes: "¡Los *interiores ahumados!* Eso es lo que está sin estudiar en España. Interiores de almas, interiores de hogares, interiores de clases, de instituciones" [*Smoky interiors!* That is yet to be studied in Spain. Interiors of souls, domestic interiors, interiors of social classes, of institutions, 4: 1; 518]. Clarín censures the national literature's inability to properly analyze Spanish society and claims that one cannot even count on "una sola descripción auténtica y artística de un salón madrileño" [one artistic and authentic description of a Madrid drawing-room] among other social environments (4: 1; 518). *La Regenta* thus sets out to do what according to the author has not yet been done in nineteenth-century Spanish literature. Hadassah Ruth Weiner reviews Clarín's critical writings and his meditations on the novel and compares the author's sense of literary integrity with his smoky interiors. Weiner concludes that for Clarín it is necessary in novelistic creation to see "los 'interiores ahumados' de los seres vivos tanto como los de las cosas inanimadas" [the "smoky interiors" of humans and those of inanimate things].[50] Indeed, fiction allows Alas to do what he promotes in his critical writing, which is to focus and explore the interior side of things and of people. The novel allows him to examine both the inner mind of the individual and the deeper composition of social, political, and cultural spaces. Alas furnishes the novel by drawing on crucial repeated images of corners, tight enclosed spaces, and the fierce act of invading and occupying these interiors. The recurring "rincón" [corner] is associated with the wider quest for meaning in the novel because—while it represents a hidden part of reality, a dead end, and a possible end point that the citizens of Vetusta can reach—it is also a synecdoche for society. Upon discovering and squeezing through to these mysterious dark interiors, one ought to find answers to reality's enigmas, but more often than not these are left unanswered. This subtle narrative technique not only highlights the fragments and cruelty that fill both the spaces and the minds of the characters but also serves as a leitmotif for the depth Clarín insists narrative must aspire to reach.

The author places his concern with the interior world at the center of *La Regenta*'s groundbreaking opening scene, which is unlike that of any contemporary realist novel. Eça's *The Maias* begins with the description of a house and Machado's *Quincas Borba* with the main character in his drawing room. The first chapters of the Portuguese and Brazilian novels are complex in their own way, but Clarín's aperture is especially avant-garde because without using the commonplace of the domestic setting it still demonstrates from the onset how interiors organize the narrative objectives. The Spanish novel starts with a poetically detailed description of the wind blowing the garbage that pollutes the empty streets of Vetusta, the Spanish provincial capital that serves as the setting and collective character of *La Regenta*. From the very beginning the narrative perspective points to the importance that the obscured details and hidden fragments have in the novel as a whole. These pieces of paper, food, and rubbish dancing in circles and concealed in the street corners are neatly tied to the realist aim of creating an illusion of reality. Directing attention to the veiled and secretive elements strengthens this illusion; it reveals that the invisible is as important as the visible. The fact that a strong narrative voice comments on these fine points reinforces the readers' faith in the reality depicted. This fragmented existence and lyrical filth represent both the moral and immoral, the ugly and the beautiful parts of life. The same way the good is inseparable from the bad, so are the shattered pieces indivisible from the whole.

If this well-known opening paragraph underscores the intent to disclose the debris that lies beneath, the rest of the first chapter emphasizes the ongoing effort to penetrate inside the different interior worlds housing the broken pieces of reality. In his discussion of how already in the eighteenth century privacy turns into both the context and the subject of the novel, Peter Brooks points to how Alain-René Lesage's *Le diable boiteux* (1707) offers a parable of the novel's subject matter with the "devil" Asmodée removing Parisian rooftops, making "us privy, precisely, to the private lives enacted under them."[51] It is known that Luis Vélez de Guevara's *El diablo cojuelo* (1641) inspired Lesage's satire of Parisian society. In this original version Cojuelo also shows Don Cleofás what is taking place inside Madrid's homes by "levantando a los techos de los edificios" [raising the rooftops of the buildings].[52] Clarín's Don Fermín seems to embody both the literary devil and the contemporary naturalist narrator as he too looks down from the cathedral's tower scrutinizing all its corners and "levantando con la imaginación los techos" [lifting roofs in his imagination, 1: 78; 28]. He examines "los rincones de las conciencias y los rincones de las casas" [the corners of consciences and the corners of houses, 1: 78; 28]. Alas's brief story "El diablo en Semana Santa" (The Devil on Holy Week) which concludes his *Solos de Clarín* (1881), constitutes in Sobejano's words, in his introduction to the critical edition, "el germen de *La Regenta*" [the seed of *La Regenta*].[53] In this story the devil invades the interior of a cathedral: "El aliento del diablo, entrando por la ventana de los vidrios rotos, bajaba hasta el altar mayor en remolinos" [The devil's breath entered through the window with broken glass panes and went down in whirls to the main alter, 4: 1; 389]. If at the beginning of the story the devil "Como un león en su jaula bostezaba" [Like a lion in his cage, yawned, 4: 1; 386], now the inhabitants of this "ciudad vetusta comenzaban a despertarse y a su vez bostezaban" [old city started to wake up one at a time and yawned, 4: 1; 388]. A mysterious anxious feeling begins "entrando por el corazón y los sentidos" [entering through the heart and senses] of the priest (4: 1; 390). In Clarín's short story then the devil penetrates not only the interior of the cathedral but also the interiority of the people inside. The story prefigures the novel in different ways, but the devilish act of invading interior spaces and interiorities seems to be the model, which both Fermín and the narrator follow in *La Regenta*. Fermín and the narrator, as the devils before them, begin to pierce, inhabit, and infuse through broken windows and lifted rooftops the various and imperfect corners of the world.

Architectural images of curves, holes, and rooftops recur throughout the novel and appear to embody the narrative secrets and the characters' consciences, as Fermín's observations quoted above indicate. Clarín's interest in exploring these dark, gray, and hazy enclosed settings surfaces in the recurring metaphors and images of rooftops and corners. From Fermín's opening geographical tour of the novel's collective protagonist, Vetusta, where he slowly moves his telescope "de tejado en tejado, de ventana en ventana, de jardín en jardín" [from roof to roof, from window to window, from garden to garden], the novel aims to approach interiors and search for the whole in the inner parts (1: 81; 31). The poorest houses of the cathedral quarter, the Encimada, not only pile one on top of the other but "se metían los tejados por los ojos, o sean las ventanas" [roofs poking into eyes: into windows, that is to say, 1: 84; 33]. The returning emigrants or "indianos" live in the new-rich neighborhood called the Colonia, and their bad taste is characterized by, among other things, the colorful rooftops of their houses: "En los tejados todos los colores del iris" [On the roof-tops all the colours of the rainbow, 1: 85; 33]. These roofs deliberately contrast with the decaying ones of the Encimada, not only in their bright colors but also especially in their uniformity, which results from Vegallana's powerful influence in town politics since according to the Marqués no roof should be above another: "los tejados deben medirse todos por un rasero" [all buildings should be of identical height, 1: 242; 159]. If the upper class and the poor live piled on top of each other and in everyone's view, the new rich are all alike and controlled by the whims of the aristocracy. The opening rooftops thus serve to expose the important power relations governing the novel and Vetustan society, and at the same time to characterize Fermín and the narrator as voyeurs and invaders of interiors.

Besides rooftops, images of corners underpin not only Fermín's desire to penetrate private worlds, but also set the tone for the narrative. If Machado asked his readers to call his life an old house, Clarín apparently finds in a dim corner the fragment that helps one make sense of reality. In the above cited piece on *Tormento* Clarín writes: "No cabe negar que en la naturaleza misma hay *rincones* que parece que están solos; suelen ser el escenario de un idilio; un aislamiento aparente; con estos *rincones* (ya de paisaje, ya sociales), se pueden hacer cuadritos de hermoso conjunto" [There is no denying the fact that in nature one finds *corners*, which appear to be all alone; often they are the setting for an idyllic place; an apparent isolation; with those *corners* (be they natural or social), one can create a beautiful collection of portraits, 4: 1; 516]. Here the corner is very clearly the piece that forms the aesthetic whole. Like Machado's threshold and Eça's movables and immovables, the corner is a synecdoche that serves the author to ask larger socio-political and artistic questions. In *La Regenta*'s rendering of a greedy, empty, and treacherous society, these corners more often than not contain undesirable and disturbing elements, yet for Clarín the horridness is inseparable from the beauty of life, and therefore these corners also locate aesthetic creation. For example, during Ana's extended and cheerful stay in the Vegallanas' summer retreat, the Vivero, she thinks that there ought to be "rincones en la tierra en que no hay nada feo, ni pobre ni triste" [corners of the earth where there's nothing ugly or poor or sad, 1: 779; 609], and in her devotion to Saint Teresa of Ávila she proclaims that she would have searched for her beloved nun "en el último rincón del mundo" [in the most remote corner of the world, 1: 616; 474]. While for Ana a lost corner of the world can reveal something beautiful, for others it functions to hide what is intolerable. Don Robustiano, the town's doctor, for instance, protests to Don Fermín about Rosita Carraspique's continuing in Salesas. Before speaking openly about the topic, he first scrutinized "a todos los rincones, a todas las puertas" [all the corners and doors in the room, 1: 348; 245]. Similarly, Glocester from the pulpit "escudriñó los rincones de la iglesia" [scrutinized every corner of the church] in search of any free-thinking character (1: 363; 258). "Rincón" in Spanish can refer to a lot more than just a corner of a room, it also indicates a remote spot or place, or even the nooks and crannies of a house, and it becomes an enduring image in the novel used throughout to conceal adverse secrets and to lodge and disclose truths.

Corners are also highly important in the narrative because characters make very practical use of them. Considering what happens in the murky places of marchioness Vegallana's yellow salon, no wonder the narrator tells us: "no había rincones seguros" [not a single nook provided safe refuge, 1: 249; 165]. Hide and seek is a favorite among the diverse childish games that the privileged society frequenting the Vivero enjoys playing. Rainy summer days oblige them to run around the house hiding and exploring its dark, inaccessible, and mysterious corners. The others slowly convince Ana to partake in these pastimes, and as she does she gradually gives in to Mesía's romantic advances as well. Ana's evolving emotions are often described with the image of a "rincón." As she starts to acknowledge her attraction for Álvaro, Ana gains consciousness of one of these significant novelistic corners, "Ana iba sintiendo emociones extrañas, nuevas del todo, una inquietud alarmante, sofocaciones repentinas y una especie de sed de todo el cuerpo que hasta le quitaba la conciencia de cuanto no fuese aquel rincón oscuro, estrecho, donde cantaban, reían, saltaban..." [She felt strange, utterly new emotions, an alarming restlessness, sudden choking sensations, and a kind of thirst throughout her body which made her oblivious to everything except that dark corner where people were singing, laughing, leaping, 1: 811; 636]. Earlier in the novel, during one of her moments of desperation, Ana takes refuge in her room and attempts in vain to flagellate herself with some feather dusters. These feather dusters are left not coincidently in the corner of her bedroom: "En un rincón del cuarto había dejado Petra olvidados los zorros con que limpiaba algunos muebles" [In a corner of the room Petra had left the whisks with which she cleaned those pieces of furniture, 1: 693; 539]. Ana searches for answers to her pain in the trivial and overlooked details hiding in the corners of her space and mind, and treats her body as one of her room's furnishings. In her effort to deal with her grief and confusion, she is unconsciously led to hidden spots. Nooks and crannies might or might not transport both characters and readers to a different, deeper, and more complex understanding of individual desires and reality, but they clearly function as spaces of possible transition and revelation.

Fermín takes great pride in believing that he has access to these interior realms; to the souls and minds of his fellow citizens. His opening surveillance of Vetusta frames the larger preoccupation that the novel places on inner and dead-end spaces, as represented in the images of corners. According to Fermín, the corners or the interior of a house conceal the thoughts and private desires of its inhabitants. Fermín's conquistador aspirations convince him that he will take his power and influence "a todos los rincones de las bien alineadas casas de la Colonia" [into every corner of La Colonia's well-regimented houses, 1: 85; 34], and of course the first place Fermín turns his attention to is the Ozores palace, Ana's home, fittingly located "en la rinconada" [in the corner] of the Plaza Nueva (1: 76; 28). As the narrative progresses, he will try to know and control Ana's soul and secrets, and the narrator describes their growing intimacy with a similar image: "creían conocerse uno a otro hasta el último rincón del alma" [They were both convinced that they knew every hidden recess of each other's souls, 1: 657; 509]. Fermín easily enters other characters' spaces, makes himself at home, and in doing so supposes he understands the deepest aspect of a person or institution: "El Magistral conocía una especie de Vetusta subterránea: era la ciudad oculta de las conciencias. Conocía el interior de todas las casas importantes y de todas las almas que podían servirle para algo" [The canon theologian knew a kind of underground Vetusta: the hidden city of consciences. He knew the inside of every important house and of every soul that could be useful to him, 1: 322; 225]. When in someone's home, De Pas is often the only person with access to the secrets hidden inside: "acaso era el único que estaba en el secreto" [in fact he was perhaps the only person present who was in the secret, 1: 323; 225]. Fermín tries to conquer interiors, his own and that of others, but his entrance into these inner worlds is limited. His attempts to infiltrate different private worlds are characterized by the image of him constantly moving through narrow alleyways and corridors. Ultimately he must settle for a limited or blurry vision of the interiors he penetrates, and this is characterized in the way he often peeks through cracks of a door, window or balcony left ajar.

The tour of Vetusta from above articulates an important narrative perspective that persists throughout the novel, but this point of view is not only about affirming Fermín's obsession for dominance. There is no doubt that control and power play a critical role in the novel, but chapter one places great emphasis on the act of piercing and permeating different inner social and psychological realities. Thus following a review of Fermín's curious afternoon routine, the narrative continues the idea of the exploration of interiors with a detailed and guided tour of the inside of the cathedral. Fermín passes rapidly from staircase to corridor, to nave, and to sacristy, where he sees *Palomo* sweeping "en un rincón las inmundicias de cierto gato" [the dirt left in a corner by a certain cat, 1: 89; 37] and delivers the narrative baton to Saturnino Bermúdez, who then leads a long-winded historic tour of the church. The visit to the dark and silent church is, like the admirable painting by the illustrious Cenceño that Bermúdez describes to the visitors, a bit "ahumado" [smoky] in the words of señor Infanzón (1: 97; 43). Clarín links the church tour to his idea of the artistic study of reality's misty interiors. This inner traveling that begins with Fermín from above and is prolonged now from below not only generates different levels of interiors and promotes their examination but also paints them as ambiguous, fragmented, hidden, and hazy spaces. To reinforce the growing dimness and multiple planes of this interior world, Bermúdez's tour takes the visitors further into the pantheon chapel where he and Obdulia bury themselves in yet another interior passage and make their way through the "estrecho pasadizo" [narrow passage, 1: 101; 47]. The image of various different levels of interiority and the Chinese-box effect of enclosed spaces, which Machado also uses to describe Sofia's depression and Eça Ega's desperation, is a strategy repeatedly employed by Alas as well. The cathedral's various interiors become darker and tighter, suggesting the sense of claustrophobia that recurs throughout the novel and, more importantly, prefiguring the discourse on death, which a closer look at Ana will show ties to the language of interiors. The frequent images focusing on narrow and dark enclosed spaces tend to hide dirt, excrement, and dust in their corners and indicate the deeper sense and inner complexity the author strives to structure into his narrative.

The attention on interiors in the opening chapter continues throughout the slower-paced first part of the novel, which describes the common characteristics of Vetusta's settings and spaces; they are dark, hazy, divided, multileveled, dusty, adulterated, and often more impenetrable than penetrable. The spatial distribution of part one of *La Regenta* reminds us of *The Maias*, in that the action of both narratives depends on the connection or passage from one space to the next. While Eça's characters feel a sudden impulse to ride their dogcarts from Ramalhete to Toca, *La Regenta* connects all its spaces like dots. Wandering the city's streets is a common activity among the characters and one of Fermín's preferred forms of contemplation and relaxation; he often needs to walk in order to think and calm down. This walking around town connects action to space, since the narrative introduces places by way of the characters' travels. For example, Mesía and Paco guide the narrative from the casino to the Vegallana palace and later accompany the reader and Ana back to the Ozores mansion. This network or labyrinth is characterized by a sense of enclosure, and the characters walking along the streets frequently feel trapped. This has the effect of turning the narrative into one large interior structure in which Vetusta's narrow roads linking the different scenes are like corridors, and indeed the city's "aceras estrechas" [narrow, worn pavements] are often compared to long and narrow hallways created by decaying houses and century-old trees (1: 344; 242).

Frank Durand attempts to solve the problem posed by Vetusta's predominant role by calling the city a dynamic axis: "The city is the force of gravity which holds the themes and action together and gives the work unity."[54] To add to the long critical discussion on how to treat Vetusta, whether as milieu, symbol, or protagonist, I propose we consider it as one of Clarín's musty interiors. This becomes especially convincing when we bear in mind that the city's exterior spaces repeatedly recall interior or domestic environments. Álvaro meets Fermín in the "salón principal del Paseo Grande" [main hall of the Esplanade] early one morning when spring is making its debut: "Los pájaros, saltando de rama en rama preparaban los nidos para los huevos de abril; se diría que eran tapiceros de la enramada que adornaban los salones del Paseo Grande para las fiestas de la Primavera" [Birds hopped from branch to branch making their nests ready for the April eggs; they were like decorators hanging out the drapery for the spring fiestas, up in the lofty trees which surrounded and covered the broad paths and turned them into great halls, 1: 729; 567]. On a later occasion, Saturno imagines a romantic encounter on the Vivero's splendid grass, which he appropriately calls *la verde alfombra* [the verdant carpet, 1: 792; 619]. These descriptions give the exte-

rior world an interior feeling, while reinforcing the nineteenth-century bourgeois obsession with landscaped gardens. These images obliterate differences between the social and the natural. Jo Labanyi explores in "City, Country and Adultery in *La Regenta*" how Ana's adultery serves as a metaphor for
the dissolution of social and moral values that results "when the boundary
between what lies inside society and what lies outside it breaks down."[55]
Scenes of nature are often found on patterns that decorate interior spaces,
bringing inside a domesticated version of nature, but Alas instead uses the
process of interiorization to characterize all his worlds be they natural, social,
interior or exterior. The descriptions of exterior places render Vetusta one
vast interior space, and not only are the city's streets like hallways, but
different salons and corridors of buildings function as public avenues. More
than one character has contemplated the utility of converting the cathedral's
long naves into a public promenade to be used during the endless rainy
season, and of course the casino's grand salon fills this function in the winter.
As the narrator hyperbolically points outs, "Veterano del casino había que
llevaba andado en aquel salón camino suficiente para llegar a la luna" [There
were some old members of the Gentlemen's Club who had walked far
enough in the ballroom to have reached the moon, 1: 566; 432]. Besides
reducing differences between exterior and interior, this imagery also transforms Vetusta, or the collective, and hence the novel, into one more interior
to explore and penetrate. Vetusta is conceptualized as an interior and as a
significant protagonist, just as Ana Ozores or Fermín de Pas, so that studying
the inner sides to the city is also part of the author's rhetorical use of interiors. The provincial capital and the novel are one vast interior that houses
many levels of interiority.

The ongoing attempt to penetrate further inside is one of the dominating
tensions governing the novel, which not only ties to Fermín's desires but also
to the objectives of all of Vetusta. The citizens of the provincial capital have
a special talent for invading privacies, and one often finds them infiltrating
through walls, climbing over balconies, and peeping through keyholes. The
archdeacon, Don Restituto Mourelo, has the habit of listening "por los aguje-
ros de las cerraduras" [at keyholes, 1: 108; 52], while Santos Barinaga listens
in at the door of the bazar *La Cruz Roja* laying "el oído al agujero de una
cerradura" [his ear to the keyhole, 1: 464; 347]. The desire to gain knowledge
about the private lives of others goes beyond the concern with representing a
gossipy, jealous, and selfish society. It is not only the novel itself that sets out
to discover what is hidden inside the characters' minds and hearts, but this
also seems to be a ubiquitous Vetustan desire. Thus the novel draws a parallel between the narrator's, Fermín's, and Vetusta's points of view and hence
comments on the limits of narrative perspective. While the novel insists on
creating different levels and on penetrating deeper inside, it also shows that
this is ultimately impossible. The interior occupation is incomplete and defi-

cient and in the end characters, readers, narrators, and narratives alike have, or provide, only a limited access to the novel or to understanding reality.

Characters might not be able to penetrate fully someone's inner world, but they can try to get as close as possible, as both Fermín and Mesía's attempts demonstrate. Álvaro and De Pas are no exceptions in the collective Vetustan role of penetrating interiorities, although the former's primarily sexual interest is clearly more literal than Fermín's, who along with the occasional body also wishes to enter people's minds. The central tension governing the plot is the rivalry between the diocese's canon and the city's Don Juan as they struggle to seduce, conquer, and manipulate Ana's soul and body. Interiors function to measure the successes and failures of their endeavors. Mesía progresses by slowly entering and frequenting the Ozores house. Even before Ana finds Álvaro comfortably sitting in her drawing-room, she fears his infiltrating inside her space, as on the night she stays home alone while everyone is at the theater. She senses Don Álvaro "se infiltraba, se infiltraba en las almas, se filtraba por las piedras; en aquella casa todo se iba llenando de él" [could filter through walls and even into souls. Everything in the house was pervaded by him, 1: 308; 213]. Álvaro slowly develops his friendship with Víctor and begins to visit the couple at home: "Poco a poco fue atreviéndose a ir a cualquier hora y Ana, sin sentirlo, se le encontró a su lado como un objeto familiar" [By degrees he made bold to go there at all times of the day and, eventually, without having noticed what had happened, Ana regarded him as a familiar object when she found him by her side, 1: 569; 434]. Without passing the garden's gate, Mesía successfully fills the Ozores palace with his presence, while later his physical attendance in the house is taken for granted and he becomes like a piece of furniture or decorative object.

If entering the Ozores palace foreshadows the sexual victory over Ana, then it also reveals that Mesía's conquest is of Ana's body, not of her thoughts. The mansion is like a body without a mind, so that Mesía might penetrate the house and Ana physically but not her mind and heart. The adultery is repeatedly described as the "asalto del caserón de los Ozores" [assault on Ozores mansion, 1: 840; 661]. Álvaro, quite unaware of the hollowness of his triumph, takes great pleasure in entering the mansion, "a Mesía le gustaba entrar en la casa de la Rinconada" [Mesía did like to go into the house in the corner of the Plaza Nueva, 1: 567; 433], but as he begins to lose ground, the Ozores palace reflects his defeat. In *The Maias* and *Quincas Borba*, failed and beaten characters also trip and fall over emblematic objects and furnishings. All three novels reinforce with an ironic tone the interdependence between interior and fiction, as material culture dominates characters and becomes the agent of narrative action. Álvaro comes to say goodbye to Víctor and Ana before he goes away for the summer season, and the gallant leaves "tropezando con el pavo real disecado y después con la puerta"

[bumping first into the stuffed peacock and then into the door, 1: 612; 472].[56]
Mesía's spatial clumsiness testifies to his misreading of Ana's interiors.
While Álvaro might use Ana as a mere sexual conquest she too objectifies
him by turning Mesía into one of her furnishings. Lucky for him objects and
furnishings can evoke deep experiences for Ana, a point which will be explored in the next chapter, and therefore Álvaro will ultimately function to
fulfill some of her dreams and desires.

Fermín is a lot more intelligent in his spatial reading and writing of his
relationship to Ana, but he too falls short and is deceived. His growing
intimacy with Ana is also conceptualized as a domestic invasion, especially
for Víctor who claims not to be strong enough "para oponerse al *jesuitismo*
que había invadido su hogar" [to oppose the Jesuitism which had invaded his
home, 1: 656; 508]. Fermín prefers to meet Ana outside the Ozores palace in
her garden's gazebo, since this is where he feels most confident and closest
to her. This garden shelter is the Regenta's designated space for thought.
Ana's first significant intellectual experience takes place during her adolescence when she lives with her father in their country estate in Loreto. Although Ana discovers Saint Augustine's *Confessions* while dusting her
father's library, the transcendental reading takes place in the "glorieta de su
huerto" [arbour in Loreto, 1: 562; 429]. Ana is of course imitating St. Augustine, who also experiences spiritual rapture in the garden, but it is not in the
open garden where she feels best, but in this covered interior space surrounded by the natural world. The "glorieta" represents a type of interior
space that combines comfort with nature, marginally removed from the
house and its sense of confinement, yet sheltered and private enough so as to
stand outside the corrupt public arena. Like Carlos and Maria Eduarda's
Japanese gazebo, the "glorieta" is an interior within an exterior: "cubierto de
espesa enredadera perenne. Las sombras de las hojuelas de la bóveda verde
jugueteaban sobre las hojas del libro, blancas y negras y brillantes" [with its
dense covering of perennial creepers. The shadows cast by the leaves in the
green vaulting played upon the pages of the book, which shone out in white
and black, 1: 157; 91]. Nature shelters and echoes Ana's interior and mental
experience, while at the same time the interior experience can also affect her
ideas. As opposed to the creative rapture she undergoes on the hilltop in
Loreto, here the enclosed setting cultivates her reflections. In her gazebo,
instead of writing poetry, Ana is often seen reading. The narrative uses this
sheltered space to bring Ana slowly and gradually deeper inside herself, and
not only to blur boundaries between the social and the natural. As the narrative evolves, Ana draws closer to her own enclosed spaces, while at the same
time striving to avoid being trapped inside others.

This special place of Ana's youth in Loreto finds its counterpart in her
adult life in the Ozores mansion's outdoor porch, and whether conscious or
not of his efforts, Fermín attempts to connect to Ana inside this specific

space. The "glorieta" incarnates Ana's intellectual growth and is associated with the development of her mind, which De Pas, at least in part, strives to commune with. When Fermín visits the Quintanar couple in the Vivero and finds no one at home, he goes straight to satisfy his thirst "en la glorieta del jardín" [into the arbour, 1: 786; 615]. The first among many intimate conversations, when Fermín makes his famous argument about how form is substance, takes place in the open air "dentro del cenador" [in the arbour, 1: 508; 384]. He sits in the rocking chair "a la entrada del cenador" [in the entrance of the arbour, 1: 511; 386] and looks up sorrowfully at the starry sky. As the conversation flows he becomes increasingly more confortable and his pleasure is directly supported by this architectural structure: "apoyaba la cabeza, oculta en la sombra, en una barra de hierro del armazón de la glorieta, en la que se enroscaban el jazmín y la madreselva" [His head, hidden in the shadows, was resting upon one of the iron bars which formed the frame of the arbour and around which jasmine and honeysuckle twined, 1: 516; 391]. Fermín performs these types of sensual gestures only when he feels extremely at home in an interior space, as when he lays his head and caresses with his hand the rich curtains in Páez's drawing-room. Here his spatial language suggests his desire to get closer to Ana's thoughts.

Invading and sensually experiencing an interior space becomes a subtext that frames the complexities, successes, and failures of the different competing forces in the novel. The tension between Ana, her husband, confessor, and lover is organized by a ubiquitous sense of deceit, which surfaces in the interior details. The rocking chair, on which both Fermín and Víctor sit, is a perfect example of how the author furnishes this falseness. As mentioned above, Fermín and Ana meet to converse in this retreat of the Ozores garden, during which time the confessor tries to comfort Ana by approaching "un poco su mecedora a la Regenta" [his rocking-chair a little closer, 1: 514; 389]. When Víctor sees Álvaro climbing out of Ana's room and faces the dreadful end of his illusionary happiness, he settles in this exact same rocking chair, which proves to be a lot more comfortable than the cold stone bench he tries initially: "Entró en el cenador y se sentó en una mecedora" [He walked into the arbour and sat in a rocking-chair, 1: 848; 668]. Later once again "Volvió a caer sentado en la mecedora" [He dropped back into the rocking-chair, 1: 849; 669]. Both Víctor and Fermín occupy the same defeated and vulnerable position. The swaying sensation of peace and reassurance provided by the chair is illusory. Similarly, as we will see in the subsequent analysis of Ana's furnishings, the rocking chair in her bedroom is also a disappointment and will not compensate for the lack of affection she experienced as a child. In their selfishness Víctor and Fermín fail to ease Ana's suffering. Besides suggesting Ana's betrayal toward both Víctor and Fermín, the chair in the gazebo functions as poetic revenge for the heroine and comments ironically on their inability to support her.

Details such as the rocking chair and specific interactions between characters and enclosed spaces corroborate the narrative focus on penetrating, invading, and conquering inner realms. Thus Alas develops an important link between rooms and furnishings and a character's inner life. But what experiences leave their mark on this interior existence? Like Machado and Eça, Clarín is also interested in connecting the private experience with public and historical events. All three novels weave nineteenth-century history into specific components of their interior representations and explore how political and social events shape the individual and collective consciences. Clarín chooses to figure Spain's colonial experience into his interior representations. A number of images found in these dark interiors allude to this historical context by representing the whole with the part, the same way the corner functions as a synecdoche. The narrative frame that organizes both the plot and content of the novel, which relies on an ongoing invasion and penetration of interior realms, also reveals important consequences that Spain's political past has had on Vetustan society.

Clearly Spain's maritime history has had a disastrous and degenerative toll on the citizens of Vetusta. The provincial town can be construed, on the one hand, as a narrow, suffocating, and obscure interior world in need of renovation and ventilation. Yet on the other hand, the collective space can also be understood as a large transatlantic ship involved in a catastrophic accident whose passengers, or characters, are either shipwrecked, seasick, or drowning in the open waters. Vetusta's endless rainy season turns the city into an ocean and its inhabitants into "anfibios" [amphibians] that live through the season swimming and "debajo de agua" [under water, 1: 468; 351]. Images connecting both the plot and its characters to the sea and to water recur throughout the novel. Still, Vetusta the interior and Vetusta the open sea are one and the same. Metaphors of maritime explorations and feelings of seasickness are closely linked to the experience of being inside closed spaces. During the guided tour of the cathedral, Bermúdez begins to feel seasick as if he were "en un barco" [aboard a ship], and the visitor Infanzón feels as if he "estaba en rigor como en alta mar" [were on the high seas, 1: 119; 60]. In Spanish the word "nave" [nave] does not only refer to a wing or corridor of the cathedral but also means ship. The sea of course immediately conjures different historical connotations within the Iberian historical context and these allusions have clearly affected the imaginary of the narrative and its characters. Saturno Bermúdez is especially sensitive to this experience the evening he attends the Carnival ball:

> Saturno entra en el salón, saludando a diestro y siniestro, y aunque parece que su propósito es enterrarse de quién está allí, en el *fuero interno* bien sabe él que lo que busca es un rincón de un diván o una silla, que le sirva de puerto en aquella arriesgada navegación por los mares del *gran mundo*. Pero poco a poco

se acostumbra al agua, es decir, al salón, y ya está allí muy tranquilo, y baila y dice galanterías en unos párrafos tan largos y complicados, que nadie se los agradece.

[Saturno enters the ballroom, saluting right and left and, although his purpose seems to be to discover who is there, in *the deepest recesses of his soul* he well knows that what he is really trying to find is a chair or a corner of a divan which can be his harbour in this hazardous navigation through the seas of the *great world*. But little by little he becomes accustomed to the water, or to the ballroom, and soon he is at his ease, and dances and passes compliments in such lengthy and complicated sentences that no lady wishes to receive them, 1: 706; 549.]

The ballroom is compared to the wild seas that have to be navigated, just as one has to learn to survive in society. While such ridiculed characters as Bermúdez more often than not drown in these dark, narrow, or rough interiors, and end up submerged in waters and rooms, others who conquer interiors are compared to great navigators who reach and capture unknown lands. Fermín, who calls Vetusta his "mezquino imperio" [wretched empire] and reminds himself that while others inherited their fortune he conquered his, is not the only conquistador in the novel (1: 79; 29). Álvaro is also often in search of newfound dominions, and his sexual conquest of Ana is like that of an explorer: "La miraba como el descubridor de una isla o un continente" [He gazed at her as an explorer gazes at an island or a continent, 1: 612; 471]. The Marquis de Vegallana's curious hobbies, like his passion for "tragarse leguas" [swallowing up the miles] or his habit of populating his properties with his bastards, is Alas's form of criticizing the "caciquismo" that dominated Spanish and Latin-American politics (1: 241; 158). *La Regenta*'s web of metaphors evoking Spain's transatlantic history draws literary connections that both foreshadow and echo the narratives of colonial exploitation. This seafaring history is an Iberian experience as both Portugal and Spain built overseas empires. The repeated references to shipwrecks in the novel recall the traditions set forth in the narration of the Portuguese seafaring disasters in the collection *História Trágico-Marítima* (1735-36)[57] and in Álvar Núñez Cabeza de Vaca's *Naufragios* (1542). Since the interior space functions as the stage for the narrative, and at the same time is the site of dissolution and of the limits of reality and of the story, the links between rooms and sea imagery tie the fiction to this historical background.

Like Eça and Machado, Clarín focuses more on how a novel might narrate, evoke, and explore the past with its narrative form and metaphorical constructions. As with Eça's southwest wind, which points geographically to the Americas, a "viento sur, caliente y perezoso" [south wind, warm and languid] opens *La Regenta* and the novel ends three years later on a fall afternoon "en que soplaba el viento sur perezoso y caliente" [when the south wind was blowing, languid and warm, 1: 65, 897; 21, 712]. Clarín and Eça not only use similar images to describe the way historical events permeate the makeup of societies and identities, but they also connect the figures—the "indianos" and the "brasileiros"—to their representation of the loss of moral values and social decay. In their insightful articles Guadalupe Gómez-Ferrer Morant and James D. Fernández explore the significantly charged figure of the "indiano" in Alas's fiction. Similar to Eça's claims about the "brasileiro" and his connection to the Portuguese, Fernández's reading of Clarín's short story "Boroña" argues that America is inside Spain, having become part of the national identity and collective imagination. [58] Alas's various representations of "indianos" in *La Regenta* also reveal how the loss of innocence is part of both Spain and the New World, and that America, and much of the violence done to it and within it, is literarily inside Spain, and inside the interior settings of the novel. Alas's narrator claims that among the "negros y negras" [Negroes and Negresses] that serve Olvido Páez, her father is her "esclavo más fiel" [most faithful slave, 1: 383; 276]. This father daughter relationship recalls the interaction between many of Machado's characters, as well as the connection between Monforte and Maria in *The Maias*, since all these relations ironically reproduce the master slave dialectic. Furthermore, Alas and Eça subtly tie the figures of the "indiano" and the "brasileiro" to a violent past. Both Monforte and Don Frutos, for example, seem to be haunted by their prior experiences. The narrative parodies Don Frutos by giving him a derogatory name and by having him be an "indiano" that has returned from Matanzas, Cuba, further associating him with the violence committed in the colonies. The name of Páez's daughter, Olvido, might also suggest the individual and institutional attempt to forget these colonial atrocities. Just as in *The Maias*, these minor figures have a major role on the development of the plot and characters in Clarín's novel.

If in *The Maias* the "brasileiros" have a strong impact on the fate of Carlos and other characters, in *La Regenta* Don Frutos plays a crucial role in dictating Ana's future. Not only is her orphaned state partly due to her father's overseas adventures, ultimately marriage to Víctor results as an escape from a forced marriage to Don Frutos Redondo, which would imply a direct connection to this evil past. During the drunken celebration in honor of atheist Don Pompeyo Guimarán, don Frutos wants to ignore his memories of "la mala vida" [the bad life] he has led (1: 606; 466). Instead he is busy "haciendo islas y continentes de vino tinto sobre el mantel" [making islands and continents of red wine upon the table-cloth, 1: 606; 466]. The tablecloth is described in great detail before the meal begins and seems to map the vestiges of the dinner guests' conquests, both sexual and geographical. The narrator explains it has "embarazosos cargados con aceite y vinagre y con más especias que un barco de Oriente" [cruet-stands, laden with oil and vinegar and more spices than a boat from the east, 1: 599; 460], and the seducer Álvaro considers the tablecloth an "anfiteatro propio del cadáver del amor carnal" [appropriate amphitheater for the corpse of carnal love, 1: 602; 463]. This scene, a parody of the last supper, employs recurring religious similes, turning the red wine into a metaphor for blood, which in the case of Don Frutos seems once again to highlight the violent deaths of the colonial enterprise. Don Frutos is not solely responsible for the bloodshed by indigenous peoples, African slaves, and victims of shipwrecks and wars, but he bears the conscious and subconscious memories that surface in the details of a domestic object. The tablecloth, a component of the interior, draws characters and readers to intimate and public experiences stained by exploitation. Frutos's violent past shares common ground with Álvaro's own exploits, suggesting that Ana, while escaping the violence of one potential lover, is unable to evade that of another. Furthermore, the subtle parallel between Álvaro and Don Frutos and their types of violent conquest, sexual and topographical, once again unites adultery with colonial exploitation. To a much lesser degree than Eça's and Machado's novels, *La Regenta* nevertheless also looks to create links between adultery and slavery. The figurative blood of Don Pompeyo's dinner ceremony surfaces again in relation to Don Frutos in a very particular image in which Ana pictures him lying dead by the seashore: "el mísero tendido sobre la arena, ahogándose en un charco de sangre, como la que ella había visto en la plaza de toros, una sangre casi negra, muy espesa y con espuma" [the wretched man stretched out upon the sand, drowning in a pool of blood, like the blood she had seen at bull fights, black blood, thick and foaming, 1: 299; 207]. A marriage to him would imply a bond with corruption, violence, and blood. As in Eça's recurring imagery of blood and the color black to signify colonial violence and the slave trade, the figure of Don Frutos is also associated with death, blackness, and aggression. These images are concealed in the details of an interior and suggest inner existence in the face of a desolate reality is similar to a futile seafaring expedition.

Metaphors of water and drowning are not the only rhetorical figures connecting the interior of rooms with acts of historical corruption. An important link exists in the novel between the inside of spaces and coal mining. This association reinforces the narrative project of burrowing deep into human interiority while criticizing specific economic conditions. The mining industry is fundamental for the industrial development in Asturias just as it is a crucial factor in the economic exploitation of the Americas. The novel connects mining to the penetration of the interior of a room, a technique that serves to reflect critically on the act of narrating as social criticism. The association between mining and the interior begins with Doña Paula's curious investigation of her son's private quarters. As a subsequent closer look at Fermín's character will show, to understand De Pas's personal thoughts and desires one must focus on the physical movement that takes place inside his rooms. Scrutinizing his interior space, looking for objects out of place, or identifying changes in the furniture's position will not reveal all that takes place inside De Pas's mind. Still, Doña Paula tries to uncover her son's feelings and secrets by examining his private rooms:

> Doña Paula había vuelto a entrar en el despacho de su hijo. Registró la alcoba. Vio la cama *levantada*, tiesa, muda, fresca, sin un pliegue; salió de la alcoba; en el despacho reparó el sofá de reps azul, las butacas, las correctas filas de libros amontonados sobre sillas y tablas por todas partes; se fijó en el orden de la mesa, en el sillón, en el de las sillas. Parecía olfatear con los ojos. Llamó a Teresina; le preguntó cualquier cosa, haciendo en su rostro excavaciones con la mirada, como quien anda a minas; se metió por los pliegues del traje, correcto, como el orden de las sillas, de los libros, de todo.

> [Doña Paula had gone back into her son's study. She inspected the bedroom with its made-up bed, stiff and fresh—it had not one crease, nothing to tell her. She walked out of the bedroom and into the study and there examined the blue rep sofa, the easy chairs, the correct lines of books piled up on chairs and shelves on every side; she scrutinized the disposition of the table, the armchair, all the other chairs. She seemed to be smelling something out with her eyes. She called Teresina and asked her a question, excavating the girl's face with her look, like someone prospecting for a mine, and plunging into the very fold of her clothes, which were in perfect order, like the chairs, the books, everything, 1: 344; 243.]

The excavation of Fermín's intimate environment tells the reader a lot more about Doña Paula than it does about her son. Doña Paula treats the components of her son's interior world as a site that she can exploit and smell, and that could theoretically communicate to her and fulfill her desires. Fermín's mother grows up in the mining region of Asturias and learns early on that the act of mining brings riches, resources, and satisfaction, and she begins her lifelong career of fraud by exploiting with her prosperous tavern the coal miners in her hometown of Matalerejo. [59] Ongoing economic metaphors relating to mining describe the way she reads the world. Doña Paula believes that everything is to be found deep within: "El dinero estaba en las entrañas de la tierra; había que cavar hondo para sacar provecho" [Money was in the bowels of the earth, one had to dig deep to get it out, 1: 446; 331]. Recurring images in the novel paint private spaces as dark and blinding caves, so that interiors are often like mines and the characters penetrating in and out of these rooms are like miners. Doña Paula controls the Bishop and his Palacio, for example, which is also compared to a cave and thus for Fermín "salir de Palacio era salir de una cueva. De tanto hablar allá dentro, tenía la boca seca y amarga y se le antojaba sentir un saborcillo a cobre" [Coming out of the palace was like emerging from a cave. So much talking in there had left him with a dry, bitter taste in his mouth—he even thought he could detect a tang of copper, 1: 381; 274]. Fermín's desire to conquer the world by penetrating inside people's thoughts and homes reproduces his mother's own understanding of having to dig to triumph over others. As an adolescent in his mother's tavern, De Pas will learn to peek in on the coal miners from his hidden corner, a position and movement he repeats as an adult. The corruption of the self and control over others, associated with mining and with Doña Paula and Fermín's desire for power, relate to the act of piercing spaces and once again underline the larger formal preoccupation in the novel with interiors.

Vetusta's casino is an excellent example of an interior setting that begins to resemble a mine and that is associated with corruption and with the sense of slavery that emerges in all three novels as an important bond regulating character relations. In its long, narrow, and decaying floor plan and architecture, the casino's tight and dim salons tend to leave its dwellers immobile, sleepy, mute, and in the dark. The novel describes the casino members as "esclavos de tamaña servidumbre" [servile slaves, 1: 205; 129], and the ombre[60] card-players as "esclavos de su vicio" [slaves of their vice, 1: 199; 125]. The casino seems to enslave the gamblers, or Vetusta's citizens, evoking not only the image of the mine but also Doña Paula's belief that things and ideas are buried inside spaces. The red parlor where the Vetustan gentlemen play ombre never receives the light of day, "siempre permanecía en tinieblas caliginosas, que hacían palpables las tristes llamas de las bujías semejantes a lámparas de minero en las entrañas de la tierra" [it was always sunk in murky shadow, which made the candles' dismal flames seem palpable, like miners' lamps in the bowels of the earth, 1: 198; 124]. By developing a link between coal mining, slavery, and the sense of enclosure, the novel seems to comment on and critique the social injustices related to slavery and the proletarian classes. Furthermore, the narrative is interested in demonstrating how economic and political events intimately distort selves and communities, how they infiltrate inside people and places.

The act of narrating is also a form of penetrating inside. The narrator is thus a sort of miner himself, who explores how exploitation works. The novel's metaphors and descriptions focus on digging deeper into a space and of forming a pattern of increasing depth. This becomes clear from the way various interior settings in the novel contain other enclosed spaces. Rooms often include other interiors: the Vegallana kitchen has a very peculiar pantry that previously served as a bedroom, Fermín uses his room's armoire to let out his feelings of jealousy, and Ana's majestic dining-room fireplace contains her sadness. Like Gaston Bachelard, who explores a desk or a dresser's many drawers as guardians of knowledge, memories, and history, *La Regenta*'s narrator is a sort of miner who keeps digging and scuffing away at reality and thus creates holes and other containers within his interior settings. On the one hand these different levels multiply the interpretive meanings, while on the other hand they suggest that the act of excavating uncovers hidden immoral actions and tragic events. In her study of Vetusta as "espacio-fuerza" [space-force] Harriet Turner claims that the novel constantly reflects and inverts its representations and that the spatial holes are there to oppose the openings:

> Desde la primera página vemos que Vetusta es, sobre todo, un mundo doblado y replegado. Sus múltiples aperturas, elevadas en forma de balcones y ventanas—promesas de luz y de libertad ascendente—se tornan abajo para angostarse en agujeros y pozos, *perforaciones* que configuran el diseño decisivo: el círculo concéntrico de la cloaca digestiva o el caracol o espiral, ilusión óptica por la que todo *subir* se torna *bajar* y vice-versa. [61]

> [From the very first page we see that Vetusta is, above all, a doubled and withdrawn world. Its multiple openings, elevated in the form of balconies and windows—promises of light and of rising freedom—turn upside down and become narrow holes and wells, *perforations* that configure the decisive design: the concentric circle of the digestive cloaca or of the snail or spiral, an optic illusion where all that *rises* also *falls* and vice-versa].

In addition to this significant technique of inversion defined by Turner, the images of holes and the move of lowering represent the idea of penetrating deeper inside; the process of interiorization. Characters are constantly and at crucial moments experiencing fears and desires in the deepest recesses of their minds and bodies. The opening references in the novel to the digestive system introduce the idea of the inside, or the entrails, as a ubiquitous and repeated image that is not limited to the body. The entrails, like the many and varied corners and narrow spaces, tie into the rendering of Vetusta as one interior space and even one body. But as we will see the novel is also interested in the insides of the inside. Once in an interior space the author probes further other possible interiors, real and metaphoric. The recurring preoccupation with the inside of furniture, stuffed objects, and rooms within other rooms parallels the constant analysis of interiorities of individuals but also that of mines and seas, all metaphorical images that point to the subconscious or interior depth that the novel explores. Along with the governing movement in the narrative of descending and inverting as identified by Turner, equally important to the novel's aesthetic concerns is the strong drive to penetrate and interiorize.

The architectural framing of the novel with openings and closings, insides and holes, also reinforces the circular structure of the plot. The novel opens with the idea of the insides of Vetustan homes, characters' bodies, and of the church, and ends with Ana locked inside Fermín's chapel, which is an interior within the church. The key to the problem of interior and interiority emerges in the novel not only figuratively, but also literarily. A real key comes up at important points of the story and becomes an emblematic figure.

Among its many rooms, the casino has a reading room, which also serves as a library, and like many other Vetustan interiors, it is "estrecho y no muy largo" [narrow and not very long, 1: 201; 126]. The reading room contains a very peculiar built-in walnut bookcase, whose most interesting books are in a locked lower compartment for which the key has apparently been lost. This non-existent key is important because it points to the significance of this reading room. During the Carnival ball the aristocracy locks itself inside this reading room to dine, revel, and dance removed from the other social classes. The plan of locking the door receives widespread approval among the ladies and gentlemen present. To keep the party happy the waiting staff must enter through a side-door "que estaba cerca del armario de libros" [near the bookcase, 1: 709; 552]. Keys to locks of doors are a central figure in the story, bearing in mind that characters peep through keyholes into the private lives of others and that the narrative is constantly interested in penetrating these spaces and in drawing characters and readers inside them. Here the misplaced key surfaces in the one that locks the group up in their isolated world and then again in the key that encloses the heroine at the end of the novel in Fermín's chapel. Celedonio arrives with his jangling keys for one final enclosing of Ana inside Vetusta and her dreadful reality.

The novel's storyline begins and ends with Ana trapped inside a dark and cold interior; first caught in Víctor's study, at the end of the novel she is locked inside the chapel. Noël Valis's splendid reading of Ana's entrapment in "Order and Meaning" reveals how *La Regenta* is concerned with the loss of meaning, the total dissolution and disintegration of reality. [62] My focus on highlighting the narrative movement toward the interior space is also an attempt to elucidate how for Clarín society's state of utter loss is in a sense impossible to narrate. The narrative perspective aims to reach deeper inside the characters, the ideas, the mystery, and enigma of life, but at the same time this constant search is also, to use Valis's own words, "an experience in entrapment." [63] The novel and narrator, like the characters, try to reach a deeper level, but often they can not penetrate fully inside, the view is incomplete and smoky. At the same time the process of interiorization is a like a dead-end street. Being in our interiors and in our inner worlds is also being unable to escape them. Interiors in *La Regenta* reproduce the depth of life, the intensity of literature, and the complexity of human psychology. *La Regenta*, like *Quincas Borba* and *Os Maias*, frames its narrative themes and concerns with the interior space so that settings are no longer only a reflection of topics, characters, and societies but give shape to the novel's purpose. Machado de Assis's relationships between spaces, things, and characters in *Quincas Borba* analyze fundamental social and political structures of Brazilian society. Similarly, Eça's novel reproduces in the nineteenth-century fascination with interior architecture and domestic environments a simile for the complex effects Portugal's history has on the stagnated status quo. Clarín explores the tension between inside and outside by asking how the external surroundings, real and imagined, past and present, affect the inner construction of the self, and of reality and art.

Notes

1. René Wellek, *Concepts of Criticism* (New Haven: Yale University Press, 1963), 236.
2. Noël Maureen Valis, *The Decadent Vision in Leopoldo Alas: A Study of* La Regenta *and* Su único hijo (Baton Rouge: Louisiana State University Press, 1981), 47.
3. Benjamin, *Arcades Project*, 220.
4. *Quincas Borba* was originally published in *A Estação* between June 15, 1886, and September 15, 1891. Machado significantly revised the work before its publication in book form in 1891. Jorge de Sena coined the term "modern quintet" to refer to Machado's last five novels. In his essay "Machado de Assis e o seu Quinteto Carioca" [Machado de Assis and his quintet], Jorge de Sena reads these texts "como um todo, e, mesmo mais, como uma unidade estética, em termos de moderna técnica de ficção novelística" [as a whole, and more, as an aesthetic unity, in terms of modern technique of novelistic fiction] (Jorge de Sena, *Estudos de Cultura e Literatura Brasileira* [Lisboa: Edições 70, 1988], 325).
5. António Cândido, *Vários Escritos* (São Paulo: Duas Cidades, 1995), 32. Some of the problems that Machado explores and António Cândido discusses in his article, which emerge as important topics in *Quincas Borba*, include defining identity and madness, the relation between the real and the imagined, the significance of the act, the impossibility of choice, and the reified individual.
6. Enylton de Sá Rego, "The Epic, the Comic and the Tragic: Tradition and Innovation in Three Late Novels of Machado de Assis," *Latin American Literary Review* 14: 27 (1986), 26.
7. Earl E. Fitz, "The *Memórias Póstumas de Brás Cubas* as (Proto)type of the Modernist Novel: A Problem in Literary History and Interpretation," *Latin American Literary Review* 18: 36 (1990), 7. Fitz identifies four essential modern characteristics in Machado's *The Posthumous Memoirs of Brás Cubas*, which in my view also describe *Quincas Borba*. He explains that the novel:

> challenges bourgeois attitudes about meaning and morality in art by being self-consciously aware of the artifice of its own composition; it is primarily concerned (thematically speaking) not with action or event in the external world, but with the representation of inward states of human motivation and consciousness; it conveys a disquieting sense of nihilism, capriciousness and disorder that lie behind the orderly and 'realistically' depicted surface of human existence; and it frees itself from dependence on linear, cause-and-effect plot structures. (ibid.)

8. Celso Favaretto, "Afterword," *Quincas Borba*, trans. Gregory Rabassa (New York: Oxford University Press, 1998), 275.
9. Ibid.
10. As António Cândido observes: "No fim, pobre e louco, ele [Rubião] morre abandonado; mas em compensação, como queria a filosofia do Humanitismo, Palha e Sofia estão ricos e considerados, dentro da mais perfeita normalidade social" [In the end, poor and crazy, he (Rubião) dies completely abandoned; but in compensation for that, as the philosophy of Humanitism would have, Palha and Sofia are rich and considered part of the most perfect social normalcy] (António Cândido, *Vários Escritos*, 35).
11. Emilia Viotti da Costa, *The Brazilian Empire: Myths and Histories* (Chapel Hill: University of North Carolina Press, 1985), 55.
12. John Gledson, *The Deceptive Realism of Machado de Assis* (Liverpool: Francis Cairns, 1984), 5.

13. For example, Rubião believes Sofia and Carlos Maria have their love nest in the "Rua da Harmonia" [Harmony Street], and the "Rua da Ajuda" [Help Street] is where Rubião first saves Deolindo's life, the boy who later joins a crowd of youth in mocking him on the same street.

14. Roberto Schwarz, "Duas notas sobre Machado de Assis," *Que horas são? Ensaios* (São Paulo: Companhia das Letras, 1987), 166. The italics are in the original.

15. Tomasi di Lampedusa, *The Leopard*, trans. Archibald Colquhoun (New York: Pantheon, 1960), 40.

16. Peter Jones, "Introduction," *Odyssey*, 59.

17. Ibid., 58-59.

18. Ibid., 231.

19. Ibid., 233.

20. Ibid., 234.

21. John Gledson, *Deceptive Realism*, 14.

22. Silviano Santiago, *Uma literatura nos trópicos: Ensaios sobre dependência cultural* (Rio de Janeiro: Rocco, 2000), 26.

23. David T. Haberly explains in *Three Sad Races* that an interior and exterior identity is present in both Machado and his characters. He argues that, unlike the interior identity, which is essential, natural, and genetic, one's exterior identity is completely socially constructed and learned. Ideally, a balance should exist between these two, but more often than not they are incompatible, contradictory, and impossible. Haberly explains that "the external identity contradicts or dwarfs the internal self, creating a destructive, antipathetic symbiosis" (David T. Haberly, *Three Sad Races: Racial Identity and National Consciousness in Brazilian Literature* [Cambridge: Cambridge University Press, 1983], 76).

24. Machado writes: "O que se deve exigir do escritor antes de tudo, é certo sentimento íntimo, que o torne homem do seu tempo e de seu país" [what one should demand of a writer above all is a certain intimate sentiment that makes him a man of his time and country, 3: 817].

25. Jürgen Habermas, *The Structural Transformation of the Public Sphere: An Inquiry into a Category of Bourgeois Society*, trans. Thomas Burger (Cambridge, MA: MIT Press, 1989), 45.

26. Richard Sennett, *The Fall of Public Man* (New York: Norton, 1974), 4.

27. Peter Brooks, *Body Work: Objects of Desire in Modern Narrctive*. Cambridge (MA: Harvard University Press, 1993), 28.

28. Ibid.

29. See João Medina's "O Pessimismo Nacional de Eça de Queirós: Estudo Sobre *Os Maias*," *Seara Nova* 1514 (1971): 21-30, or José de Almeida Moura's "*Os Maias*, Ensaio Alegórico Sobre a Decadência da Nação," *Cadernos de Literatura* 14 (1983): 46-56.

30. Alexander Coleman, *Eça de Queirós and European Realism* (New York: New York University Press, 1980), 188.

31. Isabel Pires de Lima, *As Máscaras do Desengano: Para uma Abordagem Sociológica de Os Maias de Eça de Queirós* (Lisboa: Caminho, 1987), 56.

32. Isabel Pires de Lima, "Eça e *Os Maias* pensar-se pensando Portugal," *Colóquio/Letras* 103 (1988), 22.

33. Benjamin, *Arcades Project*, 212.

34. Orest Ranum, "The Refuges of Intimacy," *A History of Private Life* (Cambridge, MA: Belknap Press of Harvard University Press, 1989), 243.

35. Benjamin, *Arcades Project*, 16.

36. See António Coimbra Martins's "O Incesto d'*Os Maias*," *Ensaios Queirosianos* (Lisboa: Europa-América, 1967), 267-287.

37. Maria Manuel Lisboa's *Teu Amor Fez de Mim um Lago Triste* suggests two different and revealing readings of the incest theme: "A primeira apreende o tema do incesto como uma metáfora de apologia da (porventura incestuosa) união ibérica de Portugal com uma Espanha entendível no passado como a mãe edipianamente descartada em 1143, e num futuro mais ou menos próximo como possível irmã no contexto peninsular" [The first understands the incest as an apologetic metaphor for the (coincidentally incestuous) Iberian union between Portugal and a Spain understood in the past as the mother oedipally discarded in 1143, and in a more or less near future as a possible sister in the peninsular context] (Maria Manuel Lisboa, *Teu Amor Fez*

de mim um Lago Ttriste: *Ensaios sobre* Os Maias [Porto: Campo das Letras, 2000], 18). In a second interpretation, Lisboa writes "o tema do incesto entre irmãos n'*Os Maias*, será considerado como tendo origem numa patologia narcísica ela própria desencadeada pela perda amorosa da mãe, e como sendo conducente a uma desintegração psíquica de implicações mais amplas (nacionais), que, porém, sugerem ser não o incesto, mas antes a perda do amor incestuoso, a causa dessa desintegração ou decadência" [The incest between the two siblings in *The Maias* will be considered to have originated in a narcissistic pathology unleashed by the loss of the mother, and as conducive of a psychological disintegration of more widespread implications (national), which however, suggest that the cause of that disintegration or decadence is not the incest but the loss of the incestuous love, 66].

38. Eça prefigures the unfortunate end of the story with the comical event resulting from the offensive letter Dâmaso writes and which is nearly made public. Because of the letter, Ega and Cruges confront Dâmaso with Carlos's challenge to a duel. Although things turn out well and no duel takes place, in Ega's words everything could have ended "numa poça de sangue!" [in a pool of blood!, 561; 487]. The novel indirectly does end in a pool of blood, but not literally, only in literary terms.

39. The man of humble origins who emigrates from the Peninsula to the Americas and returns exceedingly wealthy to his hometown is a very important Iberian cultural type in the nineteenth century and plays a prominent literary role. In Portugal he is known as "o brasileiro" and in Spain as "el indiano." During Romanticism this character is caricaturized and parodied, but with Eça and Clarín he takes on more complex and various narrative functions. Eça claims that this figure is completely original to the Peninsula's literary tradition. He writes in his preface to Luís de Magalhães's *O Brasileiro Soares* (1886), "O brasileiro, porém, era só nosso, todo nosso, deste solo que pisamos, castiço e mais originalmente português que a chalaça e a louça das Caldas" [The "brasileiro" was ours, all ours, of this ground that we step on, genuine and more originally Portuguese than the earthenware from Caldas, 8]. Not all representations of the "brasileiro" are the same, and Eça writes that Magalhães gives a very new face to this figure in the novel *O Brasileiro Soares*. As Eça points out, the protagonist, Joaquim Soares da Boa Sorte, is at the same time real and poetic, local and universal. This honest, optimistic, but incredibly ingenuous commercial success story commits suicide at the end of the novel when his bride, his much younger, beautiful, and cunning niece, flees with his administrator. Interiors play a significant role in *O Brasileiro Soares* by showing the destruction of the old aristocratic taste and ways. Soares buys the wealthiest estate in his hometown of Guardeira, whose fields and land his antecessors worked. The interior of the old country estate was completely renovated and all that was antique was substituted with the new and modern: "nada resistiu à mania do moderno do brasileiro sem gosto e dos operários especuladores" [nothing resisted the obsession with the modern of the Brazilian without taste and of the speculating workers, 49]. The new bourgeois interior filled with the latest fashions and furniture contrasts with the majestic exterior of the house. As Soares begins to fulfill his role of the "brasileiro" and flaunts his wealth he ironically gets closer to his own ruin by creating a trap for himself. He contracts an upholsterer from Porto to create an all light-blue boudoir for his bride, which later serves as the love nest for his wife and her lover.

40. Alexander Coleman, "Uma Reflexão a Respeito de Eça de Queirós e Machado de Assis," *Eça e* Os Maias: *Actas do 1º Encontro Internacional de Queirosianos* (Porto: Asa, 1990), 70.

41. João Medina, *Reler Eça de Queiroz: Das Farpas aos* Maias (Lisboa: Livros Horizonte, 2000), 73.

42. Beatriz Berrini's *Portugal de Eça de Queiroz* (Lisboa: Imprensa Nacional-Casa da Moeda, 1984) points to these and further harsh remarks concerning blacks and other ethnic groups in the novel as elements of discrimination. She claims Eça's lexicon reflects the still undeniably largely racist society of the time and the racist tendencies of the author himself (111-115). Although I do not disagree with this I also believe that Eça's merciless irony criticizes all races and nationalities and is often a very important self-critical technique that, instead of an intolerant personality, suggests the author was critical and open-minded.

43. The wind is not the only feature in the novel that repeatedly alludes to transatlantic voyages and contact with the Americas. For my argument it is a fundamental element because

the wind penetrates inside the characters' interior spaces and minds. But one would also have to emphasize the narrative insistence on different visions of the river Tagus with its many passing transatlantic ships. Following the scene when Maria Eduarda, Castro Gomes, and their black servant enter the Hotel Central is a long paragraph describing the serenity of the river and its many freight ships and extensive foreign steamers. It is also significant that Carlos returns to the Cais do Sodré and walks along the Aterro looking for Maria Eduarda, as is the fact that Afonso discovers a limited but enchanting view of the river from his rooms in the Ramalhete. It is emblematic that the Maia men are constantly fascinated by what is coming and going by sea.

44. João Camilo dos Santos, "Ramagens, Arvoredos, Folhagens...Breves reflexões sobre o campo semântico do 'Ramalhete' em *Os Maias*, de Eça de Queirós," *Queirosiana: Estudos sobre Eça de Queirós e a sua geração* (1999), 40.

45. It is important to note that the narrative line that the novel ultimately draws regarding colonization does not have to directly relate, it seems to me, to Eça's publicly pronounced political ideas on the topic. From two very early pieces in *Distrito de Évora* (1867), "Colónias" and "As conquistas," it becomes clear that the young Eça initially and naively defends a kind of just colonization based very much on an ideology of economic liberalism. In these early journalistic articles he uses the image of being asphyxiated between four walls to describe how nations and individuals become sterile and weak as they lose their political vitality and strength. Eça suggests then that the nation and the individual as represented in *The Maias* is no longer capable of historical and heroic feats such as an overseas expansion. However, it is already also clear even from this early piece that in the author's view the Iberian system and type of colonization was historically and incontestably failed and immoral.

46. Jo Labanyi, *Gender and Modernization in the Spanish Realist Novel* (Oxford: Oxford University Press, 2000), 209.

47. Gonzalo Sobejano, "Introduction," *La Regenta*, 12.

48. Gerardo Gonzalo, *Leopoldo Alas Clarín* (Madrid: Eneida, 2005), 11.

49. Dale J. Pratt, "Mapping, Realist Narrative and Cartographic Imagination in *La Regenta*," *Revista de Estudios Hispánicos* 35 (2001), 107.

50. Hadassah Ruth Weiner, "Integralismo de Clarín: Los 'interiores ahumados,'" *Los Cuadernos del Norte*. 2:7 (May-June 1981), 93.

51. Peter Brooks, *Body Work*, 30.

52. Luís Vélez de Guevara, *El diablo cojuelo*, ed. Enrique Rodríguez Cepeda (Madrid: Cátedra, 1984), 77.

53. Gonzalo Sobejano, "Introduction," *La Regenta*, 11.

54. Frank Durand, "Structural Unity in Leopoldo Alas' *La Regenta*," *Hispanic Review* 31.4 (1963), 325.

55. Jo Labanyi, "City, Country and Adultery in *La Regenta*," *Bulletin of Hispanic Studies* 63 (1986), 54. In her own analysis of patterns of imagery in *La Regenta*, Labanyi uses the words "inside" and "outside" to describe the inability to differentiate between the natural and the social, corroborating that this dilemma involves the dialectic between interiors and exteriors.

56. This is the one object in Víctor's study that Álvaro sympathizes and identifies with: "El único bicho que le era simpático a don Álvaro era un pavo real disecado por Frígilis y su amigo" [The only creature there with any appeal for Don Álvaro was a peacock which Frillity and his friend has stuffed, 567; 434]. This emblematic object involves a number of male figures all importantly related to Ana, Frígilis and Víctor, who dissect it or disembody it, and Fermín, who imitates its aesthetic qualities since the rhythm of the swaying and swinging of this cloak at times looks like "cola de pavo real" [a peacock's tail, 87; 36]. This simultaneously empty and impregnated symbol embodying and disembodying Mesía and his opponents contributes along with the Ozores mansion to the subtext signifying Álvaro's defeat and deception.

57. Although the *História Trágico-Marítima* (Tragic History of the Sea) was not published until the mid eighteenth century, most of the narratives are from the sixteenth and seventeenth centuries.

58. James D. Fernández, "America Is in Spain: A Reading of Clarín's 'Boroña,'" *Bridging the Atlantic: Toward a Reassessment of Iberian and Latin American Cultural Ties* (Albany: SUNY Press, 1996), 40-41.

59. The name of Doña Paula's native village, Matalerejo, sarcastically reminds us of where Don Frutos returns from in Cuba, Matanzas.

60. Ombre is a card game of Spanish origin in the whist family.

61. Harriet Turner, "Vetusta: espacio-fuerza en *La Regenta*," *Clarín y su obra: en el centenario de* La Regenta, ed. Antonio Vilanova (Barcelona: Universidad de Barcelona, 1985), 34-35.

62. Noël Valis, *Reading the Nineteenth-Century Spanish Novel: Selected Essays* (Newark, DE: Juan de la Cuesta, 2005), 27-28.

63. Ibid., 17.

Part Two: Interiors and Interiority

Critics credit realist-naturalist narratives with establishing as a necessary one the connection between characters and their social and historical milieus. Erich Auerbach explains in his reading of *Old Goriot* (1854) that Balzac's description of Madame Vauquer's room and person is controlled by a leading motif, which he calls the motif of "the harmony between her person and what we (and Balzac too, occasionally) call her milieu."[1] Or in Balzac's words: "enfin toute sa personne explique la pension, comme la pension implique sa personne" [she makes the boarding house what it is and the boarding house makes her what she is].[2] Gérard Genette also draws on Balzac to explain how description in literature is both explanatory and symbolic. He writes: "physical portraits, descriptions of dress and furniture tend, in Balzac and his realist successors, to reveal and at the same time justify the psychology of the characters, of which they are at once the sign, the cause, and the effect."[3] The dynamics between Eça's, Clarín's, and Machado's interiors and their characters are not always harmonious. Nor is there a simple cause and effect between the two. The furniture and objects are indeed impregnated with important historical and social milieus, but the energy that exists between interiors and characters suggests these novels are focused on interiors as representations of conscious and subconscious thoughts. *La Regenta's* protagonist, Fermín, already seems to think that interiors reveal the consciences of the characters. Moreover, while some characters in these novels manipulate, invent, dialogue with, and contradict their spaces, their rooms and furnishings in turn begin to dictate characters' feelings and actions. The narratives explore the psychological and emotional complexity both of major and minor characters by having them interact, echo, and challenge their private spaces and those of other characters. Interiors become a viable path to the characters' inner selves and to their struggle with memory and the passage of time.

The representation of interiors in these novels brings readers closer to the intimate thoughts of characters. The settings enhance character development because they point to how the interior minds of primarily major characters evolve in the narrative. The complex interaction that exists in these novels between interiors and characters reveals how the authors explore interiority in narrative. In this chapter I will examine the interiors of the novels' protagonists and those of some very important minor characters. The novels pay significant attention to the inner worlds of secondary figures. By describing the interior space associated with a minor character, the authors can efficiently hint at untold stories belonging to these additional characters, which they do not otherwise elaborate. Not every secondary figure is introduced along with his or her private milieu. The ones that are, therefore, have a specific function within the novel's larger framework; they are closer to the private desires of other characters, narrators, and even authors. Furthermore, they are personalities whose public persona contrasts dramatically with their private identity. These minor characters keep secrets hidden in their interior spaces, and the veiled details and obscurities uncovered there help decipher questions about the story and the protagonists.

There are relevant differences between major and minor interior spaces.[4] While major characters commonly have a variety of settings associated with them, there is usually only one interior that relates and is important to a minor character. Furthermore, the reader is most often introduced to this specific room merely once or twice in the novel, and very seldom does the space evolve substantially throughout the storyline. Still, a minor interior not only expands the role of the minor character but also suggests the complexity that interiors imply for the narrative as a whole. The authors seem to set up a parallel between the function of minor characters and that of interior settings since both interiors and minor characters serve the larger narrative through their subtlety. In other words, there is nothing minor about these subordinate figures the same way the particulars of interiors and decorative styles are pointedly significant. Both costitute the fine points in the plot design and elucidate the major thematic lines of the novel.

INSIDE THE MINDS AND HEARTS OF MACHADO'S CHARACTERS

In *Quincas Borba* the reader penetrates the interior surroundings of two significant minor characters. Dona Tonica and Teófilo are key figures in the novel not only because they connect to other characters and to the action, but also because they evoke important facets of Machado's own private life. Dona Tonica and Teófilo have a considerable amount in common with the protagonist, Rubião. All three characters are at the same time comic and tragic figures, and the narrative documents the progression of their increasing incompatibility with society. Their destinies are by no means equally tragic, but in all of the cases the narrative is mostly concerned with the last phase of the downfall, as if to suggest that the situation had been hopeless from the onset. In the course of the novel, Rubião loses his sanity and dies, while Tonica's eyes change from "olhos pretos, cansados de esperar" [dark eyes that were weary from waiting, 1: 665; 45] to "olhos tão vermelhos, que pareciam doentes" [eyes so red that they looked ill, 1: 801; 264]. The total absence of development in Teófilo's character alludes to the futility behind the politician's professional dedication. The readers penetrate the private spaces of these two minor figures in order to detect the important points they have in common with Rubião.

Chapter XLIII leads one inside the bedroom and mind of Dona Tonica. The narrator's sarcastic description and remarks of her intimate space tend to leave an initial negative impression of Dona Tonica. A closer reading, however, reveals that she represents, as many of Machado's minor female characters, an opportunity lost for the protagonist. The function of this unmarried almost forty-year old woman is to present a possibility of normality and happiness for Rubião, had he fallen in love with her instead of with Sofia. It is no coincidence that both Rubião and Dona Tonica, utterly defeated characters by the end of the narrative, end up linked by a detail concerning their dwelling places; as mentioned earlier while she relocates to "Rua da Princesa," Rubião moves to a house on "Rua do Príncipe." While on the one hand, the unreliable narrator treats with indifference the pathetic fates of these two characters; the narrative itself draws fundamental connections between Rubião and Dona Tonica through different residential details. [5] Although not as young or beautiful as Sofia, Dona Tonica is still, at the start of the novel, an attractive woman disinterested in Rubião's money; with her as his mate, Rubião's sanity and wealth might have endured. A more intimate look into her private space confirms these speculations, while also revealing hidden sides to her personality.

The narrator takes the reader into Dona Tonica's bedroom where her subconscious and intimate thoughts surface. Upon her return from the dinner party at Santa Teresa, where Dona Tonica first meets Rubião and witnesses the flirtation between him and Sofia, the narrator explains that Dona Tonica, engrossed in her thoughts, is "metida em si mesma" [wrapped up in herself] and experiencing an "explosão de raiva interior" [explosion of inner rage, 1: 673-674; 58]. However, the anger Dona Tonica apparently directs at Sofia is more emblematic of an inner sense of unhappiness and self-resentment. As a single middle-class woman in nineteenth-century Brazil, she suffers from the need to appease society and "resolver o problema do matrimônio" [to solve her marriage problem, 1: 668; 49], and her seemingly strong feelings of jealously clash profoundly with the innocence of her environment. Machado provides little detail about interior spaces, but he never fails to include an emblematic visual image: a bust, a painting, or a statue. Dona Tonica's representative image is of the Virgin, and the diminutive is used repeatedly to describe her space and emphasize the innocence of her character. She sits on a "cadeirinha" [small chair] and her lonely bedroom is always "arrumadinha com arte" [artistically arranged]. The care Dona Tonica gives to her interior is "dessa arte engenhosa que faz da chita seda e de um retalho velho uma fita, que recama, enlaça, alegra o mais que pode a nudez das cousas, enfeita as paredes tristes, aprimora os trastes modestos e poucos" [that ingenious art which turns cotton into silk and an old swatch into a ribbon, as much as possible, adorns sad walls, beautifies the few modest pieces, 1: 673-674; 58].[6] This attention to detail recalls Carolina's special care of the Machado household. Identifying Dona Tonica with Carolina underscores the sympathy for this character, making it easy for the reader to forgive and understand Dona Tonica's thoughts toward Sofia.

As we will see later with major characters like Clarín's Ana Ozores and Machado's Rubião, the authors rely on the interior to recreate the past and develop the link between memory and space. The case of Dona Tonica shows that this is a significant function of the private space, since the most characteristic element of her private thoughts is the act of remembering. When Dona Tonica begins to look intensely around her bedroom she recalls a past personal love experience. Despite the narrator's focus on Dona Tonica's sexual frustration and bitter jealousy, her care in her bedroom's arrangement and the fact that it is "feito para receber um noivo amado" [made to receive a loving bridegroom, 1: 674; 58] evoke a strong sense of sensuality. Dona Tonica's thoughts of her first love are far stronger than her supposed fit of anger. To underline her main mental act during this scene, the prefix "re" is repeated throughout in different verbs such as *recalling* and *recomposing*: "remoendo," "recompondo," "rebaixar," "recama," "remira," "recorda," "reverdeceu," and "recordou" (1: 673-674). This prefix points to the act of remembering and perhaps to her desire to repeat the romantic act. Memory, innocence, and the potential for love permeate Dona Tonica's private setting. Machado's "deceptive" narrator, to use John Gledson's famous term, in one of his typical heartless dispositions prefers to paint a picture of a bitter and frustrated woman; the interior setting, however, hides her important sympathetic qualities.[7]

The narrator treats Teófilo's interior space more objectively than Dona Tonica's. The late introduction of Dona Fernanda's husband into the novel is distinctly staged in chapter CXIX, and focuses on Teófilo's fixation with his exterior image. Still, although engrossed in his political work and preoccupied with his reputation, Teófilo unexpectedly surprises the reader and his wife with his perceptiveness. At the end of this brief first encounter he immediately identifies Maria Benedita's secret love for Carlos Maria. This begins to point to an inner side of Teófilo's personality, one that is not simply obsessed with his own public figure. The story reveals this complexity through Teófilo's interaction with his interior space. When the new government declines to name him minister Teófilo is devastated, and only Dona Fernanda's nurture can placate her husband's fit of rage. A confidential dialogue takes place inside the couple's private chambers, to which Rubião and the house's servants are denied access. The reader and narrator, on the other hand, are the only ones that are admitted to this private space to witness the couple's intimate encounter and learn more about Teófilo and Brazilian political life.

The dialogue between husband and wife begins in the couple's bedroom and continues in his study, which along with the drawing-room are the most important rooms of the bourgeois home at this time. The drawing-room was the social center of the house where the family gathered and the most public of rooms since it received and hosted guests. The office was a reflection of the power-status of the head of the household. More often than not the gentleman's study was located near the living and dinning areas, but Teófilo's is instead situated right next to the master bedroom, which recalls the floorplan of Machado and Carolina's home. This unexpected detail suggests the intimacy that exists between the couple and points to the valuable role Dona Fernanda plays in her husband's professional life. A series of spatial shifts characterizes this scene, as husband and wife change from sitting to standing positions, from a "canapé" [settee] to a "poltrona" [armchair] and then to a "cadeira" [chair, 1: 786-787; 241-242]. The characters also move from the bedroom to the study: "ergueu-se e foi ao gabinete de trabalho, que ficava ao pé do quarto" [he arose and went to his study, which was next door to the bedroom, 1: 787; 242]. This constant movement not only reflects Teófilo's anxious state of mind and Dona Fernanda's sympathy for his distress, but also mirrors the chaos of the nation's state of affairs. With these changes, the text moves from a private to a public world and brings the Brazilian political condition into Teófilo's interior space. As he looks around him, Teófilo is reminded of the recent political events. He hears in his private objects the voices of his colleagues and the echoes of their political discussions. The shelves topped with books, official papers, files, magazines, and other bureaucratic documents stand metonymically for the whole Brazilian government. The weekly newspapers are temporarily framed and then properly catalogued. While the private and the public collide in this interior, the order in Teófilo's environment contrasts with the state's inefficiency and disorder. Everything is arranged "metodicamente" [methodically] and the desk "estava em ordem" [was orderly]: "Tudo ali respirava atenção, cuidado, trabalho assíduo, meticuloso e útil" [Everything there breathed attention, care: assiduous, meticulous, and useful work, 1: 787-788; 243]. The representative image or decorative piece, typical of Machado's descriptions of interior settings, is nonexistent in this case. The narrator explains that the study contains nothing superfluous: "Nenhum quadro ou busto, adereço, nada para recrear, nada para admirar;" [No picture or bust, decoration, nothing for recreation, nothing to admire—everything dry, exact, administrative, 1: 788; 243]. This interior space not only evokes the psychological antagonism that subsists between Teófilo's private person and public persona, but also suggests that there is a fundamental incompatibility between private work and public office, an important contradiction that preoccupied Machado throughout his life. Later in the novel, Teófilo must temporarily leave Rio and he gives a special farewell to his study: "Parado no centro, circulou a vista pelas estantes, e dispersou a alma por todas elas" [Standing in the middle of the room, he ran his eyes around the shelves and spread his soul over all of them, 1: 791; 247]. The admiration he expresses toward his books, or what he calls his saints and his friends, recalls Machado's own appreciation of privacy and love of books. Teófilo's study evokes the author's own working space overflowing with books and papers. Both Dona Tonica's and Teófilo's interior spaces refer to some of Machado's own personal experiences, but more importantly they function to expose a not so obvious side of a minor character and to reflect a private and public memory with significant ties to the larger narrative.

Dona Tonica and Teófilo are also important examples of how the act of reminiscing central to the novel always takes place in interior settings. Characters tend to remember and contemplate while inhabiting their intimate spaces, even if some of the elements that stimulate the private thoughts of the characters come from the exterior world. Machado uses the representation of interiors to ultimately explore how memory works in narrative. Rooms and salons resemble a mind in the act of remembering because, as memory, theses spaces are also composed of fragments juxtaposing different time periods and social conflicts. Machado not only connects memory to the inner space, but also relies on the private setting to discover his own narrative style. Thus for Machado writing memory and interiority define the new task of the author. There is a parallel development between the author's representation of interiors and his search for a narrative voice, especially in some of his significant early short stories.

Machado was almost certainly one of the founders of the modern short story and perhaps the greatest writer of this genre in Portuguese. A large majority of the protagonists of his short stories are bourgeois women living in Rio de Janeiro during the Second Empire (1840-1889). Female characters are extremely important in his novels as well, but the focus of a number of the short stories is a woman's mind and her domestic atmosphere. If we accept that the short story is in part an exercise in narrative creation, then women and interior spaces challenge and help Machado's narrators with the poetic construction. Machado's short-story narrator also harks back to his life-long career as a writer of newspaper articles and editorials, since the narrator of these stories often reports to a larger audience on the life, habits, and changing roles of the bourgeois woman in nineteenth-century Brazil. The level of comfort the narrator experiences inside these feminine living quarters is often representative of the degree to which he understands or misunderstands his subjects and subject matter.

A brief look at three of the author's short stories will elucidate how a link develops between narrative control and comprehending a woman and her space. The narrator of Machado's short story "D. Benedita: Um Retrato" (D. Benedita: A Portrait) paints an incoherent picture of the female protagonist. D. Benedita's inability to make decisions emerges in the narrator's own failure to decide over her actions. This perplexity surfaces in the fact that the narrator is as confused about her personality as he is about her interior space. This is probably why he is incapable of describing D. Benedita's house in great detail:

> Deixemo-las almoçar à vontade; descansemos nessa outra sala, a de visitas, sem aliás inventariar os móveis dela, como o não fizemos em nenhuma outra sala ou quarto. Não é que êles não prestem, ou sejam de mau gôsto; ao contrário, são bons. Mas a impressão geral que se recebe é esquisita, como se ao trastejar daquela casa houvesse presidido um plano truncado, ou uma sucessão de planos truncados. (2: 312)

> [Let us allow them to savor their lunch at ease; let us rest in this other room, the drawing-room, without besides taking an inventory of its furnishings, just as we did not do in any of the other rooms. It is not that the furnishings are worthless, or of bad taste; quite the contrary, they are good. But the general impression one gets is peculiar, as if a truncated plan had presided over the furnishing of that house, or a succession of truncated plans].

The narrator makes himself at home in D. Benedita's house and invites the readers to join him and share his burden of trying to make sense of it. His problem with describing her interior relates to the need he feels to write in a different style. The story, D. Benedita, and her interiors are all partially incomplete and truncated. The story's abrupt ending and D. Benedita's mysterious character relate to the impossibility of narrating her interiors and to a comparable learning process of the narrative creation. D. Benedita's engagement with her interior space is furthermore representative of the way she connects or does not connect with her society and her own private life, revealing what seem to be deep-rooted feelings of frustration and disappointment.

In this respect D. Benedita has a lot in common with D. Conceição from "Missa do Galo" (Midnight Mass). Both are women, who despite their husband's unfaithfulness, are highly admired in society for their goodness and devotion to their spouses. Their relation to their domestic interiors, however, brings out important conflicts they face with themselves and others. If the interiors reveal a woman's frustration, they also demonstrate the writer's challenges. Not unlike the novels, Machado's short stories focus on the writing of fiction and become meta-literary constructions that depend formally on interior spaces. For example, the nocturnal domestic setting structuring "Midnight Mass" functions to seduce both the narrator and the reader. The story consists of a conversation the first-person narrator remembers having years ago with his hostess, D. Conceição, in her "sala de visitas" [drawing-room]. In a middle-class home such as this one on the Rua do Senado, the "sala da frente" [front room] is typically the best situated and most elaborately decorated space. Here is where the narrator waits for midnight mass reading at a table in the center of the room until D. Conceição interrupts him. The reader supposes that D. Conceição is attempting to seduce Sr. Nogueira because of the way she sensually interacts with the room's furnishings. D. Conceição moves from one piece of furniture to another trying to get closer to the narrator using her body to touch different decorative objects.

It is also from this interior movement that the reader probes the mind of D. Conceição. Once she sits in the chair where the narrator sat originally her thoughts take a turn. The narrator is forced to confer center stage to the female protagonist. From her position, D. Conceição looks into a mirror that stands above the narrator. Therefore, she sees the narrator and herself as one. The true narrator of the story, then, D. Conceição begins to reflect on how her life with an unfaithful husband is symbolically represented by what surrounds and faces her. She attempts to indirectly communicate her feelings to Sr. Nogueira and the reader by discussing the two paintings that hang over the settee and then deliberating on whether or not to get new wallpaper. D. Conceição's impatience and anxieties surface in her engagement with her interior, prompting her not only to seduce the apparently unaware and unresponsive narrator, but also to self-reflect. The narrator seems blind to this metaphoric interior exercise that clearly stands for both D. Conceição's desires and the story itself. The short story, like D. Conceição, is also self reflective, finding its real source in the woman and her account. This highly complex tale whose vocabulary reinforces a sense of confinement, constructs a dreamy atmosphere and mixes erotic symbols with religion and the imagination. It is an excellent example of how Machado begins to develop narrators that inevitably lose control of their narration and misread the intentions of other characters. The narrator unwittingly gives prominence to D. Conceição and her interior environment, suggesting that her emotions, thoughts, and experiences are the true focus of the story.

In "Capítulo dos Chapéus" (The Chapter on Hats), Machado turns to a female's sense of interior space to question the opposition between consistency and transformation. Machado often deals with this tension in his writing, which ultimately refers to modernity's stresses on both a social and aesthetic level. The story's protagonist, Mariana, finds her sense of reality and self in the permanence of her home. The outside world's pressures for change lead to a quarrel between Mariana and her husband, and she sets out to distract herself with her friend Sofia and with a walk in town. She is clearly incompatible with the different public spaces that they frequent: the shops of the Rua do Ouvidor, the dentist's office, and Parliament. Her distress increases when faced with past experiences that might have altered her destiny, and instead she takes comfort in invoking her house ("contemplava" [contemplated] and "recordava" [remembered]) and once finally approaching it "sentia-se restituída a si mesma" [felt she returned to herself]. She creates an order of things in her home which represents "o seu mundo" [her world, 2: 410], and as most of Machado's female characters, Mariana is also childless, but as the narrator explains, "Móveis, cortinas, ornatos supriam-lhe os filhos; tinha-lhes um amor de mãe; e tal era a concordância da pessoa com o meio, que ela saboreava os trastes na posição ocupada, as cortinas com as dobras do costume, e assim o resto" [Furnishings, curtains, ornaments substituted for children; she loved them as a mother loves her child; and such was the harmony between person and environment, that she savored the furnishings in their occupied position, the curtains with their usual folds, and similarly the rest, 2: 402]. While Mariana prefers the continuity of her furnishings, which seem to embody her identity, her friend Sofia, who accompanied her, feels at home in the growing modernity of Rio's public life. In Machado, the metaphysical crisis that an individual undergoes in modern times is very often a female experience. In this case, the narrator uses two women to consider how the conflicts of modernity reflect on the individual. Women and their interiors and interior lives not only help the narrative make sense or not of an evolving society, but also manipulate the story's formal progress.

Interior scenes, thus, help the narrator uncover his tactics as he turns the inner space into a place where the development of fiction and the identification of the self coincide. In *Quincas Borba*, characters interact with their interior worlds in order to define their sense of existence. Machado's novel, like Eça's and Clarín's, equates interior space and character interiority. Interiors help explain how memory and the inner thoughts of Rubião and Sofia work or fail to work. The novel elaborates more intensely the private lives, nightmares, and fantasies of these two major characters, developing a complex relationship between their minds and their settings. Rubião's difficult psychological state is the one that most clearly deteriorates in the story. Despite the fact that it is never really clear why his mental condition fails or if it does, the connection between Rubião and his physical surroundings uncovers some of the mysteries of his mind. Sofia saves most of her secret thoughts for her bedroom, while Rubião's private setting is the sitting-room of his new home in Botafogo. Although one protagonist is female and the other male, both Rubião's and Sofia's spaces and interior experiences contain at the same time elements typically characterized as masculine and as feminine. Like Eça and Clarín, Machado challenges and explores issues of gender by creating a variety of interactions between interiors and the minds of male and female characters. Realist narratives frequently link female characters to bedrooms or *boudoirs* and male characters to their studies. Rubião's situation is unique since he connects mainly to his drawing-room. The novel opens with the Botafogo sitting-room as the center of Rubião's new reality, rendering the space crucial both for the narrative and his existence and identity. Although the most static and exhibitionist of the house's rooms, the living room is also where Rubião retreats for privacy and reflection. Rubião "meteu-se na sala" [went into the parlor] to reread the letter he receives from Sofia sent along with some strawberries (1: 665; 44). This is the setting that most inspires Rubião to immerse himself in his thoughts and explore his inner feelings.

Rubião reserves the sitting-room for his memories and intimate moments, while he entertains his guests mostly in the dining-room. The drawing-room, like Sofia's private quarters, is a place for reflection and sensuality, where Rubião often lounges and parades about in his robe and slippers. He evidently enjoys touching and caressing these and other articles in the room. This form of being within his space reinforces Rubião's sensitivity and connection to his physical self. He is indeed one of the few characters in the novel that become emotionally involved with the world around him. In fact, many of Machado's, Eça's, and Clarín's sensitive characters that search for meaning in their surroundings become incompatible with their societies. Interior spaces help the authors structure the crises that their characters undergo, which involve a search for meaning in both the self and one's surroundings. The sense of solidarity the characters experience toward their interior space begins to point to the inseparability of the individual from the social, and of emotion from the intellect. Hence, this struggle appears linked to qualities traditionally characterized as feminine. Examples of the feminization of male characters pervade late-nineteenth-century literature as do the writings of the authors studied here. In the novels I analyze, however, what strikes us about the male protagonists in that interior is how a sense of privacy pervades the way of thinking and feeling of these male characters.

Thus the characters that find their way into Rubião's sitting-room invade his most private of atmospheres. It is as if they were entering a woman's space. This becomes clear in an important scene when Palha visits Rubião and discovers to his surprise "na sala um homem mirando os quadros" [a man in the room looking at the pictures]. Rubião's new-found acquaintance, Camacho, is indeed highly attentive to the drawing-room and its art and decorative objects. By observing the components of the room, Camacho appears to study a body, which in this case could only be Rubião's. The tension between Palha, Dr. Camacho, and Rubião creates an uncomfortable silence in the room as feelings of jealousy seize the two guests. The characters' mode of being in the room suggests an important erotic pressure. Moreover, the three seated men form a triangle: "Estavam os três sentados, Rubião no canapé, Palha e Camacho em cadeiras defronte um do outro" [The three of them sat there, Rubião on the couch, Palha and Camacho in chairs facing each other]. The love triangle suits the circumstances perfectly, since both men compete to seduce Rubião and control him and his money.[8] Camacho's attitude further reinforces the erotic suggestions of the scene: "Camacho que conservara a bengala na mão, pô-la verticalmente nos joelhos" [Camacho, who'd kept his cane in his hand, held it upright between his knees]. He soon experiences a sense of imprisonment and walks over to the window to announce the coming out of the moon: "Lá vem o luar entrando" [There's the moon coming out!] The moon, which Rubião invites the two guests to stay and admire, overshadows the whole interior scene, and the verb "entrar" is not fortuitous since in Portuguese it means both coming out and entering. This erotic and feminine symbol penetrates the highly marked interior, and Rubião appears to invite the men inside the world he inhabits, a sensual, female world lit by the moon. The narrative intensifies the frame of the interior space by contrasting its silence with the noise coming from the outside: "Fora, rumor de carros, tropel de cavalos e algumas vozes" [Outside the sound of carts, a troop of horses, and voices, 1: 686; 78]. Camacho and Palha gain access to Rubião's most sensual and vulnerable side. This scene begins to reveal, however, that Camacho and Palha's successful manipulation of the protagonist is not due merely to Rubião's weakness, but more so to the fact that the protagonist undergoes a crisis throughout the narrative. This happens to him because unlike the majority of characters that protect themselves in their selfish society, the hero makes himself receptive and available emotionally to others.

As with Dona Tonica, the narrative uses the sitting-room to reveal different levels of Rubião's personality. Despite the narrator's insistence on presenting an arrogant and naïve man in love with a married woman, obsessed with his new luxuries and controlled by others, the interior settings point to a much more complex character. Rubião's doubts emerge in the objects, people, and experiences that populate his surroundings. The narrator does not hide the influence Palha exerts over Rubião. In the opening description of the Botafogo drawing-room there are three different references made to Palha. Rubião is wearing "umas chinelas de Tunes, que lhe deu recente amigo, Cristiano Palha," [slippers from Tunis that his new friend Cristiano Palha had given him] and even though he does not like bronze, Rubião has two figures in the salon because "o amigo Palha disse-lhe que era matéria de preço" [his friend Palha told him that it was valuable] and finally, Rubião accepts the Spanish butler against his wishes because "o amigo Palha insistiu" [His friend Palha insisted].[9] More than dictating Rubião's taste, Palha is making his presence felt in the most private elements of Rubião's life. Rubião chooses not to contradict Cristiano on some decorative choices, but he maintains his own preferences too. His "crioulos de Minas" [blacks from Minas Gerais] and his favorite metals, silver and gold, remain important components of his sitting-room (1: 641; 5-6). Rubião recognizes the fleeting nature of Palha's foreign selections, while his personal choice is partial to native elements. He often prefers what is Brazilian made instead of following the fad of the time which was to revere European goods and styles. Even the ironic narrator seems to credit Rubião for appreciating the timelessness of things when he refers, at the end of the novel, to the diamond jewelery Rubião gives Sofia over the years: "tão certo é que, neste gênero de atavios, as modas conservam-se mais" [in the case of this type of adornment, style stays the same for long periods, 1: 801; 264].

The narrative depicts through the representation of the Botafogo salon an independent thinker in the protagonist with his own original perspective. The purpose of Rubião's intense involvement with the space enclosing him is not to emphasize his materialistic nature, but to suggest aspects of the inner crisis haunting him. He contemplates his recent social advancement and struggles, with his limited capabilities, to identify his reality and its meanings. Like many of Machado's meditative characters, Rubião focuses on the room and its walls and searches for sense, insight, and freedom. The significance of the furniture and decorative objects lies in their power to stir Rubião's ideas about his past and future self. Most importantly, he understands that the silver platter, the English engravings, and the two bronze figures are symbols embodying his new reality. It is the sense of sight that more effectively helps Rubião observe his interior space and penetrate his inner world. Rubião relies on other senses to embrace his interior and exterior worlds, which in turn highlight his sensuality, but sight predominates. At the beginning of the novel Rubião "fitava a enseada" [was staring at the cove, 1: 641; 5] and moments later is caught "disfarçadamente mirando" [surreptitiously looking, 1: 641; 6] at his silver tray; he questions his Spanish butler, "lançando um ultimo olhar" [casting a last glance] at the tray and stays longer in the living room, "a olhar para os móveis" [gazing at the furniture] before sitting on his *pouf* "olhando para longe" [staring off into the distance, 1: 642; 7]. At the end of the flashback in chapter XXVII Rubião is still sitting "a olhar para longe, muito longe" [looking far away, very far away, 1: 659; 35], and at a later point when trying to decide whether to return to Santa Teresa, Rubião "deixou-se estar na sala, no *pouf* central, olhando" [sat there on the couch in the parlor watching, 1: 694; 90-91].

Peter Brooks writes that "realism more than almost any other mode of literature makes sight paramount" and that "our sense of sight is the most reliable guide to the world as it most immediately affects us."[10] Sight is undoubtedly the most prevalent sense used in *Quincas Borba*, as the narrator, the reader, and the characters depend on the sense of sight. With vision, the narrative designs a dialectics for the understanding of the exterior world, or reality, and of the interior world of the mind and heart. Machado's dynamics between interiors and exteriors suggest that by observing what is outside, one draws nearer the interiority of persons and things. The references to sight in the narrative reinforce Rubião's visionary imagination, and point to his search for meaning in his society. The interior prompts him to see beyond and inside himself using the space as a vessel. Toward the end of the novel, Dona Fernanda and Sofia make an important visit to Rubião's dog. Dona Fernanda is able to see inside Quincas Borba: "ele ficou a olhar para ela, e ela para ele, tão fixos e tão profundos, que pareciam penetrar no íntimo um do outro" [he stayed looking at her and she at him, so steadily and deeply that they seemed to be penetrating each other's intimacy, 1: 799; 262]. This scene is highly significant because it shows that the same intense stare that is used in the novel to look around a space is also the one that sees inside a soul, be it human or animal.

Dona Fernanda penetrates a very peculiar soul, that of a dog reminiscent of the holy trinity, since three entities appear to share it: the philosopher, the dog, and the protagonist. Helen Caldwell writes, "the animal symbolized some quality of soul shared by the two men."[11] In this scene, however, Dona Fernanda is not only inside the thoughts and feelings of the dog, but she also finds herself inside Rubião's last humble abode, a small sea-side house on Rua do Príncipe, where Palha "meteu o nosso Rubião" [installed our Rubião, 1: 779; 228]. This is the last interior the protagonist occupies before his death, and while she looks around at the neglected and miserable quarters she approaches Rubião's inner world: "Aquele espetáculo não lhe trazia um tema de reflexões gerais, não lhe ensinava a fragilidade dos tempos, nem a tristeza do mundo, dizia-lhe tão-somente a moléstia de um homem" [That spectacle didn't bring her any generalized reflections, it didn't point out the fragility of the times or the sad state of the world. It only bespoke the illness of a man]. Penetrating various interiors, Rubião's abandoned home and the dog's captivating mind, profoundly moves Dona Fernanda. Despite the narrator's emphasis on her practically-minded personality, it is evident that the experience of being in Rubião's space forces her to face undesirable emotions and experiences: "E ia ficando e olhando, sem pensar, sem deduzir, metida em si mesma, dolente e muda" [And she stayed there looking, not thinking, not deducing anything, withdrawn into herself, pained and mute, 1: 799; 261]. This is not a typical reaction of Dona Fernanda's character, but rather proves that she becomes more skeptical toward the end of the novel. In her sincere concern for Rubião and his condition she shows herself to be anything but ingenuous and develops a better understanding of the selfishness so prevalent in her society.

Rubião undergoes a much more dramatic change throughout the story, but like Dona Fernanda, he too grows incompatible with society, and this estrangement surfaces in the parallel between the failure of this sanity and an increasing indifference toward his interiors. Rubião's transition to madness can be read ironically as a rising awareness of the reality surrounding him. While becoming increasingly delusional, Rubião strengthens his understanding of the essence of things and the real motives behind objects and people. If in the beginning, the interior space transported him to his inner world, toward the end of the narrative Rubião lives only in his mind and the interiors it imagines. The narrative is explicit in showing that while he escapes to the interior space of his inner world he also begins to lose interest in the material world enclosing him. The day after the events in Santa Teresa marks a notable change in Rubião's mind set: "Não cuidou de nada; calçou as chinelas africanas sem interesse, não mirou as alfaias belas, ou simplesmente ricas, que lhe enchiam a casa" [He put on his African slippers without interest, didn't look at the beautiful or simply expensive furniture that filled his house, 1: 687; 79]. When Rubião escapes into a stronger sense of self and into his imperial fantasies he is physically attached to a piece of furniture: "Estava em uma longa cadeira de extensão, ermo do espírito, que rompera o tecto e se perdera no ar" [He was on a chaise longue, bereft of his spirit, which had broken through the ceiling and had been lost in the air, 1: 763; 204], and later "atirou-se a uma poltrona, e viu passar muitas coisas suntuosas" [dropped into an armchair and watched all sorts of sumptuous things pass by, 1: 765; 207]. Although comfortably reclining on furnishings it is the departing of the interior setting, breaking through walls and ceilings, that defines his spiritual development and imagination. Furthermore, he becomes dispassionate toward his new residences, so that when Palha moves him to the small house on Rua do Príncipe, Rubião "adotou a mudança sem desgosto" [adjusted to the move without any displeasure, 1: 779; 228], and when he finally occupies "uma sala e um quarto especiais" [a living room and a bedroom, especially arranged] in a "casa de saúde" [hospital], once again he does not resist the move and: "entrou nos seus aposentos, como se os conhecesse desde muito" [went into his quarters as if they'd been long familiar to him, 1: 797; 258]. Despite his failing sanity, Rubião apparently gains an understanding of how the objects that compose his new life are in effect props on a stage of a fictional representation, and, ironically a growing sense of the difference between reality and fiction leads him to blur evermore the lines between the two. As Rubião grows madder, he also sees clearer through the falsity of others and himself.

If at the beginning of the story, the interior space invented Rubião's reality, now he uses his imagination to transform his surroundings. He even reinvents exterior spaces and turns them into luxurious and elaborate interiors, as when he walks through the Rua da Ajuda and believes he passes over

carpets and through "muitas salas e galerias" [many rooms and galleries, 1:
797; 257]. The degeneration of Rubião's mind parallels the falling apart of
his homes and interior spaces, and his inner world needs fictional interiors.
As noted earlier, Rubião's last residence reveals a complete state of neglect:
"O interior da casa tinha a feição do abandono, sem a fixidez e regularidade
das cousas, que parecem conservar um resto da vida interrompida" [The
inside of the house had a look of abandonment, with no permanence or
regularity of things that seemed to hold a remnant of an interrupted life, 1:
798]. He further loses his things throughout the narrative, and as Peter
Brooks reminds us when writing of Balzac's Coralie, "Lack of things is the
immediate precursor of death."[12] Rubião interrupts his new wealthy life, his
fictional existence as a newfound capitalist, and discovers his real self and
the truth of his society. Unable to cope with this failure and ubiquitous
malevolence he turns inward first to a more sensitive and sensual understanding of the world, and finally enclosing himself entirely in the sumptuous and
grand interiors of his mind.

In the beginning Rubião connects with his Botafogo interiors, but as the
narrative progresses other people and his own feelings and illusions exile
him from specific interiors. Rubião's initial attachment to his drawing-room
reminds one of a very important analogy Sigmund Freud draws between the
unconscious and a bourgeois interior:

> Let us therefore compare the system of the unconscious to a large entrance
> hall, in which the mental impulses jostle one another like separate individuals.
> Adjoining this entrance hall there is a second, narrower, room—a kind of
> drawing-room—in which consciousness, too, resides. But on the threshold
> between these two rooms a watchman performs his function: he examines the
> different mental impulses, acts as a censor, and will not admit them into the
> drawing-room if they displease him.[13]

In *The Sense of an Interior*, Diana Fuss claims that Freud's comparison
between the mind and the interior space reveals how interiority is much more
than a metaphor, but in fact a "mental structure constructed over time, with
inner chambers and inner walls."[14] Machado's narrative reinforces both
Freud's and Fuss's ideas because it attempts to build a discourse of the mind
with architectural images. In Rubião's case, people and objects emblematic
of his corrupt society invade his rooms. These forces disfigure his unconscious, forcing him into madness. In order to compensate for this, he begins
to create more rooms in his head, or other unconscious spaces that he might
possibly inhabit. Rooms are very much part of Rubião's external and internal
life; grand expanding galleries with high ceilings provide him with a sense of
a limitless existence. The development of Sofia's sense of interior space, on
the other hand, grows smaller and closes in on her as the narrative develops,
indicating her increasingly closed mind and heart versus Rubião's open and

generous one. Initially Sofia explores her conscious thoughts and reveals her fear and loneliness through her interaction with the interior. As opposed to Rubião, however, Sofia is ultimately incapable of living honestly with her interior feelings. The narrator explains that when Sofia returns from her reclusive moods, "estados de consciência vagos e obscuros" [vague and obscure states of consciousness], she always tries to flee them (1: 776; 224). While both Rubião and Sofia penetrate their own inner worlds, Rubião never returns from his and is unable to coexist with his exterior world and society. Sofia, on the other hand, apparently focuses less and less on her real inner feelings and instead becomes a leading player in her corrupt society.

A contradiction develops from the onset between Sofia's apparent confidence and her vulnerable side. This ambiguity surfaces in Sofia's interaction with her domestic environment. It appears that Sofia is more confident and outspoken at home: "Sofia era, em casa, muito melhor que no trem de ferro" [Sofia was much better at home than on the train]. In her own house Sofia speaks more openly as she is "dona da casa" [lady of the house, 1: 658; 33], and can protect herself from outside pressures and her own actions. In Santa Teresa, after Siqueira interrupts Rubião's declaration of love in the garden, Sofia knows how to maneuver around her house and behavior: "não entrou pela porta da sala de visitas, mas por outra que dava para a de jantar; de maneira que, quando chegou àquela pelo interior, era como se acabasse de dar ordens para o chá" [She didn't go in through the parlor door but through another that opened into the dining room, so that when she reached the parlor from inside it was as if she'd just given orders for tea, 1: 671; 55]. Sofia depends on her home to stage manage her deceptive life and gain power to perform her role in society.

Sofia demonstrates her dramatic talents during the first private meeting that the readers witness between her and her husband. Chapter L is one of the most striking theatrical scenes in the novel. The interior is portrayed like a minimalist, dark stage set with a light coming from "um bico de gás" [a gas jet]; a piano, a mirror, and the pivotal settee make up its central furnishings (1: 679; 68). The sofa keeps the characters apart more than holds them together, although it gives the scene unity with its continuous presence. Sofia is at first "reclinada no canapé" [reclining on the settee, 1: 680; 68] until Palha "Sentou-se no canapé" [sat down on the settee] after which she gets up (1: 681; 70). Later Sofia "Voltou ao canapé" [returned to the settee] and lastly Palha, (1: 681; 70) "com a cabeça reclinada nas costas do sofá" [his head resting on the back of the sofa], imitates Sofia's previous sensual actions on the couch (1: 683; 73). They change accordingly from standing to sitting positions as they battle for dominance over one another. Sofia attempts by her physical interaction with the "canapé" to savor Palha's discomfort by getting evermore comfortable and letting her hair down. This endeavor to control the circumstances seems to be an attempt to compensate for her feelings of apprehension. Palha's psychological abuse and ability to instill fear in Sofia is clear from this very first moment of this pivotal meeting: "A mulher ia a sair, o marido deteve-a, ela estremeceu" [The wife was about to leave the room; the husband held her back. She trembled, 1: 680; 68]. Palha orders the servant to leave them alone, trapping Sofia inside the dark room. He intimidates her with stories about dead women and husbands who devour their wives. Sofia makes an important digression over to the piano and mirror. Earlier in the evening Palha accompanied a woman singing at the piano, consequently the musical instrument is instilled with his presence. Sofia's gesture then communicates her resentment toward her husband, while in the mirror she sees her alienated self.

Sofia, as many of Machado's characters, relies on her interior surroundings for support. Many characters, and especially female characters, need furnishings to fall back on. Female characters in particular fall literally back on their furnishings for reassurance. In Machado's first novel, *Ressurreição*, the interior already serves to invite the reader inside Lívia's state of mind and to reveal how indecisiveness in male characters connects to the delicate fate of female characters. Félix's constant doubting has tragic consequences for Lívia, who eventually dies of despair and of her frustrated love for him. Lívia grows hopeless throughout the narrative because of Félix's suspicions and attacks, and she increasingly needs to hold onto objects in order to attach herself to reality. When Félix confronts Lívia with his jealousy, she looked "assustada para todas as portas, deixou-se cair frouxamente numa cadeira e tapou o rosto com as mãos" [scared at all the doors, she let herself fall flabbily on a chair and covered her face with her hands, 1: 160]. This gesture reveals on the one hand a wish to escape the imprisonment that Félix's love creates for her, and, on another, a form of retreating into her own space and self. After reading the letter where Félix breaks off the wedding, Lívia looks around again to regain consciousness, and once more "se deixou cair na cadeira" [she let herself fall on the chair, 1: 182]. In her despair she tries to remain in contact with the real and searches for objects, walls, doors, and windows. Her intense search of her interior space, however, ultimately drives her into a deeper emotional inner realm, which brings her closer to her imminent death.

As Lívia, Sofia also faces moments of despair, but manages to escape them with a little help from Rubião. He communicates his solidarity to her through the important indirect role he plays in Sofia's interior space. Sofia and Palha's domestic environments grow more luxurious throughout the narrative, as they prosper from investments made with Rubião's money. Yet, if Palha attempts to be part of Rubião's intimate settings, it looks as if he is largely absent in the objects that make up his wife's private quarters. Rubião, on the other hand, showers Sofia with timeless gifts that she takes along to her most intimate places. He populates Sofia's empty world with vivid reminders of his and her interior lives. The diamond jewelry Rubião gives Sofia is consistently a solitary rock suggesting that Rubião can read Sofia's feelings of isolation. The reader seldom witnesses Rubião presenting his gifts to Sofia; instead more often than not she unwraps and takes pleasure in her gifts once left alone in her private chambers. On her birthday, Sofia "só, no quarto de vestir" [alone in her boudoir] opens Rubião's magnificent diamond: "uma bela pedra, no centro de um colar" [a beautiful stone in the center of a necklace, 1: 738; 162].

The solitary stone, central to the scene above, prompts Sofia to reminisce: "Deteve-se algum tempo, sentada, sozinha, recordando cousas idas" [She remained sitting there for some time, remembering past things, 1: 738; 162]. When Sofia is alone, Rubião's gifts repeatedly trigger her memory and private thoughts. The day the newlyweds Carlos Maria and Maria Benedita part for Europe, Sofia shuts herself in her bedroom with a recent novel Rubião gave her, and other things around her "lembravam o mesmo homem" [reminded her of the same man], not to mention his words that echo throughout the room and form part of Sofia's "inventário de recordações" [inventory of memories]. Out of all her recollections "Rubião é que persistia" [Rubião was the one who persisted], and, unable to continue her reading, Sofia "fechou o livro, fechou os olhos, e perdeu-se em si mesma" [closed the book, closed her eyes, and became lost in herself, 1: 751; 183]. Lying on her bed alone in her room reminded by objects of Rubião's enduring love and genuine character, Sofia attempts to reach inside herself. The same way that Rubião's preferences next to Palha's contain more eternal qualities, Rubião's recurring emergence on Sofia's mind points to her subconscious wish to love as he does, and to the grief she must feel when faced with Rubião's authentic self juxtaposed to her own false character.

Sofia's memories not only disturb the life and person she defines for herself but also connect to the passage of time. During a very important visit to Sofia, Rubião nearly tempts her into joining him on a romantic daytrip to Tijuca. Machado indicates the passage of time here as he does in other scenes throughout his work by a timelessness that is interrupted. Rubião and Sofia "alheios e remotos um do outro" [alien and remote from one another] sit quietly together for an indeterminate time: "Não se pode dizer, ao certo, que tempo estiveram assim calados" [It can't be said for certain how long they were silent like that], until Rubião interrupts time with time by taking out his pocket watch (1: 760; 199). The two are in Sofia's "saleta de trabalho," a small sitting-room where Sofia, as Penelope, does her needle and lacework. Meanwhile Rubião's imagination thrives, incited by two roses he sees through the window in Sofia's garden. Once Rubião leaves, Sofia returns to the exact same corner of the window and imitates Rubião in imagining a dialogue between the two flowers. The roses could of course symbolize the brevity of beauty and of life, but Sofia actually grows more attractive with age. It is not beauty that appears to flee but instead her last chance for true love. Although it would seem Carlos Maria is the target of her affections, Rubião is the one who once again persists in his direct and indirect presence. The wicker basket where Sofia keeps her sewing things, "ainda uma lembrança de Rubião" [one more remembrance from Rubião] strategically opens and closes her conscious thoughts, framing this way the dialogue between the two protagonists and between the roses (1: 761; 200). Its reappearance, however, suggests Sofia's unconscious desire for Rubião and the genuine affection he represents which is lacking in her relationship to Palha and to her world. These interior details and the strategic architectural framing of the interior portray different levels of meaning of Sofia's character.

This is not the first or the last time Sofia confounds Rubião and Carlos Maria. Sofia spends a rainy day, just as *La Regenta*'s Ana Ozores, shut up inside her house lost in her thoughts and dreams. Machado's female characters have a tendency to close themselves in their rooms to contemplate. Guiomar from *A Mão e a Luva* (*The Hand and the Glove* 1874) hides "na alcova, solitária e tôda consigo, sentada na poltrona rasa ao lado da cama, com... os olhos vagando de objeto em objeto, como se reproduzissem fora as atitudes interiores do pensamento" [in her room, alone and all into herself, sitting on the low armchair next to the bed, with... her eyes idling from object to object, as if they reproduced outside the interior attitudes of her thoughts, 1: 226]. Like Lívia and Guiomar, Sofia too relies on the objects and frames enclosing her sense of existence to explore her desires and fears. This solitary rainy day sets up different levels of interiority that show how interiors create depth in narrative, both in a space and in the mind of a character. All three authors use this technique of interiors within interiors to build multiple points of significance in their novels. The weather outside forces Sofia to stay inside and resign herself to reclusion. In the exterior natural environment the sea and the sky blend and close in on each other. The narrative insists on the melancholic weather repeating how the sea and sky appear as one, and how the thick haze and low clouds shut the world out. The closed and blinding sensation outside reflects Sofia's own entrapment inside her house and mind, and she in turn seems to interpret these different inner levels: "Sofia meteu a alma em um caixão de cedro, encerrou o de cedro no caixão de chumbo do dia, e deixou-se estar sinceramente defunta" [Sofia put her soul into a cedar casket, closed the cedar one up in the lead casket of the day, and left it there, sincerely deceased, 1: 775; 222]. Sofia buries herself in this sort of Chinese box the same way she moves from the sitting-room to her bedroom where she throws herself on the bed and sleeps.

These different levels surface in yet another interior realm as she passes from a daydream to a real dream. In her dream she mixes the "espetáculo exterior" [spectacle outside] with her interior thoughts. She faces a similar *"parede* de cerração" [wall of mist, 1: 776; 225],[15] and it would seem impossible to escape the confinement, but all of a sudden a figure dressed in Carlos Maria's body and Rubião's words rips and splits apart the wall, penetrating her interior and saving her from death and filling her with love. The complex dream that the narrator tells with the usual lighthearted and sarcastic tone ends violently, commenting powerfully on Sofia's disturbed emotions. After Sofia wakes up, the novel further alludes to Palha's masochist tendencies. The dream is only part of the larger design of multiple inner realms, and the recurring key word "cerração," which in Portuguese besides meaning mist or haze also conveys a sense of closing in, refers to both the importance of enclosing one in and to the blurring of one's vision. Once again sight in *Quincas Borba* emerges connected to interiors. Characters close their eyes to sleep or to think and retreat into an inner world but do not always penetrate this inner space. They also look intensely around their rooms and objects and do not achieve the inner connection or understanding that they are searching for. The haziness of the "cerração" surfaces as the only alternative or possibility one has available to reach a deeper level of interiority. This vagueness recalls Machado's constant effort to create thresholds and ambiguities, but also resembles the faint, scarcely described, interior settings of the novel, where incompatible elements and objects confound and merge. Sofia's interior experiences end up confusing dream and reality, Carlos Maria and Rubião, inside and outside, mind and body, self and other, and female and male characteristics and desires.

Confounding gender differences in interior spaces is the opposite of what most realist and naturalist texts tend to do with domestic spaces. There is extensive critical work on the engendering of interior spaces in nineteenth-century literature, especially in the Victorian novel. [16] Even though the novels studied here were all written by relatively powerful male authors who had complicated, and often contradictory, personal views on gender roles, the narratives actually disguise and challenge the idea of female and male spaces. In *Quincas Borba*, *La Regenta*, and *The Maias* gender differences play an important role, but both male and female characters undergo within their private space significant interior experiences. The authors underline instead the qualities that emerge in these spaces, such as sensitivity and vulnerability. Furthermore, they relate the interior milieu to the important modern ideas of reflection, creativity, and interiority, which were seldom associated with women. Rubião, Fermín, and Carlos are all male characters whose way of being in their interior is primarily sensual and an experience of both the body and heart, despite the fact that none of them succeed in harmonizing the two. Verena Tarrant in Henry James's *Bostonians* claims that if men "had the intelligence of the heart, the world would be very different now." [17] Such a platform seems to be what these Luso-Hispanic novels contend is necessary for the new modern existence. This also recalls Noël Valis's wholly convincing argument that what is largely absent in *La Regenta*, but which Clarín wanted, is a "thinking heart."[18]

Nancy Armstrong's history of domestic fiction, *Desire and Domestic Fiction: A Political History of the Novel*, argues that the rise in the domestic woman and in domestic fiction not only develops the qualities of female subjectivity but also makes subjectivity a female domain and that therefore "the modern individual was first and foremost a woman."[19] In order to explain the rise in the writing by, for, and about women in nineteenth-century England, Armstrong claims that the domesticity of the subject and of the novel's subject matter must have caused modernity's obsession with the individual. In line with her argument, I suggest more generally that the modern individual was first and foremost a creature of the interior, regardless of gender. But, that clearly the qualities and sensibilities that the interior develops in the individual are traditionally more feminine in nature. Being able to invent, interpret, and create one's interior is a form of understanding both an inner world and how it connects to exterior experiences. Along with developing the individual, however, the novels studied here are also highly interested in cultivating the sense of collectivity. Therefore the preoccupation with interiors is also a meditation on reality, a consideration of how historical experiences affect interiorities and subjectivities, and an analysis of how space and material objects locate memories and feelings. The fixation of the modernist writer on interiority and subjectivity would never have developed without nineteenth-century realism's obsession with interiors.

EÇA'S INTERIOR DECORATORS

In Eça de Queirós's *The Maias*, characters are particularly infatuated with interiors. Spaces end up substituting their passions, personal objectives, and intellectual pursuits. Almost all of the characters one way or another interact on different levels with their interior space. This ubiquitous attention to the interior surroundings also equals the novel's narrative technique of developing the psychology and inner life of its characters. The narrative focuses on the relationship between a character and his or her space in an attempt to approach the workings of their conscious and subconscious thoughts. This allows the narrator to maintain an impersonal and objective tone and at the same time penetrate the interiority of the characters. In Eça's case, piercing a character's mind is often compared to accessing their private quarters, but there are different levels of invading the privacy and unraveling the intimacy of a character. This technique is used in the novel to reveal the inner side of a character, and, more importantly, to explore the ways this private experience connects to the larger public and national dimensions.

The case of Vilaça senior is a perfect example of how the representation of an interior space makes clear that the self is linked to the national and to the aesthetic development of the novel itself. It also proves how, like Machado, Eça creates important links between minor characters and the greater narrative agenda. Upon arriving at the Santa Olávia estate for his visit, Vilaça not only carefully observes the all-blue guestroom where he will be staying, but he also touches and feels the objects and furnishings: "Foi logo apalpar os cretones, esfregou o mármore da cómoda, provou a solidez das cadeiras" [He immediately went over and felt the cretonne, stroked the marble top of the chest of drawers and tested the solidity of the chairs, 56-57; 47]. Chapter III is narrated from Vilaça's perspective and spans his entire life as a character, since it concludes with his death. Thus during the Santa Olávia episode the only private setting the reader is taken into is Vilaça's bedroom because he and his world are the focus of this chapter. His actions and care while in the blue room, for whose decoration he himself is responsible, adequately reveal Vilaça's attachment to the Maia family. Despite his and later his son's pragmatic minds, the interior scene reveals a more sensual side to Vilaça that is not otherwise evident. The objective of the interior narrated here is to reveal how the sentimental inner lives of characters like Vilaça strongly impact the history of the Maia family and of Portuguese society in general. The form of this chapter further reinforces how significant a character like Vilaça is in the narrative because it reproduces the structure of the novel. Vilaça's death at the end is followed by a separate section, a number of brief paragraphs, which narrates an event some time after his death and serves to reflect on Vilaça's life and on this episode in the novel. Similarly, Afonso dies in the penultimate chapter of *The Maias* and the closing section makes crucial comments on the narrative as a whole making the Vilaça-centered chapter a type of novel within the novel. Afonso's existence is compared to Vilaça's in the same way that Carlos's life is measured up with Manuel Vilaça's or Vilaça junior. Furthermore, the lives of these two pairs are connected through death. One of the underlining themes in this chapter is expressed at one point during the soirée by three different characters. The widow Dona Eugénia murmurs "—Cada um tem os seus mortos" [We all have our dead to remember, 71; 59] and the Viscountess and another faithful family friend, the public prosecutor, echo her by each in turn repeating her exact words. These three mortal blows announce Vilaça's death at the end of the chapter and further draw attention to the question of burial. The young Carlos is the one who ultimately buries Vilaça senior, since he convinces his grandfather to build the Vilaça family a vault in Lisbon's prestigious cemetery, while at the end of the novel Vilaça junior ends up burying Afonso since the old man's body is temporarily stored in the Vilaça vault before being moved to Santa Olávia. The link between the narrative structure of the novel and of this episode suggests a sort of social cycle of life and death, showing that the interior or the intimacy of a character is a collective experience that relies on certain bonds that exist between different social classes.

By entering a character's private lodgings, narrators and readers attempt to penetrate and interpret the mind of a character. At the same time, to understand someone on a more intimate level is to enter, observe, and experience his or her interior space. This is why Ega only feels at ease with Maria Eduarda after meeting her in her intimate space. He finally visits Maria Eduarda in Olivais long after her affair with Carlos has started and is extremely curious to see her "no seu interior" [at home, 519; 449]. A tour of the newly redecorated Toca and a lighthearted "discussão sobre bricabraque" [conversation about bric-à-brac] breaks the ice between Ega and Maria Eduarda and marks the beginning of their friendship (520; 450). Similarly, Carlos's friend Cruges poses a challenge to him because Carlos knows nothing about Cruges's past, inner life, and more importantly his home. In fact Carlos is extremely insulted when Cruges moves residences and does not tell him about it. Cruges's timid personality does not allow his best friends or readers to enter his space. Ironically, it is exactly at Cruges's house where Maria Eduarda temporarily resides. His secretive and shy mind and vague house in turn hide what Carlos most desires to discover: Maria's whereabouts. Cruges's impenetrability is reflected in his concealed interiors. As Cruges, Afonso's mind is also increasingly mysterious as the novel progresses, and toward the end of the story the reader rarely accesses his private rooms or thoughts. At a late point in the novel Afonso decides to renovate his Santa Olávia estate and a newfound passion for redecorating takes over him: "ultimamente invadira-o a paixão de edificar—sentindo-se remoçar, como ele dizia, no contacto das madeiras novas e no cheiro vivo das tintas" [he had been filled, lately, with a passion for building; the rough touch of new wood and the sharp smell of paint made him feel younger, he said, 529; 458]. This new desire to renovate expresses his fear of aging and of death, while also suggesting that the growing distance between grandfather and grandson begins to unease Afonso. As he is gradually more disconnected from Carlos, Afonso attempts to recuperate their intimacy by involving himself as his grandson does with redecorating activities. He hopes that by doing what Carlos loves best their closeness might be restored. Even the minor function of interiors connects meaningfully to the greater sense of the novel and to the portrayal of the characters' motives, desires, and fears.

To identify a character's growing preoccupations or changing feelings implies looking inside their rooms and at the way they interact with their interior surroundings. In *The Maias* there is an interesting inversion that Carlos Reis points out in the relation between characters and their interior environments: "Um condicionamento que, nos romances naturalistas, ia do meio para as personagens...agora vai das personagens para o meio, projectando-se neste o que caracteriza aquelas" [A conditioning that in naturalist novels would go from the environment to the characters... now goes from the characters to the environment, projecting on the latter what characterizes the former, 188]. Ega and Carlos maintain a much more complex and wider relationship with interiors than other characters throughout the narrative. This is because the novel deals more closely with the inner worlds of these two main characters. The central contradiction that the novel attempts to sort out between movement and stagnation also lies at the core of the novel's development of character interiority. The two protagonists, Carlos da Maia and João da Ega, the would-be movers and shakers of Lisbon society, never realize any of their many creative, intellectual, and scientific future projects. Instead they consume themselves with interiors, creating and inventing their inner selves and their feelings by imagining and redecorating interior spaces. The acquisition of *móveis* or furnishings is intended to bring movement into their lives and empower them through a fulfillment of their artistic desires. Ega and Carlos are fascinated with interiors because they see them as an expression of a rich and full inner life. Their interest in interiors represents their dedication to aesthetics and symbolizes intellectual progress. Ultimately, however, they frustrate any development of their thoughts and emotions, and interiors end up replacing their memories and ideas. They live closeted up in their salons and buried in their divans with the illusion of an inner life and do not succeed in involving themselves with their reality or in contributing to the world around them.

While the majority of Lisbon society does not seem to disapprove of Carlos and Ega's lethargy, the Maia family members are increasingly critical and aware of their idleness. Maria Eduarda and her grandfather have a lot in common, especially in aesthetic taste, but they also agree on a very important issue. They both want the two protagonists to be more productive and do something useful with their lives. When the move to Olivais is first considered, Maria Eduarda assumes, to Carlos's delight, that it will not be a problem for him to continue his daily visits since he seems to have "quase nada que fazer" [very little to do, 408; 351]. She is constantly reminding Carlos that he has nothing to do: "Tu não tens nada que fazer, não?" [You haven't anything else to do, have you?, 505; 436]. Afonso's famous words are quite in line with Maria Eduarda's thinking. He says to Carlos and Ega "—Pois então façam vocês essa revolução. Mas pelo amor de Deus, façam alguma coisa!" [Then why don't you two do something to bring about that revolution? Why, for God's sake, don't you do something, anything?, 385; 332]. Even little Rosa seems to understand Carlos's lack of occupation. When Rosa is reprimanded by her mother during one of Carlos's last visits to Rua de São Francisco, she says to him "Também nunca fazes nada!...Sensaborão!" [You never do anything anyways! You bore!, 657].

The novel criticizes Carlos and Ega's apathy via an ironic and ambiguous design with interior spaces because, although the protagonists never realize any of their grand schemes and plans, they do manage to take a very important first step. They always find a home and create the perfect interior atmosphere for the potential materialization of their objectives. Carlos opens and elaborately arranges the interiors of his consulting rooms and laboratory, and Ega creates working environments both in his Vila Balzac and in Ramalhete to accommodate the writing of his planned ambitious work. Despite these seemingly perfect working conditions, Ega and Carlos make little progress on their intellectual projects. Hence, one must ask if the space itself is not, however, their true creation. For example, they have ongoing plans to start a critical cultural magazine that they never manage to write for, but "Uma coisa porém ficou decidida: a casa da redacção. Devia ser mobilada luxuosamente" [They did decide on one thing: the editorial office. It would have to be luxuriously furnished, 567; 492]. Carlos reacts to this idea full of passion and is emotionally moved. Ega agrees enthusiastically: "E móveis! E máquinas!" [furniture and machinery, 566; 491]. If Machado de Assis spends a significant part of his life struggling to house the Academy of Letters, Carlos and Ega so consume themselves with accommodations that they achieve very little in the realm of letters. Their main motivation behind all their professional and even romantic plans seems to be the acquiring and decorating of new spaces. They are closeted interior decorators, and it will become clear that, just as with Rubião, Carlos's and Ega's whims for interior creativity ultimately reflect a deeper search for personal fulfillment and self understanding.

At the beginning of the story, Carlos struggles to be useful to his fellow countrymen and moves to the capital city motivated to help modernize and revolutionize Lisbon. He insists on serving others with his scientific knowledge: "A ciência como mera ornamentação interior do espírito, mais inútil para os outros que as próprias tapeçarias do seu quarto, parecia-lhe apenas um luxo de solitário: desejava ser útil" [Science as a mere ornament of the spirit, as useless to others as the tapestries adorning his bedroom, seemed to him the luxury of the recluse; he wanted to be useful, 97; 82]. As long as he has redecorating plans to care for he is excited and resolved to work. When these are over, however, and he sits hours in his newly renovated consulting rooms waiting for the patients who never come, he begins to confound the interior world of his office and inner desires with the exterior reality of a provincial European capital. It becomes difficult to distinguish between the interior of his medical practice and the lazy sounds and sensations of the Rossio plaza. The "veludos pesados" [heavy velvets] of his office's upholstery and the "ar aveludado de clima rico" [soft air of a benevolent climate] of the outside world are one and the same (103; 87). Apparently Carlos does not wish for his scientific knowledge to be, as his bedroom's tapestry, mere adornment for the spirit, but this is ultimately the protagonist's main and sole achievement. Interior décor, on the other hand, is the one activity Carlos never tires of and that he actually develops throughout the narrative, the one thing with which he most successfully impresses his fellow countrymen. The only revolution and modernization that Carlos brings to Lisbon does not concern a scientific or medical breakthrough, but has to do with his knowledge, appreciation, and skill for interior design. Furthermore, the topic of interiors sets the tone for Carlos's new friendships and love affairs.

One of Carlos's new Lisbon acquaintances, the greatly ridiculed and caricaturized Dâmaso Cândido de Salcede, quickly develops a passion for the protagonist through a variety of dealings related to interiors. To impress Carlos, Dâmaso begins a spirited devotion to the decorative arts: "Lançara-se no bricabraque. Trazia sempre o *coupé* cheio de lixos arqueológicos, ferragens velhas, um bocado de tijolo, a asa rachada de um bule" [He threw himself into collecting antiques. His coupé was always full of archeological detritus, rusty metal fittings, bits of old brick or tile, the broken handle from a teapot, 190]. The arrangement of his own interiors makes his affection for Carlos particularly evident while revealing other important details about their friendship. The visit of Ega and Cruges to Dâmaso's home unveils not only the latter's adoration of Carlos, but also the protagonist's esteem for interior decorating. Earlier Dâmaso and Carlos were supposse to visit the house of the ladies Medeiros to go look at some bedspreads in order to advance on another of Carlos's many decorative projects: the creation of a special *boudoir* for himself that would be lined with these antique coverings. Much to Dâmaso's despair, they never did make it to the ladies' house that day, but a closer attention to Dâmaso's rooms suggests that they eventually indeed make it out together to Lumiar:

> O tapete era exactamente igual aos dos quartos de Carlos no Ramalhete. E em redor abundavam os vestígios da antiga amizade com o Maia: o retrato de Carlos a cavalo, num vistoso caixilho de flores em faiança: uma das colchas da Índia das senhoras Medeiros, branca e verde, enroupando o piano, arranjada por Carlos com alfinetes....

> [The carpet was exactly the same as the one in Carlos' rooms at Ramalhete. And all around were abundant signs of his former friendship with Carlos: the portrait of Carlos on horseback in a showy frame of faience-ware flowers; one of the white and green Indian bedspreads bought from the Medeiros sisters and subsequently draped over the piano and pinned into position by Carlos..., 551-552; 478]

Not only does Dâmaso participate in the private affair of renovating Carlos's dressing room, but the protagonist himself has left his own very personal touch on Dâmaso's interior world. These interior particulars, which bind these two characters together, are not only very feminine in nature [the flower pattern of the picture frame, their dealings with ladies, the pins], but they also suggest a sensual intimacy [bedspreads are made to cover beds]. Dâmaso seems to be quite aware and conscious of Carlos's presence inside his bedrooms. Ega's challenge to a duel rouses Dâmaso to such a degree the he begins not only bumping clumsily into the furniture but also hopping "através do tapete" [on the carpet, 555; 481] demanding to see Carlos immediately. When pressured to sign the horrid confession letter, Dâmaso, "atirando um olhar tonto e vago por sobre os móveis" [casting a vacant glance about the room], searches in his interior for an explanation to this betrayal (556; 482). Whether these and other details, such as the symmetry between Dâmaso and Maria Eduarda's devotion to copying Carlos's scholarly work, point to homoerotic desires seems less interesting than the fact that private rooms reveal not only the psychology of minor characters but also secrets about the protagonists themselves. Cruges's interiors reinforce the fact that Carlos repeatedly relates to others through the composition of interior spaces.

Carlos also begins a friendship with Craft with great ease mainly because of a shared interest in shopping for knick knacks, a common taste in antiques, and a passion for collecting. He is immediately welcomed into the Maia family and becomes one of Carlos's regular friends due to "similitudes de gostos e de ideias, o mesmo fervor pelo bricabraque e pelo *bibelot*" [similar tastes and ideas, the same enthusiasm for bric-à-brac and antiques, 186; 161]. On his way to Ega's dinner party, Carlos fittingly runs into Craft at the antique shop of the old Jew Abraão. They instantly start up a conversation about Craft's experience as a collector and later in the evening they momentarily escape the dinner crowd and walk over to the veranda to continue their discussion about Craft's collection in his home in Olivais. Craft's name is especially appropriate since it alludes to the English Arts and Crafts movement of the second half of the nineteenth century, which championed a new appreciation of the decorative arts considered by many critics to be under threat by industrialization. This aesthetic development in the history of the decorative arts parallels concerns of the realist genre, mainly the wish to reconcile social responsibility and egalitarian objectives with an artistic agenda. Craft's ideas on collecting and craftsmanship inspire Carlos the very same evening that the protagonist sees Maria Eduarda and her beauty begins to captivate him. At this point begins the significant analogy in the novel between Carlos's obsession for different homes and the renovation of their interiors and his love for Maria.

If Craft charms Carlos with his aesthetic plans, Maia's own possessions in turn seduce other characters. For example, when Teles da Gama visits Ramalhete with the solemn and determined purpose of confronting Carlos and defending his recently offended and threatened friend Dâmaso, he is quickly fascinated and distracted by the décor around him. Teles da Gama becomes so preoccupied with the "faianças holandesas" [examples of Dutch faience-ware] that fill Carlos's lovely rooms that he forgets his duty to Dâmaso (428;

369). He promises Carlos to return when he has more time in order to better study the rich collection. The protagonist allures Teles da Gama with his rooms and interiors the same way he leads Maria Eduarda on a seductive tour of the Toca. The couple's first visit to the Olivais home with its long architectural foreplay immediately follows this meeting with Teles da Gama. The juxtaposition of these two scenes once again reinforces the analogy between Carlos's two love affairs: interior décor and Maria Eduarda.

The entire liaison between Carlos and Maria Eduarda has a corresponding design history involving a number of different domestic spaces. The relationship between the two can be traced to a affection Carlos maintains with different homes and interiors. His love for her parallels his attachment to different furnishings and spaces. In nineteenth-century novels, characters rountinely search for remote homes and rooms to accommodate and hide their adulterous affairs. In *The Maias* it is almost as if characters invent forbidden relationships to suit their architectural projects. The adoration for Maria Eduarda begins on the memorable day when Carlos visits her hotel rooms for the first time to check on the health of her daughter Rosa. Although he is called upon for his medical qualifications, Carlos never uses these; no intricate medical examination takes place, instead Carlos "examinou um momento o quarto" [examined the room, 263; 227]. He scrutinizes the objects and the tastefully arranged room and fancies the interior space long before he ever meets the woman and falls in love with her.

On his first visit to Maria Eduarda's rented floor in Cruges's house, Carlos stands on the landing observing the solitude and impenetrability of the three blue doors that lead to her apartment. His desire to finally and personally know Maria Eduarda is expressed in architectural terms and staged at this significant threshold. He imagines her directing him through the "corredores interiores daquela casa" [inner corridors of that house] and fantasizes about her inviting him inside: "abria-lhe a sua porta" [she was opening her door to him, 344; 298]. The idea of penetrating Maria Eduarda's interiors is also without a doubt a very clear and important erotic symbol. Carlos Santos Vargas's study on this topic identifies how space is often sexualized in the novel and points out the number of times the adverb "penetrating" and the verb "to penetrate" are repeated throughout the text.[20] Still, the relationship between the two lovers and their interiors goes far beyond symbolism. This analogy is a lot more complex if we consider the role furnishings and interior decorating play in Carlos's life, in his position in public life, and in the ironic development of the plot. Interiors set the tone of the relationship between Carlos and Maria Eduarda from the very beginning. The topic of their first conversation quickly turns to houses and their comfort or lack thereof: "Maria Eduarda queixava-se sobretudo das casas, tão faltas de comodidade, tão despidas de gosto, tão desleixadas" [Maria Eduarda's main complaint was the quality of the houses, so lacking in comfort, so devoid of taste, so neglected, 356; 308]. When he reminisces about his visits to the Rua de São Francisco he specifically thinks about her drawing-room and imagines every detail of the "larga sala de repes vermelho" [large red-upholstered room, 364; 315). Carlos is quickly fascinated with his assigned corner of the room where he sits near a rosewood desk on the "mais velha, a mais cómoda das poltronas de repes vermelho" [oldest and most comfortable of the red-upholstered armchairs, 367; 317]. Maria Eduarda's wish to rent a different home for the summer months convinces Carlos to rent the Olivais estate and buy its collection of antiques and furnishings from Craft. The day he decides this he no longer enjoys the red-upholstered salon with the same fervor, is unable to sit still in his designated seat, and instead paces about the room. His appreciation for this interior diminishes: "Pobre senhora! Tão delicada, e ali enterrada entre aqueles repes" [The poor woman! She had such delicate tastes and yet there she was buried among all that cheap red upholstery, 407; 351]. His mind has moved on to future plans to acquire and remodel Craft's house. The excitement with which he confesses his love to Maria Eduarda is the same enthusiasm he feels toward his soon to be new home: "era como se a casa, os móveis, as árvores fossem já seus, fossem já dela. E teve ali um momento delicioso" [it was as if the Olivais house, with its furniture and its trees, were already his—already hers. And he spent a delicious moment, 408; 352]. Her beauty is enhanced by the exquisiteness of the decorative arts for she would look grander and ever more beautiful "no meio desses móveis de Renascença, severos e nobres!" [among all that severe, noble Renaissance furniture!, 407; 351].

The plans to move to Olivais fill Carlos with newfound artistic energy. Long before imagining himself making love to Maria Eduarda, Carlos fantasizes about and awaits anxiously the architectural tour of the house that they take together: "Mas, o que mais lhe apetecia era percorrer com ela as duas salas de Craft, parando ambos diante de uma bela faiança ou de um móvel raro" [What he most wanted, however, was to stroll with her through Craft's two drawing-rooms and for them to linger together before some beautiful faience-ware or a rare piece of furniture, 307; 266]. Throughout Eça's writing, furnishings function as euphemisms for the sexual activities that take place on them. Characters measure the quality of a couch or a divan on its ability to hold out through ardent lovemaking. But, Carlos and Maria Eduarda are in fact interested in the interior for the interior's sake. Their tour of Olivais more than confirms their passion for interior architecture. Maria begins eyeing every detail of the house right away and insists twice on seeing the house immediately: "Vamos ver a casa" [Let's go and see the house, 431; 371]. She continues attentively through the rooms "examinando a acomodação dos armários, palpando a elasticidade dos colchões, atenta, cuidadosa, toda no desvelo de alojar bem a sua gente" [assessing the size of wardrobes and testing the springiness of mattresses, eager to ensure that the people in her charge would be comfortably lodged, 431; 372]. Carlos is beside himself with excitement especially at the chance to renovate and redo the rooms to her liking. He exclaims "Muda-se!" [We'll change it!] and "Deita-se abaixo!" [We'll knock it down!] rubbing his hands with glee while Maria accepts all his modifications (432; 372). The idea of a collective redecorating project inspires him above all as he asks her: "Para que serve o nosso génio decorativo?" [What else are our decorative talents for?, 435; 374]. The enthusiasm of the two lovers is rendered in the language they know best, the language of interiors. This is a climactic moment for they are meeting in private in their new abode for the first time and what most moves them emotionally is their passion for the interior details of the house and its furnishings. Homes, furnishings, and interior décor trace the development of their love throughout the novel and this climax is just one step in this process.

The Olivais home will prove insufficient for such a creative and furniture-crazed mind as Carlos's. Dissatisfied with the long travel he must undergo almost daily from Lisbon to Olivais in order to see Maria Eduarda, Carlos decides to rent a small cottage nearby for himself. He quickly becomes very fond of his new refuge referring to it tenderly in the diminutive and as his "choupana" [cabin]. Baptista immediately arrives with a cart full of furniture to adorn "este novo ninho" [the new nest]. Maria's reaction is unenthusiastic: "Mais outra casa!" [Not another house!, 460; 396]. She realizes she must compete with this new home for Carlos's attention and affection. His luxurious Ramalhete interiors represent a part of Carlos's intimacy that she has hitherto not accessed. This is why she insists on visiting the mansion and once there impatiently tours, touches, and takes in every detail of his rooms, the house, and the garden. As friends begin to know about the affair and the couple starts to host *soirées* at Olivais, Carlos's main concern becomes to improve and beautify the Toca: "nunca voltava de Lisboa sem trazer alguma figurinha de Saxe, um marfim, um faiança, como noivo feliz que aperfeiçoa o seu ninho" [he never came back from Lisbon without bringing with him some Saxe figurine, and ivory carving, or a piece of faience-ware, 528; 457]. The steps that their liaison take are measured by the acquisition of homes and spaces moving from Cruges's house to Olivais and its Japanese gazebo in the garden to Carlos's cottage and Ramalhete and finally returning to Rua de São Francisco where it all started. Just as the novel opens and closes with the family mansion, the couple's architectural love narrative tour also makes a full circle.

Slowly interiors become Carlos's epistemological understanding of the world. They replace his language for reading and interpreting his feelings. Carlos saves his most intimate reflections for when he is alone in his bed-chambers. His private thoughts and ideas are often equated with furnishings and objects that fill an empty space. His vision, for example, of Maria Eduarda and her entourage "tomou cor, encheu todo o aposento" [took on colour and filled the whole room, 184; 159]. His memory in this scene is furthermore framed by a significant piece of furniture. He sits on his *chaise longue* smoking Alencar's cigar and remembering his past. Carlos seems more often than not to ignore his parents' difficult history, and the reader has little access to the protagonist's feelings about such painful events. After a flashback where Carlos revisits this terrible past, the narrative returns to the present and focuses once again on the *chaise longue*. It is as if the severity of Carlos's memory were alleviated by the comfort of the chair. Carlos's subconscious thoughts are substituted with the luxury, beauty, and comfort of furnishings and interiors. By making a fetish of the décor, Carlos refurbishes and adorns his thoughts as well; reupholstering and covering up any difficult memory or feeling. Upon discovering that Maria Eduarda is his sister, Carlos decides to confront her with this truth. As he approaches the house on the Rua de São Francisco he is unable to enter because he is reminded of certain details of the house: "o sofá largo e profundo com almofadas de seda" [the broad generous sofa with its silk cushions] and "o cortinado branco da cama dela" [the white curtains around her bed, 654; 570]. At such a moment one is surprised to see Carlos pondering these material details, but the text insists on the comfort and splendor of the interior not only because it might lure Carlos away from facing the horrid reality and seduce him to love her still despite his knowledge, but more importantly because the protagonist can only articulate and give shape to his feelings via the language of décor.

Ega's relationship to interiors likewise reveals a great deal about his failed desires. He too can trace the core of his affair with Raquel Cohen to his Vila Balzac, whose creation eventually usurps his own possibilities for work or love. The name of this architectural project alludes to "Les Jardies," a rather fantastic house that Honoré de Balzac builds in Sèvres in 1838 and leaves in 1840. This imitation of a model writer's own architectural and decorative adventure reinforces the idea that Ega's attempt to bring mobility and progress into his life is reminiscent of the frustrations of authors as well. Balzac apparently moves into the house before he manages to furnish most of the rooms. Biographers point out how the French author used his imagination to fill the emptiness of the house by writing on the walls with charcoal what he intended the interior decoration of his house to look like. Balzac literally writes his interior décor, reinforcing the fundamental connection between writing and interior renovating. Ega's Vila Balzac is also apparently set up as a haven for literary production. Carlos's best friend is motivated to find a secluded place conducive to writing in order to finish his *Memories of an Atom* and barely has time to socialize because he is busy "estudando mobílias" [studying how best to furnish, the house, 130; 110]. Ultimately, he falls short of writing a single chapter of his book, but he successfully furnishes, decorates, and moves into his new home. Ega is first impressed with the way Carlos arranges his consulting rooms and begins to scrutinize with his monocle the furniture and decorative objects. Vilaça admits to everyone that Ega has inquired about Carlos's purchases especially the "mobília de veludo" [velvet-upholstered furniture, 116; 98]. Ega manages to realize his Vila Balzac project, an accomplishment he has been preparing and undertaking throughout the narrative. Hence character development in *The Maias* seems to equal making progress on decorative art projects.

Carlos's visit to Vila Balzac makes it clear that the home's central function is not to facilitate Ega's writing. The bedroom dominates the house and its very large bed fills and dominates the room: "Parecia ser o motivo, o centro da Vila Balzac; e nele se esgotara a imaginação artística do Ega" [The bed appeared to be the *raison d'être*, the very centre of Villa Balzac, and into it Ega had poured all his artistic imagination, 147; 125]. Carlos asks Ega where he produces his great art and Ega points to his bed. Vila Balzac is in reality a love nest that accommodates Ega's adulterous affair with Raquel, and sex has substituted for his work as a writer. The artistic imagination can refer both to the energy necessary to write a masterpiece as it can to Ega's talent as an interior decorator. By drowning the room with the bed Ega has failed in subtlety. He later explains to Carlos and Craft how Raquel always entered Vila Balzac through a back door and how everything had been organized "com uma arte muito subtil" [with the most subtle and impenetrable skill, 284; 246]. The lack of elusiveness in the interior decoration of Vila Balzac is replaced with the subtlety used to hide his romantic liaison with Raquel. Still in the end the affair becomes public, the same way Ega's short-lived creative project also collapses. Vila Balzac is not a delicate well-designed interior, but an erratic reflection of its real purpose, just as the mirror on the bed's headboard paints a clear image of what is normally reflected on it. As Carlos, Ega is unsuccessful at separating his true feelings for Raquel from his decorative project. After the affair is catastrophically broken up, Ega often thinks back with nostalgia to the furnishings of his house, especially to the large bed and its black-satin bedspread.

Ega's interaction with and views on interior decoration reveal on the one hand his insecurities and disappointments, while acting on the other hand as a form of communication between him and Carlos. As with other subject matter, Ega maintains zealous opinions on the decorative arts. According to him an interior should reproduce the dweller's ideas and beliefs; during Carlos's visit to Vila Balzac, Ega professes: "eu não tolero o *bibelot*, o bricabraque, a cadeira arqueológica, essas mobílias de arte…Que diabo, o móvel deve estar em harmonia com a ideia e o sentir do homem que o usa!" [I can't stand knick knacks and bric-à-brac, antique chairs and "artistic" furniture…Furniture should be in harmony with the ideas and feelings of the man using it, damn it!, 149; 127]. This speech is a way of covering up and justifying the obvious functions of his new home. Likewise, when Carlos keeps his affair with Maria secret and Ega begins to suffer from his friend's neglect, he expresses his frustration by criticizing the Olivais collection. He disapproves of Carlos's impulsive purchase and highlights the home's inconveniences. Ega's discontentment with the Olivais period style and design points to his discontent toward Carlos. In other words by taking it out on the furniture Ega confirms that it is through the language of décor that the two protagonists connect.

> —Essa concepção do Paraíso—exclamou ele—parece-me de um estofador da Rua Augusta! Como Natureza, couves galegas; como decoração, os velhos cretones do gabinete, desbotados já por três barrelas... Um quarto de dormir lúgubre como uma capela de santuário... Um salão confuso como o armazém de um cara-de-pau, e onde não é possível conversar... A não ser o armário holandês, e um ou outro prato, tudo aquilo é um lixo arqueológico.

> ["Your idea of Paradise," he exclaimed, "seems to me worthy of an upholsterer in Rua Augusta! For nature, a few rows of cabbages, for decoration, the old cretonne in the study, faded from one too many washings. A bedroom as gloomy as a church chapel. A drawing-room as cluttered as a junk-dealer's warehouse and where it is impossible even to hold a decent conversation. Apart from the Dutch dresser and the odd plate, it's just a pile of archaeological rubbish," 416; 358.]

This typical reaction from Ega discloses his feelings of jealousy, and, like Carlos, he only knows how to articulate his emotions in terms of judgments and ideas about interior decoration. He tries here to emphasize his more modern preferences for fresh, new, and harmonious interiors favorable to dialogue, and to oppose these tendencies to Carlos's and Craft's more old-fashioned predilections, which he considers more traditionally Portuguese.

Ega's desire for harmony between the interior space and the inner mind is nonetheless just one of his many illusions. Interiors play an extremely important role in the narrative exploration of the inner lives of Ega and Carlos by showing how the protagonists develop new etymologies and epistemologies to interconnect with each other and the world. In Ega's case they emphasize the friction that exists between him and his desires and truncated plans while also alluding to important subconscious weaknesses and contradictions. From the moment Ega learns Maria Eduarda is Carlos's sister, he dominates the narrative perspective. He is ultimately too weak to face Carlos with what he has learned, and Vilaça must take the responsibility of informing Carlos; not only can Ega not tell Carlos the truth, his only way to frame and comprehend the tragic turn of events is in terms of interiors. As he enters Ramalhete, Ega's thoughts articulate the tragedy of the incest by wandering from room to room and by tripping over furniture and by fixating his attention on the details of Carlos's private quarters: "entreabriu o reposteiro dos aposentos de

Carlos; deu alguns passos tímidos no tapete, que pareceram já soar triste-
mente. Um reflexo de espelho alvejou ao fundo na sombra da alcova. E a luz
caiu sobre o leito intacto, com a sua longa colcha lisa, entre os cortinados de
seda" [He lit a candle and drew aside the curtain at the door that led into
Carlos' rooms; he took a few timid steps across the rug, footsteps that already
seemed to have a sad echo. A mirror glinted palely in the shadows. And the
candle light fell on the untouched bed with its broad smooth bedspread and
silk drapes, 624; 542]. Ega requires furnishings and adornments to frame and
cope with the tragic turn of events.

The two main characters of *The Maias* are the interior architects of their
own lives. They translate their knowledge of reality, art, and love into a
language of interiors. The fact that they search for a deeper understanding of
themselves and others in terms of interior decorating connects them, as
Rubião in Machado's novel, with the feminine. Carlos and Ega are sugges-
tively feminized throughout the narrative. As pointed out earlier, women
spearhead the profession of interior decorating, while also being the protagonists of the new cultural emphasis on the inner world and its stress on the
more sensual and vulnerable sides of an individual. As with Rubião, Ega and
Carlos are also associated with female attributes. For example, many characters and the narrator himself constantly point to the feminine qualities of
Carlos's private rooms. The silk-covered walls of his Ramalhete bedrooms
make Vilaça remark "aquilo não eram aposentos de médico—mas de
dançarina!" [that they were more like a dancer's boudoir than a doctor's
private apartments!, 10; 5]. Carlos also has an ongoing idea of creating a
special *boudoir* for himself of antique bedspreads, which we discover
through his interactions with Dâmaso. When preparing to go to sleep, Carlos's turned-down bed "entreaberto mostrava, sob a seda dos cortinados, um
luxo afeminado de bretanhas, bordados e rendas" [revealed, beneath the silk
hangings, an almost effeminate luxuriance of Breton linen, lace, and embroidery, 138; 118]. Novels at this time very often place female characters in
boudoirs, but in *The Maias* the reader often finds Carlos in his private closet.
As he prepares for the Cohen ball the narrator highlights the sensuality of the
materials and the pleasing aromas of soaps and cigars that float in his dressing room: "Sobre duas cómodas de pau-preto, marchetadas a marfim, duas
serpentinas de velho bronze erguiam os seus molhos de velas acesas, pondo
largos reflexos doces sobre a seda castanha das paredes" [On two Indian
rosewood chests of drawers, inlaid with ivory, two old bronze candelabra
proffered bunches of lit candles, which cast a golden light on the brown silk
of the walls, 268; 232]. Carlos is not only preoccupied with the beauty of
things and materials, but the character's entire emotional and intellectual
depth is tied to his perception of interior detail. The pleasure that the protagonist derives from his interior world recalls the narrator's delight in describing
rich interior environments.

Compared to Clarín's protagonist, Ana Ozores, and many of Machado's female characters, the more prominent women in Eça's fiction—Amélia, Juliana, Luísa—seem to readers to be far less complex. Most critics, however, focus on these female characters of Eça's earlier fiction to show the author's sensitivity to the female condition. Yet his more mysterious, vague, and later characters, Gouvarinho, Maria Eduarda, and Maria da Graça, play less of a role in the novels but pose a greater challenge to the reader, to other characters, and to the narrator himself. It is significantly more difficult to penetrate their interiority than it is to enter Carlos's or Ega's inner worlds, but this is precisely because the narrator, like his predominantly male characters, is unable to fully understand the inside world of these female characters. This does not mean, however, that the women don't make their independent thoughts and feelings known to the reader. They do this primarily through the way they interact with their interior setting. Maria Eduarda and Gouvarinho recall female characters like Machado's Flora or Fidélia because the distance created between them and the reader is formally structured into the novel's discourse on interiors. This allows the female characters to make a strong impression in spite of their indefinite and ambiguous qualities. Despite the fact that most of the characters in *The Maias* are men, one can better understand Gouvarinho's and Maria Eduarda's personas by looking inside their spaces and at how they live in relation to their interiors.

Sensitivity to decorative detail, apparently the duty of both narrator and dandy, is also a woman's talent. Maria Eduarda and Countess Gouvarinho portray the strength of their personalities through their manipulation and understanding of their interiors and those of other characters. Their interaction with Carlos via the interior space is crucial. As we have seen the protagonist's entire relationship to Maria Eduarda is narrated in terms of homes and rooms, but she recognizes that through interiors she can understand the mechanism of Carlos's inner mind and desires. Of all the places Maria Eduarda inhabits, the house on Rua de São Francisco is the only one that is originally her own. The décor of this rented apartment reveals that what is most characteristic of Maria's taste is the fact that it reminds one of the Maia family's own preferences. The description could very well be of a Ramalhete interior or of one in another Maia house. Maria Eduarda has a similar taste for objects of art and for oriental pieces, "um pequeno contador árabe" [a small Moorish chest of drawers], "taças japonesas de bronze" [bronze Japanese goblets], "um vaso do Japão" [a Japanese vase, 347; 301] and a yellow vase from India as well as an Indian rosewood desk. The "biombo de linho cru, com ramalhetes bordados" [lovely screen in raw linen embroidered with bouquets of flowers] not only reminds us of the comfortable niche Afonso creates for himself by the fireplace in Ramalhete but also alludes with its bouquets of flowers by name to the Lisbon mansion. Even the Reverendo Bonifácio has a counterpart in Maria Eduarda's interiors, the "cadelinha escocesa" [little griffon dog] Niniche (348; 301). The bullfighter's panoply in the corridor in the Toca, which so enchants Maria Eduarda, reflects Afonso's preference for a traditional bullfight instead of the disastrous horse races. In taste and aesthetic inspiration Maria Eduarda is clearly part of the family. Her care for her interior world is described as a "hábito inquieto de recompor constantemente a simetria das coisas" [restless habit of constantly trying to restore things to symmetry, 366; 316]. The unconscious equilibrium she aims to maintain is not only the one that exists within her own space, but more importantly the symmetry between her world and Ramalhete's, which represents the identity and existence denied to her. The Olivais country home receives her special touch, which softens the excessive, cold, and museum-like quality of the house. Unlike Carlos, Maria Eduarda controls her decoration and does not let the interior take over her sense of the world. Maria Eduarda's interiors make evident the workings of her own subconscious desires to belong to her natural family.

Similarly, Gouvarinho's interaction with interiors reveals her strength over the protagonist. Carlos assesses the significance of the passionate but short-lived adulterous liaison he maintains with Countess Gouvarinho once again in terms of interiors. To Maria Eduarda he later confesses that his past relationships with other women are merely "quartos de estalagem onde se dorme uma vez" [rooms in an inn where one sleeps only once, 468; 403]. When Carlos pictures himself making love to Gouvarinho, he associates her body with materials that more often upholster his rooms and furnishings: "enrolava-se-lhe no cetim das formas" [he undressed her, became lost in her satiny curves, 211; 183]. Still, Gouvarinho's resilience and assertiveness, which she uses to resist her melancholy, ultimately expose Carlos's weaknesses. Carlos, as Ega, has not always been especially gifted at creating subtlety in interior décor. His consulting rooms reinforce his tendency to exaggerate. Afonso already felt that his grandson embellished too much in Ramalhete, in the old man's opinion Carlos's love for the luxury of cold climates led him to overstress on the tapestries, velvets, and curtains. Gouvarinho also makes Carlos aware of the inadequacy of the décor of his consulting rooms. She hesitates before sitting on what seems to be a very inappropriate divan for a medical office, and when she sees the piano she asks ironically: "Os seus doentes dançam quadrilhas?" [Do your patients dance quadrilles?, 207; 180]. The visit to the consulting rooms attests to her audacity and makes it clear that she can see through Carlos's sense of interior space.

The central figure framing Carlos's relationship to Gouvarinho is the sofa where they first kiss. This sofa not only eventually usurps his entire memory of their time together, but also represents the challenge that Gouvarinho herself proposes to him and he fails to meet. She initiates their affair by first visiting him in his office and then by luring him into her *boudoir* for their first romantic encounter. As Carlos kisses her he searches for a couch nearby:

Ele deu um passo, tendo-a assim enlaçada, e como morta; o seu joelho encontrou um sofá baixo, que rolou e fugiu. Com a cauda de seda enrolada nos pés, Carlos seguiu, tropeçando, o largo sofá, que rolou, fugiu ainda, até que esbarrou contra o pedestal onde o senhor conde erguia a fronte inspirada.

[With her limp body clasped in his arms, he took a step forward, but his knee collided with a low sofa, which rolled away from him. The silk train of her dress became tangled about his feet, and Carlos stumbled after the sofa, which only fled still further off, until it, at last, bumped against the pedestal on which the Count raised his inspired brow heavenwards, 297; 257-258.]

When characters are feeling weak, insecure, or frightened they characteristically trip and stumble over their furnishings. Ega wakes up in Craft's house after the Cohen ball and jumps out of bed stunned and disheveled "tropeçando contra os móveis" [barking his bare shins on the furniture, 280; 242]. When Ega and Cruges visit Dâmaso in his own house in order to challenge him to a duel with Carlos, in his bewilderment he bumps "nos móveis" [clumsily into the furniture, 554; 480]. Similarly Gouvarinho destabilizes Carlos and this surfaces in his inability to control the moving sofa. The chapter of Carlos's and Gouvarinho's first kiss ends with a final mention of the fleeing couch which characterizes and sets the tone for their entire relationship. When Carlos begins to regret his involvement with Gouvarinho he starts to curse the couch that brought them together. The fugitive sofa triggers his memory, and he thinks back to the past and "revia o sofá onde ela caíra com um rumor de sedas amarrotadas" [recalled the sofa onto which she had fallen with a whisper of crumpled silk, 655; 570]. His memory is increasingly vague and remote but the sofa's presence persists along with a recollection of silk. This evokes the fleeting and weak character of both the relationship and Carlos and the protagonist's materialization of the Countess.

The novel is explicit in showing how Gouvarinho intimidates Carlos with her tenacity: "ela era o homem, o sedutor, com a sua veemência de paixão activa, tentando-o, soprando-lhe o desejo; enquanto ele parecia a mulher, hesitante e assustada" [she appeared to take the role of the man, the seducer, tempting him, inflaming him, while he was more like the woman, 340; 294]. Gouvarinho's control over her own passion reflects the way she manipulates her interior to seduce Carlos. Both the Countess and Maria Eduarda prove to be aware and in control of the novel's ubiquitous language of furnishings, which dominates the characterization of the protagonists. The majority of the male characters are ultimately usurped and manipulated by their domestic environments. They identify with interiors and depend on the furnishing and creation of space to give sense to their lives. The women, on the other hand, seem to express conscious and subconscious desires through a more active involvement with the spaces around them. *The Maias* by no means engenders domestic interiors in a dogmatic manner. Instead, it is interested in elaborating new psychologies and epistemologies that reflect on the society of the time. The novel looks to develop both an aesthetic and a material narrative that penetrates and stimulates its characters.

MEMORY AND MOVEMENT: ANA'S AND FERMÍN'S INTERIORS

Clarín's heroine, Ana Ozores, is central to *La Regenta*'s various constructions with interior settings. While Machado and Eça turn to female characters to determine the fate of the plot and of the protagonists of their novels, Clarín places a woman at the center of his novel. Independently of whether the interior space belongs to a female or male character, what is associated with the interior world is characteristically a more female and sensual experience. This inner experience is at the heart of the individual crisis of modernity and is characterized by the breakdown these characters undergo living in a society and time when individual and collective values have all but disappeared. The three novels focus on women and on interiors to show how the turn inward requires an alternative world view, one that adopts a different ontological understanding of our surroundings and takes into consideration both emotion and knowledge in comprehending human action. Interior life is not a clear escape from the moral and political decomposition and does not always save individuals from exterior reality. The turn inward depends on the connection between interior and exterior and on the concept of using both intellect and body in defining the self. The interconnectedness between interior and exterior, individual and collective, and sensation and idea, so essential in the novels, shows that the inner crisis the protagonists undergo involves both selves and societies.

In his pioneering essay on the structure of *La Regenta*, Emilio Alarcos Llorach calls the Ozores palace and Doña Paula's house "dos islotes" [two islands] within the larger narrative.[21] Indeed Ana and Fermín's domestic spaces emerge as isolated from their society, but these interior settings are both autonomous and interdependent from the rest of the novel's spatial divisions. If in *Quincas Borba* Rubião and Sofia play the major role, and in *The Maias* Carlos and Ega maintain the greater complex relationship between interior space and character, *La Regenta* explores more intensively the psychologies and inner feelings of Ana Ozores and Fermín de Pas and not surprisingly pays particular attention to their sense of place. Ana's and Fermín's spaces are like islands because the protagonists often feel trapped, isolated, and exiled within them. Yet, like *Quincas Borba* and *The Maias*, Clarín's novel also draws important connections between Ana, De Pas, and the spaces of minor characters. Saturnino Bermudez, introduced in chapter I, for example, prefigures the protagonists not only in his failed dreams, sexual repression, and frustrated attempts to read and write his life story, but also because Saturnino is sensitive to his material and private world. Once alone in his rooms getting ready for bed he enjoys "la sensación agradable del calorcillo del suave y blando lecho" [the pleasurable warmth of his soft, soothing bed, 1: 93; 41]. Saturno's need for comfort and softness evokes the protagonists' own desires, especially Ana's, and although nothing ultimately prepares the reader for the dismal state of the heroine's mind and heart introduced in chapter III, Saturno's inner thoughts and private quarters provide a chance for the readers to wet their feet in the sea of complex inner worlds that the narrative portrays.

An examination of Ana's private rooms immediately invokes the extensive readings that have focused on Ana's adultery, the relation between her sexual desires and confession and religion, and the importance of her body in the development of the plot.[22] Noël Valis's "Aspects of an Improper Birth," which explores how Ana's body "figuratively and literally—lies at the very center" of Clarín's masterpiece, elucidates the significant complex nexus in the novel between body and imagination.[23] Like Valis's reading, I also look closer inside Ana's selves and rooms to show how the narrative of Ana's interiors, both mind and place, furnish her memory while also designing an interior architecture that attempts to confront the irresolvable complexities of life and death. As Ana prepares for her "examen de conciencia" [examination of conscience] the narrative takes the reader into her bedroom for the first time. Like many of the other domestic spaces in the novel and like her own house, Ana's private quarters are also divided into two sections. The boudoir is separated from the sleeping room by "un intercolumnio con elegantes colgaduras de *satín* granate" [elegant drapery of garnet-red sateen hanging between two columns], and this partition seems to preoccupy her thoughts (1: 124; 64). Initially she makes a conscious effort not to go into her bedroom, "se sentó en una mecedora junto a su tocador, en el gabinete, lejos del lecho" [she sat in a rocking-chair near the dressing-table in her boudoir, at some distance from her bed, 1: 123; 64]. Eventually, however, she gives in and moves toward the room. Once inside, Ana "corrió con mucho cuidado las colgaduras granate, como si alguien pudiera verla desde el tocador" [closed the garnet-red drapery with great care, as if someone might see her from the boudoir, 1: 125; 65]. This defining line between spaces turns the bedroom into a second interior, a more profound refuge of privacy. In fact, later in the story, her boudoir becomes a "tocador-oratorio" [boudoir-oratory], confining this part of her quarters and mind to her more ceremonial and external expressions of religious devotion, while her sleeping area is associated with her inner more sensual self (1: 631; 487). It is no coincidence that once inside the bedroom the narrative begins to penetrate deeper into Ana's thoughts and memories. The rocking chair, a reference to the emotional comforts absent from her childhood, and the devotional book, both which are left on the other side of the curtains, prove insufficient substitutes for her spiritual and emo-

tional needs. This spatial division suggests her mind is torn just as it seems to
Ana that "su vida se había partido en dos" [her own life had been divided into
two parts, 1: 127; 67]. The bedroom is the consecrated place for Ana as a
child, while in her boudoir the adult Ana unsuccessfully attempts to content
herself with her fate.

The bedroom subsequently narrates her childhood both figuratively and
literally as the room, its objects, and furniture slowly extend into Ana's past
childhood experiences, creating a fundamental continuity between past and
present and between space and memory. Ana's gilt "vulgarísima cama de
matrimonio" [commonplace double bed, 1: 124; 64] becomes "la barca de
Trébol" [the ferry-boat at Trébol, 1: 127; 67] that navigates the reader to the
climactic childhood event that traumatizes her. By spending a harmless night
with her friend Germán as a child Ana is marked unjustly as a sinner, loses
her innocence, and is forced to face the cruel realities of life. As she begins to
remember this event, instead of being alone in her bed, her cheeks rubbing
against the soft sheets while keeping her "ojos muy abiertos" [eyes wide
open, 1: 125; 65], Ana finds herself cuddling with Germán in the boat and
once again with "los ojos muy abiertos" [her eyes wide open, 1: 128; 68].
The bed sheets and covers transform into a canvas sack "como si fuera una
colcha" [as if it were a counterpane] that protects them from the cold (1: 128;
67). Once this improvised coverlet turns back into her own bedspread, the
Regenta returns from her memories: "apartó de sí la colcha pesada" [pushed
the heavy counterpane aside] and as the bedcover "quedó arrugada a los
pies" [lay crumpled at her feet] those painful memories of her childhood
disappear (1: 132; 70). If in her room she buries her small bare feet "en la
espesura de las manchas pardas" [in the fur with its brown makings] of her
infamous "piel de tigre" [tiger-skin, 1: 125; 65], in her memories she remembers cuddling with a noble, black, long-haired dog and how she hid "el rostro
en la lana suave y caliente" [her face in smooth, warm hair, 1: 126; 66]. The
river's soft tide substitutes the unsatisfactory rocking chair with "un rumor
dulce que la arrullaba como para adormecerla" [a gentle murmuring, sweetly
lulling, as if to send her to sleep, 1: 128; 68]. Gaston Bachelard notes in
Poetics of Space that a house is an embodiment of dreams, and it is on the
level of the daydream that "childhood remains alive and poetically useful."[24]
Ana was denied a happy childhood in her family's home, and so in her
unconscious effort to fill this absence she turns her room, its furnishings, and
materials into the absent emotions and missing feelings. She converts her
space into Bachelard's oneiric house and relives in it the poetry of the past
that was never present. The physical interaction between Ana and the textures of her room's objects give shape and tone to her memories and feelings
not simply by symbolizing them, but by reenacting and interpreting her
memories, building points of rupture as well as of continuity.

The double bed as ferryboat is reinforced by another significant image of Ana using her childhood bed as a means to escape the loneliness she feels when living with her aunts in Vetusta. The narrator describes Ana while lying in bed relishing in the early hours of the morning: "Ella se dejaba columpiar dentro de la blanda barquilla en aquel navegar aéreo de sus ensueños" [She would abandon herself to the swaying of that soft little boat, as her day-dreams took her sailing through the sky, 1: 174; 105]. The bed is the vessel that transports her to the past and fulfills her dreams of childhood. The furnishing transformed into boat substitutes the cradling warmth of her mother's womb and becomes the site of life or birth, and yet, as I will explore subsequently, it also brings Ana close to death. The idea that a birth brings a death and vice-versa occurs with the death of Ana's mother at childbirth as well. The cycle of life, which is also the link between fiction and reality and past and present, is expressed through points of continuity between the interior and Ana's self and existence. Important connections between her childhood and adult life articulate how Ana's bedroom reproduces the story of her inner feelings as they evolve throughout the narrative, and how the Ozores mansion frames her life story. When Ana first moves to her family's estate to live with her spinster aunts, she spends hours alone during her illness because "la alcoba de la sobrina estaba al otro extremo de la casa" [their niece's bedroom was at the other end of the house, 1: 169; 100]. Ana repeats the traumatic childhood experience of loneliness in her adult life. Ana and Víctor divided the marriage bed years ago, and she moved her room "al otro extremo del caserón" [to the other end of the house, 1: 138; 76]. As a child, however, she sleeps on a "pobre lecho" [humble bed], which has now been converted into a rich matrimonial bed as if this could in some way compensate for her past solitude (1: 170; 101). There are some furnishings that stay the same. Her bedside table, another commonplace piece of furniture that irritates Obdulia, is the same one on which her astonished aunt Anuncia finds "un cuaderno de versos, un tintero y una pluma" [a notebook full of poems, an inkwell and a pen, 1: 183; 112]. The considerable upgrade in her bed rectifies the injustices done to the little girl while ironically predicting its future utility as her and Álvaro's love nest, while keeping the same night table is Ana's form of holding on to the literary aspirations denied her by society's contempt and jealousy.

These furniture connections between past and present reinforce the importance of Ana's bedroom and house. Most critics point out that the Ozores mansion works to confine the heroine. Her home is at times compared to a prison and even a tomb; Sobejano refers to the palace as Ana's "casa-sepulcro" [house-tomb].[25] Her house and especially her bed do on different occasions begin what seems like to bury Ana but the recurring connection between interior and captivity is the narrative's form of exploring the individual's interiority, which takes place in enclosed settings. At the same time her home is a metaphor for her inner life as interiors are a form that the novel uses for its search for human interiority. Furthermore, it is true that Ana often dreams of escaping the walls of her family's mansion and confesses to Fermín her "anhelo de volar más allá de las estrechas paredes de su caserón" [desire to soar beyond the narrow confines of her old house, 1: 518; 393]. Yet, the metaphor of flying is an abstract image that Ana uses to escape intellectually and with her imagination her misery and loneliness. This theoretical flight is more important than the actual breaking out of her home, just as when she was small she fancied having wings and flying above rooftops.[26] The Ozores palace plays a major role in Ana's life but its interiors do not only function to imprison Ana, but also to help the heroine escape her reality. They likewise serve as a place of refuge from her corrupt society while locating her interiority, intimate thoughts, and wishes for freedom.

The Ozores manor, its garden, and her bedroom serve thus as Ana's primary and only shelters. The complex real estate history of the Ozores mansion reminds us of the continuous injustices Ana suffers both as a child and as an adult. Her father's mistakes and selfishness culminate with the abandonment of his daughter in total economic destitution and vulnerability upon his death. Ana's mission in life is and continues throughout the narrative to be an unyielding attempt to battle for freedom, which for her is psychological and spiritual growth. She is painfully aware, however, that "No bastaba la fuerza de sufrir en silencio, ni el refugiarse en la vida interior; necesitaba del mundo, un asilo" [The fortitude which silent suffering inspires was not enough, nor was it sufficient for her to shelter in her own inner life: she needed a refuge in the world]. Her greatest fear upon her father's death is expressed in terms of enslavement, "se sintió esclava de los demás" [she felt herself to be everybody's slave, 1: 166; 97]. Ana is deprived of her childhood's innocence the same way she is left without her inheritance, since her father undersells the Ozores mansion to his sisters. Víctor is able to buy the mansion back as a small retribution for Ana, and Frígilis struggles at the end of the novel to make sure Ana keeps the house, which "era de Ana legalmente y moralmente" [belonged to Ana both legally and morally, 1: 895; 711]. Because she has her own home, she is able to hide in it and keep others out, and she often prefers "la soledad de su caserón" [the solitude of her vast old house] to Vetustan company (1: 615; 472). While her aunts spend long hours "fuera del triste caserón" [away from their sad ancestral mansion, 1: 169; 100], and Don Víctor "no paraba en casa" [did not stay long in the house, 1: 540; 409], Ana spends increasingly more time alone indoors, and the thought of leaving her house frightens her. Her home is the only thing she has in the end, but if she had owned it from the beginning, she might have been able to choose a different destiny. Like *The Maias* and *Quincas Borba*, *La Regenta* relies on an elaborate real-estate history to reflect the fortunes and misfortunes of its characters.

The spaces associated with the protagonist, the Ozores palace and her sleeping quarters, demonstrate how interiors interpret Ana's background and fate, while at the same time begin to develop the novel's spatial narrative discourse. When Ana closes the garnet-red draperies in her bedroom she also shuts out Obdulia's perspective and opinion of her bedroom and begins her own private unveiling as she lets her blue dressing-gown fall to her feet. By including the widow's point of view of the Regenta's private quarters in the presentation of the heroine's domestic spaces, the novel connects Vetusta's effort to penetrate interiors to the narrator's own objectives. Ana rejects her provincial city by drawing the curtains, and Clarín seems to suggest that only the novel can create a private backstage scene that allows a deeper insight into character and thought. What follows depends on different levels of veiling and unveiling of Ana's secrets and past; from the "colgaduras granate" [garnet-red drapery] to her "bata azul" [blue dressing-gown] to her bed's "pabellón blanco" [white canopy] and the silky softness of her sheets and bedcovers, there are various coverings that both conceal and uncover what is happening in this scene (1: 124-125; 64-65). Standing naked and then over the bed delighting in the comfort of her bedclothes Ana apparently masturbates, so the novel seems to suggest, since she comes back from her thoughts "algo avergonzada" [somewhat ashamed, 1: 127; 67]. These various decorative materials function then to create different levels of Ana Ozores's sensuality and self-understanding. They generate multiple possible readings and interpretations of the events being narrated as well. During her period of religious fervor, Ana adopts a similar technique but in reverse form. She now removes layers and veils. First she prays on top of her soft bed sheets, she then rouses herself, kneels, and prays, "sobre las sabanas tibias" [on the warm sheets] and her rounded knees sink "en la blandura apetecible" [into the welcoming softness]. When her health is stronger she moves from this comfort to the harder floor and prays on the tiger-skin. But she still wants a firmer surface and "y separaba la piel y sobre la moqueta que forraba el pavimento hincaba las rodillas" [she pushed the skin aside and knelt on the moquette-carpet, 1: 635; 489]. Ana covers and removes the veils that represent the various intricate understandings of her desires and thoughts. Alas constructs an interior world with multiple partitions, the divided mansion, the separation between the boudoir and the bedroom, the different levels of the floor and the bed, and the variety of material veils and coverings. Thus the author uses interior architecture to structure the depth and complexity of both Ana's emotions and the novel's narrative project.

The presentation of Ana's character and her interiors portrays the various levels of the heroine's interiority, but this opening scene in her bedroom functions also as a prelude to the important later events centered on her bed. The time Ana spends in the bedroom is associated in the novel with the workings of Ana's consciousness, her memory, meditations, and desires.

Ana's bed is the site where life greets death and where the past haunts the present affecting her sense of self both in this life and in a world beyond.[27] She undergoes throughout the novel a series of symbolic deaths and resurrections. Different events and periods of illness confine her to bed from which she struggles to survive. Her bedroom and more specifically her "lecho" or bed serve as the vehicles that transport her to other times and spiritual stages, or in her idol Saint Teresa's architectural term, to other "moradas" or dwellings. The images used to describe Ana's alienation, metaphors of exile, shipwreck, reclusion, suffocation, submersion, and others, are all ideas of being buried alive. In *La Regenta* death is part of life, and part of Ana's life in particular. The scenes that take place in her bedroom when she is alone accentuate the tension between life and death. From the very first time we meet her, she finds it necessary to measure her pulse to verify that she is alive. As she feels a beat, she comes back from the past and from her memories and returns to her present life, but then again she moves at this point into her dark bedroom and into thoughts of the ferryboat, which is also symbolic of her moving toward the underworld. The boat transports her to some in-between place where her earlier life and her current reality clash. The ambiguity of life and deah is one of the central themes in the novel and it relies on furnishings and rooms to give it structure. It is important, therefore, to trace Ana's four symbolic deaths in order to observe how interiors profile these experiences.

The first and last of Ana's figurative deaths are caused by real ones. The former takes place after her father's death, and the latter after Víctor's death, her husband and father figure. The other two also center around two male figures: Fermín de Pas and Álvaro Mesía. These two turning points in her life stand out less as near-death experiences and are more important as representations of types of resurrections. Ana first experiences a rebirth to religion and devotes herself entirely to spiritual quests and her confessor's wishes, and in the second experience she is born again for her lover and concentrates on her physical health and happiness. Ana feels that as a child she was stronger than now and measures this power of being able to withstand society's cruelly with the particular ability to jump out of bed: "La niña que saltaba del lecho a oscuras era más enérgica que esta Anita de ahora, tenía una fuerza interior pasmosa" [The girl who used to jump out of bed in the dark had been more vigorous than this Anita of the present: she had possessed an extraordinary inner strength, 1: 127; 67]. As the novel progresses, the capacity to free herself from her bed will become a matter of life and death. A few days after her father's funeral Ana wanted to get up but could not, "El lecho la sujetaba con brazos invisibles" [Her bed was holding her down with invisible arms] and it takes a month before Ana can leave her bed (1: 166; 98). When Ana overhears her aunts' slanderous conversation about her childhood trauma, she jumps out of bed "Pálida como una muerta" [As pale as death] and realizes the vulnerability of her situation (1: 170; 101). The leap gives her newfound energy to live a life in which ultimately her spirit is dead. Because Ana discovers and refines her imagination in bed, this piece of furniture will always be associated with both pain and pleasure. While Ana's bed transports her back and forth from the past to the future and from life to death, it is also a medium between fiction and reality. Her bed allows her to escape the surrounding melancholy, "Para ella su lecho no estaba ya en aquel caserón de sus mayores, ni en Vetusta, ni en la tierra; estaba flotando en el aire, no sabía donde" [Ana's bed was not then in that ancestral mansion, or in Vetusta, or indeed anywhere on earth; it was floating through the air, she knew not whither, 1: 174; 105]. Ana likes to sleep in and enjoys spending the morning hours in bed. This is the site of her past, her only sense of warmth, and the one place where she can experience and live her dreams and hopes. While abandoning her bed would imply a return to life, it also implies having to face reality, and often Ana prefers to escape her existence which she sees as another form of death.

According to Don Robustiano Somoza, a spring fever is to blame for the months the Regenta spends in bed struggling for her life for the second time in the story. Again she is left alone in this dreary state; she struggles over her sense of self, suffers with her imagination, doubts, and thoughts, and contemplates whether and how to come back to life. Here again she sees clearly that the reality and people around her wear a superficial mask and concern themselves only with "lo de fuera" [what was happening outside] while she is devoted to what she believes is true and found in the inside. This time fiction does not bring Ana solace, she thinks people enter and leave her bedchamber "como en el escenario de un teatro" [as if it were a stage in a theatre] and ironically her sense of reality is what will give her strength to live again (1: 562; 428). Her bedroom and bed once more frame this spiritual crisis, bringing her ever closer to dying. In her dark bedroom Ana feels completely desolate, alone, and in incurable pain. The many pillows on her bed are like massive walls and life is the color of lead. This piece of furniture is transformed into the grave that starts to bury her. Life is like being buried alive and her multilayerd bed emblematically becomes the transport between reality and death. When releasing her grip on the sheets and weeping with despair "resbaló en el lecho, y quedó supina mientras el muro de almohadas se desmoronaba" [she slipped down into the bed and lay there as the wall of pillows crumbled into ruin, 1: 562; 429]. Eventually, however, she regains her strength and awakes from her nightmares. Her bed is no longer her tomb, but instead furnishes its expected relief, that "melancólico regalo" [melancholy comfort] she is so familiar with and life begins to stir again in her ravaged mind and body (1: 564; 431). She resuscitates from this second death to experience a spiritual rebirth and so begins her wholehearted commitment to her religious passion and to Fermín de Pas, whom she will consider for a time as her soulmate.

The third death occurs after Ana's participation in the Holy Friday procession in what marks the climax of her devotion to Fermín and is seen through the perspective of other characters. Víctor, alone with Mesía on the casino's balcony, watches without being seen the event that he interprets as his wife's funeral: "a don Víctor sí le sonaba aquello a himno de muerte; se le figuraba ya que llevaban a su mujer al patíbulo" [To Don Víctor it sounded like a dirge, and he imagined that his wife was being taken to the scaffold, 1: 758; 593]. Mesía appropriately dressed all in black tells Víctor that he is confident and certain that Ana "está muerta de vergüenza" [is dying of shame, 1: 758; 592]. The multitude of noiseless figures that accompany the procession "no parecían seres vivos" [did not look like living beings, 1: 760; 593], and Víctor hears the death march and imagines he is a "viudo" [widow] watching "el entierro de su mujer" [the burial of his wife, 1: 764; 597]. Obdulia is also convinced that Ana "va muerta" [is dying] of shame (1: 762; 596). Clarín relates through one of the typical long flashbacks that narrate a large part of *La Regenta* the period of illness and depression that follows the procession. After this shameful event Ana spends days motionless in an easy chair before getting so sick that she is once again confined to her bed. This time her recovery takes place in the Vegallanas' contry villa, El Vivero, inside a new room. Once again furnishings and interiors give shape to her evolving psychological phases. The heroine is now encouraged to indulge in writing and to articulate her thoughts and feelings and does this in a fresh spacious stuccoed bedroom, which she now shares with her husband. Her "lecho blanco" [cheerful white bed] and "escritorio de palisandro" [rosewood escritoire, 1: 772; 603] create a different lifestyle for Ana, one where she returns to the power of fiction to brighten her spirits and bring her hope and happiness: "se me antoja todo el Vivero escenario de una comedia o de una novela" [I think of El Vivero as the setting for a play or a novel, 1: 780; 610].

After Álvaro kills Víctor in a duel, Frígilis finds Ana on her bed one last time "como muerta, supina" [lying on her back as if she were dead]. For a week "había estado Ana entre la vida y la muerte" [Ana had hovered between life and death] and once more is restricted to her bed for an entire month before she is out of danger (1: 888; 704). Ana spends the same amount of time recovering from her first shock, her father's death, and the Vetustans by shunning her now fulfill what at the beginning of the novel the doctor feared would happen to Anita: "La dejarán a usted morir, hija mía" [They're going to let you die, my girl, 1: 167; 98]. As the novel comes to a close, Ana keeps struggling with her inner voice, which the narrator describes as having someone arguing inside her or experiencing in her brain a "especie de *terremoto* interior" [kind of inner earthaquake, 1: 889; 705]. Although her body has survived, Benitez and Frígilis believe that this last death finally kills her intellectual spirit and it seems that "lo mejor de su alma" [the best part of her soul] will sleep forever and that she is on her way to death (1: 893; 708). Indeed Crespo compares Ana's self-imposed reclusion to suicide, while Benitez insists on taking care of her health first and foremost "si no hemos de suicidarnos" [if we aren't going to commit suicide, 1: 890; 706]. In Noël Valis's view, Ana's repeated exaltation of self "conceals a very real though latent suicidal urge."[28] Throughout the novel, Ana's ambivalent near-death experiences are also meditations on suicide. The similarities between the first and last near-death experiences encircle the narrative, connecting beginnings and endings to rebirths and deaths. This last death, on the other hand, kills the fiction inside her: "Aborrecía los libros" [She hated all books now, 1: 893; 708]. As an adolescent she uses fantasy as a means of survival, while during her spring illness she instead learns to deplore her society's constant fictional performances. In El Vivero Ana reinvents and writes a new libretto for her existence, but at the end of the novel she seems to abandon imagination for good. The bed and the enclosed space lead Ana to and from her oppressive mind and take the narrative between fiction and reality. Ana's continued crises in search for an inner life form a cycle that frames both the heroine's mental development and *La Regenta*'s narrative discourse. Interiority is the novel's own quest, and hence its structure encloses and circles around the constant recycling of Ana's inner life (or death).

Fermín also feels in his and in the interiors of others similar emotions of confinement and solitude as Ana. Unlike the narrative's exploration of Ana's interior space, which focuses primarily on the individual's spiritual crisis and her interiority, the purpose of De Pas's sense of the interior is to emphasize the interconnectedness between him and his society's corruption. To a certain degree Fermín is a lot more sensual than Ana, who interprets and redefines her interior on an abstract level, while Fermín depends on the material comfort and on the sensations surrounding him in order to experience his desired sense of self. The presentation of Fermín's imposing character in the opening chapter establishes the important connection between the inner self and the interior of a place. As we have seen from the very beginning it becomes clear that the link between self and space relies on thoughts, emotions, and physiological experiences. While the exterior sensations penetrate the soul and the body of an individual, a character's ideas, dreams, desires, and memories in turn are transformed into material objects that fill a space.

The first portrait of Fermín exemplifies the novel's technique of relating space to feelings. As Harriet Turner has noted the sexual dominates the description and representation of Fermín's charater. The initial presentation is filled with references and images that ultimately paint a picture of a protagonist at the point of orgasm. He climbs to the top of the cathedral tower, takes out his "cañon chico" [small cannon], a slowly-expanding telescope he uses to observe the city from above (1: 74; 27). Climbing is one of his favorite pastimes and to reach the peak of a mountaintop is always a great pleasure for him, "un triunfo voluptuoso" [a voluptuous triumph 1: 75; 27]. The narrator tells us that Fermín's reddish complexion is the type sometimes caused by orgasm, and finally thoughts of his childhood dreams culminate with a kind of ecstasy that Fermín also often experiences when preaching. The strength of the emotions he feels in the pulpit at times is incredibly strong and intense: "le ahogaba el placer" [choking and speechless from the sheer joy of it all, 1: 80; 30]. The narrative's presentation of Fermín differs from Ana's since the interior and his surroundings have a stronger physical effect on De Pas, while the Regenta uses her body and interior largely as a vehicle to her mind. Yet the narrator chooses to tie a bodily experience, namely masturbation, to the presentation of both protagonists and their sense of interior space.

María del Carmen Bobes Naves takes Fermín's moment of elation in this opening descripriton of his sermoning as a typical scene in the novel when "La narración se detiene, se espacializa, para dar cuenta de las actitudes y para describir el ambiente mediante las sensaciones diversas y simultáneas" [The narration stops and becomes spatial in order to consider the attitudes and in order to describe the atmosphere with diverse and simultaneous sensations].[29] Indeed, the sensations, smells, noises, and feelings that describe this scene fill the cathedral, and this is a spatial technique that repeats throughout the novel. Interiors come into a sort of narrative existence only when a variety of sensations consume the space. However, it seems especially important that what fills the space also enters the body, and that the warm and voluptuous aromas and feelings "que le rodeaban" [rising all around him, 1: 80; 30] are the same that "llenaban la soledad de su espíritu inquieto" [filled the solitude of his restless spirit, 1: 81; 31]. The midnight mass Ana attends represents another scene when emotional disturbances fill the magnificent dark cathedral and her heart at the same time. There is no barrier between the church and the world as different sounds and smells penetrate her passionately, and Ana "Apenas pensaba ya, no hacía más que sentir" [hardly thinking now; she was only feeling, 1: 683; 530]. This happens again when Ana hears Álvaro's declaration of love in the summer house, El Vivero; here once more noises mark the climax of the emotions felt, as she confuses the words of her future lover with the bustle, chattle, and racket of the merry-makers below.[30] The inner consciousness of self relies intimately on sensory perception, and Fermín's extreme pleasure suggests that one's sense of place is not only a spiritual and psychological experience but also one that involves the body.

Physical action characterizes Fermín's interiors and is crucial for understanding his psychological complexity. If Ana's body is more often paralyzed, what distinguishes De Pas's is constant movement. This plays out in the energy governing their actions while enclosed in their designated spaces. Ana spends a great amount of time immobile and confined to bed, while impatience, ambition, and excitement follow De Pas around Vetusta and to the spaces that trap him, such as his confessional, often compared to a prison the same way the Ozores mansion is sometimes Ana's "cárcel demasiado estrecha" [narrow, cramped prison, 1: 896; 712]. Stuck within the four wooden walls of his confessional-box he compares himself to a "criminal metido en el cepo" [criminal in the stocks, 1: 546; 415]. When inside Fermín moves his body around incessantly, tosses and turns on his bench, and is incapable of sitting still in his stall especially when hearing Ana's confession. When she talks to him about her dreams, Don Fermín's hard leather seat feels to him as if it were "lleno de brasas y de espinas" [covered with thorns and fiery coals, 1: 477; 359]. His body is often compared to a lion's locked in a cage with limited space to express his power and strength. In his private bedrooms he is often and constantly walking back and forth along the paths created by the books and papers left on the floor, and once he learns of Ana's affair with Álvaro, Fermín hides in his bedroom, restless, pacing about nonstop. After rejecting Vegallana's invitation to their country estate, Fermín spends the rest of that October afternoon wandering the streets of Vetusta aimlessly. The drifting from place to place reflects his scattered thoughts and allows him to physically express and hide his emotions at the same time.

The latter section of part one of *La Regenta* narrates a day in the life of De Pas and shows how significantly space and geographical and corporeal movements mark Fermín's existence and character. His daily routine begins with visits to the new-rich homes of La Colonia and continues with a detailed penetration through "pasillos estrechos y enrevesados" [narrow, maze-like corridors] of the Bishop's palace (1: 372; 266). Fermín feels the need to physically cover and tread all the territory over which he dominates or presumes to control, and his presence in a particular interior space is a form of making it his own. The more he feels at home, as in the luxurious interiors of his friends Francisco and Olvido Páez, the clearer his true self emerges:

> Pisando aquellas alfombras, viéndose en aquellos espejos tan grandes como las puertas, hundiendo el cuerpo, voluptuosamente, en aquellas blanduras del lujo cómodo, ostentoso, francamente loco, pródigo y deslumbrador, el Magistral se sentía trasladado a regiones que creía adecuadas a su gran espíritu; él, lo pensaba con orgullo, había nacido para aquello.

> [As the canon theologian trod those carpets, looked at himself in those mirrors as large as the doors, let his body sensually sink into the yielding softness of that ostentatious luxury, openly extravagant and overwhelming, he felt himself transported to regions which he believed to be appropriate for his lofty spirit. Surely, he thought with pride, he had been born for such surroundings. 1: 385; 277]

In this sort of dwelling, contrary to his own private quarters, De Pas is completely still and does not feel the need to move, allowing himself to experience sensual pleasure and revealing his true character, desirous of power and particularly physical. His need to occupy the spaces of others is a search for his "ambiente natural" [natural environment]. A physical touch and grace combine with the elegance of Fermín's body to disclose the decisive characteristics of the real De Pas that will materialize again in other interior spaces. Upon leaving Páez's house, Fermín stands "en el umbral de una puerta, con una colgadura de terciopelo cogida y arrugada por su blanca mano" [in a doorway, his fair hand holding a velvet curtain and drawing it into creases, 1: 385; 277]. Fermín often positions himself on the brink of an interior in scenes with an erotic subtext, as when "Apoyando una mano en el dintel de la puerta de la alcoba" [Resting one hand on the lintel of the bedroom door] he smiles pleadingly to Teresa, his servant girl (1: 329; 231), or when he stands on the threshold of the Ozores palace's gazebo. Paez's curtains further recall the drapery dividing Ana's sleeping quarters, and one can not help relate Fermín's soft caresses of the velvet draperies to his affection and desires for the heroine. There are important interior details such as this one that draw connections not only between character and interior, but also between one room and another in the novel. In the last chapter I explore these points in common and argue that these links figure prominently in the novel's overall discourse of interiors.

De Pas's sensitivity to luxury is also apparent in the pleasure he takes in his administrative duties in the offices of ecclesiastical governance. Fermín's feelings of grandeur surface as he sits in his well-appointed office "en un sillón de terciopelo carmesí detrás de una mesa de ministro" [on an armchair of crimson velvet behind a secretaire, 1: 373; 267], while the inferior room where the church bureaucracy works "no ostentaba el lujo del despacho" [did not display the luxury of the canon's room or anything like it, 1: 379; 272]. Fermín enjoys living in comfortable interior conditions, but his mother's home must deliberately exhibit to the outside world an artificial humility. Like the presentation of Ana's interior space, a minor character, Ripamilán also introduces Fermín and Doña Paula's humble abode. But, if Obdulia exaggerated the eccentric and masculine qualities of Ana's sleeping quarters, Ripamilán, perhaps underestimates the modesty of Doña Paula's residence, which according to him is filled with apparently decaying furnishings and broken objects. With the exception of Petra and Teresa, few enter the private areas of the house, and most people only know the salon which "poco menos que a oscuras" [being kept in near darkness] is obscured to visitors (1: 316; 219). The Arcipreste's description of the drawing-room's destitution reveals how the novel's dialectic between surface and profundity ties to furnishings and interior spaces. Ripamilán asks his fellow gossiping citizens, "¿Quién nos dice que las sillas de damasco verde no tienen abiertas las entrañas? ¿Las han visto ustedes alguna vez sin funda? ¿Y la consola panzuda, antiquísima, de un dorado que fue, con su reloj de música y sin cuerda?" [Who is to say that the insides are not hanging out of the green damask chairs? Have you ever seen them without their covers? And what of that ancient, bulging console table, which was once gilt; and what of that musical-box on top of it, with neither music nor spring?, 1: 317; 220]. Fermín's furnishings, as others in the novel, the woodwork on Fortunato's furniture makes "curvas panzudas" [bulging curves, 1: 357; 253] and Doña Rufina's sofa has a "panza anchísima y turgente" [bulging belly, 1: 244; 161], are bloated and pregnant with hidden meanings and secrets. Alison Sinclair's study of liminal anxieties in *La Regenta* compares Fermín's chairs to the Marquesa's and argues that this and other similarities between their rooms confirms the presence of sexuality in Fermín's life.[31] But, the primary function of the narrative's focus on the insides of Doña Paula's chairs is also to evoke her economical exploits, since the insides of furnishings recall the insides of the figurative caves and mines exploited by Fermín and his mother. Fermín's sexuality is a lot more present in his sensual interior language than in the moldering furniture. *La Regenta*'s interiors repeatedly comment ironically on the traditional realist-naturalist representation and function of interior settings. Rooms and salons are purposely presented to the reader in order to provide a fuller portrait of its inhabitants, yet they do not always do this, but instead comment on another event or character in the novel. Spaces are significant not only by what they reflect but more importantly in the way they interact with other narrative elements. Fermín's important interior movements and his interactions with other people's interiors work in conjunction to define his character.

Doña Paula's domination at home fuels her son's spatial conceptualization of the world and his sense of self. The fact that he lacks his own space makes the conquest of the interiors of other people imperative, especially the interiors of those he wishes to develop special relationships with, such as with Ana Ozores. He highly esteems, for example, the ease with which he comes and goes out of the homes of influential individuals. His thoughts and feelings become more and more spatially shaped as the narrative evolves; he is exceedingly sensitive to interior comfort and luxury, interacts with the sensations that fill an interior space, and his lack of place orients his perception of the influence he aspires to have over others. Unlike Ana, Fermín cannot find solace or be alone in the privacy of his own home because of his mother's overpowering presence, and to his understanding, individual power and intellectual development require spatial independence: "Él, aunque viviera con su madre querida, no tenía hogar, hogar suyo, y eso debía ser la dicha suprema de las almas serias, de las almas que pretendían merecer el nombre de grandes" [Although he lived with his dear mother he had no home, no home of his own, and that must be the supreme joy for serious spirits, spirits aspiring to greatness, 1: 457; 340]. In his conquest of Ana, he attempts to acquire his own interior in Doña Petronila Rianzares's house, which serves as a secret meeting place for Ana and Fermín. He occupies the space for himself and stands planted "como con raíces, en medio de la sala" [in the middle of the sitting-room as if rooted there, 1: 720; 560]. Ana hesitates before regularly meeting him there; she seems to understand that Fermín reigns over this dominion, and when she begins distancing herself from him she refuses to return to this house. The way in which the sitting-room suffocates Ana represents Fermín trying to control her. Adolfo Sotelo Vázquez's study, which describes some of the emblematic ingredients of Doña Petronila's salon, compares the room to a "cajón almohadillado" [pin-cushioned box] and claims its darkness and discomfort results in asphyxiating Ana.[32] The images of the many pillows recall Ana's bed when it begins to bury her and tie Petronila's sitting-room to its counterpart space: Doña Rufina's pillow-packed yellow salon where Mesía, Fermín's rival, will dominate.

Ana's absence from Doña Petronila's house parallels Fermín's loss of influence over the heroine. In fact, as with other characters, one can trace Fermín's growing disappointments to his increasingly violent and unsettled experiences within interior spaces. When his efforts to seduce Ana fail, Mesía trips over the furnishings in the Ozores mansion and bangs into its doors. Similarly inconsolable and disoriented, Fermín paces in his interiors around tables and chairs. On the day after Ana falls into Álvaro's arms at the ball, Fermín wanders the cathedral's naves impatiently and hesitantly unable to "encontrar la puerta" [find the door, 1: 718; 558]. Later in Doña Petronila's house during the heated discussion with Ana, Fermín passionately "descargó un puñetazo de Hércules sobre el testero del sofá" [struck the sofa a herculean blow with his fist] and fumbles to the door. As he walks away from the house he "miró a los balcones" [looked up at the balcony windows] that to his dismay remain closed (1: 723; 563). As Carlos and Ega, Fermín translates his desperation, anger, and pain into a language of the interior that expresses his weakness and aggression and shows that, just as in Eça's novel, furnishings begin to dictate a character's feelings. Petronila's interior, for example, begins to speak to Fermín: "El sofá donde solía sentarse Ana llamó al Magistral con la voz de los recuerdos" [The sofa in which Ana always sat was calling to him with the voice of memory, 1: 718; 559]. If Ana commonly sits here, it is unsettling to consider his aggressive actions toward the sofa described above. Fermín begins to fail within the spaces he tries to make his own, and in being excluded from an interior, as in the case of having absolutely no influence over Fortunato's choice of décor for his salon, the narrative reveals how Fermín's power is limited and challenged. The novel suggests that Ana is ultimately incapable of surpassing her cyclical spiritual inner crisis, while Fermín, like Sofia, is too selfish and tied to society's immorality to penetrate and accept his true inner self. Fermín falls short of his interior experiences, and his physical interaction with rooms and objects begins to reveal how he betrays himself and others.

The novel further figures Fermín's frustrated and failed attempts to love Ana with metaphors of rooms and sensations of being enclosed. To describe his experience with Ana, Fermín repeatedly relies on images related to important senses of space. When she opens herself up to him he thinks to himself: "yo no soy digno de que la majestad de su secreto entre en mi pobre morada;" [I am not worthy to welcome the majesty of your secret into my wretched dwelling, 1: 343; 242]. He claims the world without her friendship is uninhabitable and to live in Vetusta as the rest of its common citizens "era como encerrarse en un cuarto estrecho con un brasero. Era el suicidio por asfixia" [was like locking oneself up with a brazier in a tiny room. It was suicide by suffocation]. He compares their friendship to the opening of a "ventana que tenía vistas al cielo" [window which gave a view of heaven, 1: 629; 484]. These metaphors show that Fermín comprehends his intimacy with Ana in terms of interior spaces. They also begin to reveal that ultimately he fails in his desire for authority over her. A burning sensation he feels while inside his confessional is used to describe the loss of their friendship. The window to which he refers, a recurring emblematic image in the novel, will remain mostly closed except when he himself violently opens it, epitomizing Fermín's aggressiveness. His final cruel treatment of Ana exemplified in her being locked inside one of the church's chapels, demonstrates that hostility is the only emotion the canon is capable of showing despite the love he feels for her.

If Fermín's interior experiences reflect his growing disappointments and failures, Ana's involvements with her private spaces on occasion point to the upcoming and growing intimacy between the two. As they each face their self-crises, Ana and Fermín undergo a parallel interaction with their inner worlds. Ana spends the long rainy days alone inside her gloomy dining room attached to the "chimenea taciturna, de figuras de yeso ahumado" [morose fireplace with its smoky plaster figures, 1: 541; 410]. The monumental fireplace is one of these important interiors that contain yet another interior, and it also recalls the crucial event in Ana's life when in front of this "chimenea pseudofeudal" [pseudo-feudal fireplace] her aunts give her the ultimatum concerning Frutos's proposal of marriage (1: 191; 119). Faced without much of a choice, it was in this interior setting that she received her life-long sentence of solitude. At this point of the novel and in the midst of this rainy November Ana is slowly convincing herself of the need to devote herself fully to Fermín and church affairs. The interior space reveals her change of attitude with respect to De Pas. Thus Ana's wanderings about her rooms remind the reader of Fermín's movements. Ana begins an aggressive, heavy-footed walk about her house:

Entonces Ana se ponía en pie, recorría el comedor a grandes pasos, hundida la cabeza en el embozo del chal apretado al cuerpo, daba vuelta alrededor de la mesa oval, y acababa por acercarse a los vidrios del balcón y apretar contra ellos la frente. Salía, cruzando el estrado triste, pasillos y galerías, llegaba a su gabinete y también allí se apretaba contra los vidrios y miraba con ojos distraídos, muy abiertos y fijos, las ramas desnudas de los castaños de Indias, y los soberbios eucaliptos, cubiertos de hojas largas, metálicas, de un verde mate, temblorosas y resonantes.

[But she would jump to her feet, pace about the dining-room with her head sunk in the shawl gathered tight to her body, walk around the oval table to the balcony window and press her forehead against the glass. Then she would leave the dining-room and walk through the dismal drawing-room and along galleries and passages to her boudoir and there, too, press her face to the window and stare with vacant eyes at the naked branches of the horse-chest-nuts and at the proud eucalyptuses, with their covering of long, metallic, dull green leaves, shaking, tinkling, 1: 541 410.]

With the exception of her wide-open eyes, a distinguishing characteristic of Ana Ozores, the rest of her actions recall De Pas's movements. Ana is grow-ing more in tune with Fermín and preparing for what will be her futile imitation of Vetusta's zealously pious women. The horse-chestnuts and proud eucalyptuses evoke the haunting historical memory of Don Frutos penetrating her interior world. As Ana walks around her dining-room, con-fined and confused by her emotions, she is walking figuratively toward Fermín, reproducing his own interior actions. Thus this chapter closes with the lady and the priest finally meeting in Doña Petronila's melancholic salon: "en el salón sombrío, de damasco verde oscuro y de papel gris y oro. Ana se sentó en el sofá, el Magistral a su lado en un sillón. Las maderas de los balcones entornados dejaban pasar rayos estrechos de la luz del día moribun-do; apenas se veían Ana y De Pas" [in the murky sitting-room, decorated with dark green damask and grey and gold wallpaper. Ana sat on the sofa, the canon by her side on an armchair. The wooden balcony-shutters were ajar, letting narrow shafts of the light of the dying day into the room, 1: 549; 418]. This room has many typical qualities of a Vetustan interior; it is dark, silent, narrow, smelly, and the sunlight barely shines in through the half-opened balconies. But if the sadness Ana feels in her dining-room foreshadows her encounter with Fermín, which marks the culminating meeting of the two and the beginning of their intimate relationship, then it also makes an ironic comment on Fermín's failure as a lover. Because a similar, albeit distinct, climactic event will take place in the room that serves as a counterpart to Petronila's salon, the marchioness's silent, dark, yellow salon, where Ana's affair with Álvaro begins. The subtext of these parallel interiors highlights Fermín's lack of conquest, but also suggests that their friendship and Ana's new religiously devout life will ultimately prove fruitless.

Fermín is a much more conspicuous wanderer than Ana. He walks continuously the streets of Vetusta, the naves of the majestic cathedral, and the
space in his office and private rooms. He expresses, for example, his anger
by pacing "alrededor de la mesa" [around the table] of his study (1: 718;
558). The day Petra confirms Ana's adultery to Fermín revealing all the
secret details, De Pas will repeat some of these distinguishing movements
that recall and yet differentiate themselves from Ana's. After listening to
Petra, Fermín "giró sobre los talones, como si fuera a caer desplomado, dio
dos pasos inciertos y llegó al balcón contra cuyos cristales apoyó la frente.
Parecía mirar a la calle. Pero tenía los ojos cerrados" [turned on his heel as if
about to collapse, took two wavering steps towards the balcony, and leaned
his forehead against the window. He seemed to be looking out, but his eyes
were closed, 1: 840; 661]. This important scene is typical of Fermín's growing unsettledness in his interiors and underlines his suffering and inability to
face the truth. Closed up inside and too weak to move despite the fact that he
wishes to express himself physically, to run, scream and protest, he will not
move a finger, "ni un pie fuera de casa" [not set foot in the street]. The
window to their friendship, which he leans on, remains closed and their
intimacy will not develop further. The ice-cold glass of the windowpane
painfully presses against his forehead as the impossibility of this love invades him with evil and violence. He hears the devil's demoniacal laughter
attacking his "entrañas" [bowels]. Fermín, not able to force Ana to love him,
will instead act cruelly against her inside Vetusta's social codes. It is after
this realization that he dramatically "Abrió el balcón de un puñetazo"
[punched the balcony window open, 1: 841; 663]. Fermín's aggressiveness in
opening the window foreshadows the injustice he does to Ana at the end of
the novel. The glass's knife-like coldness prefigures De Pas's hunting dagger
in a subsequent scene, when Fermín locks himself up in his study, and
feverishly and restlessly struggles over Ana's betrayal. Lodged inside his
room he finds in the armoire his old hunting attire, which he desperately and
quickly changes into, while grabbing a hunting-knife with which he contemplates murdering Mesía. Once again the design of the room with its various
levels of interiors communicates to him and to the readers, and although he
contemplates, at least temporarily, searching and killing the culprit, he can
hear his mother moving overhead, "Crujieron las tablas del techo" [boards
creaked in the ceiling, 1: 870; 687]. The noise from the floor above indirectly
reminds him of his reality and of the socially acceptable path with which to
take his revenge. While in this case Doña Paula uses the room architecturally
to remind her son of what he must do, Frígilis's final presence in the Ozores
mansion, although reminiscent of the actions of Doña Paula, has a very
different purpose. Frígilis will set up his bedroom right underneath the Regenta's and instead of pacing about like Fermín's mother he coughs loudly to
give Ana a sense of security and let her know of his presence. Contrary to

Doña Paula's signal to her son, Frígilis uses the space to send a loving, albeit late, message to his friend. These types of parallels between different rooms and similar architectural moves are central to the overall discursive message the novel writes with its interior spaces.

The highly significant movements taking place inside closed spaces do not only show Fermín's feelings of love toward Ana but also his other sexual desires and relationships. Few people visit Fermín in his bedroom and study, and the ones that do are all women: Doña Paula, Teresa, his maid, and occasionally Petra, Ana's housekeeper. But Teresa, even more than Fermín's mother, has the right to move about, touch and feel the objects and furnishings in his quarters. Teresa's physical movements suggest that the interior hides a sexually charged subplot. The maid sleeps adjacent to Fermín's rooms and comes and goes as she pleases to clean and arrange his private lodgings. The narrative implies that a sexual relationship between Teresa and Fermín ensues via a particular interior movement, which seems to confirm the consummation of the sexual act by proxy. Teresa prepares Fermín's bed with such physical efforts and places herself in difficult and erotic poses that appear to reenact an encounter that might have already occurred or is still to take place between her and Fermín. From his armchair he can see Teresa's every move: "Desde allí veía, distraído, los movimientos rápidos de la falda negra de Teresa, que apretaba las piernas contra la cama para hacer fuerza al manejar los pesados colchones. Ella azotaba la lana con vigor y la falda subía y bajaba a cada golpe con violenta sacudida" [The rapid movements of Teresina's black skirt caught his glance as she pressed her thighs against the bed, gaining leverage to lift the heavy mattresses. As she pounded their woolen surface, each blow made her skirt jump]. Fermín watches this scene with both pleasure and irritation, and the aggressiveness of Teresa's movements suggests not only the eroticism but also the masochist qualities of the sexual desires involved. In one of her movements, she lies almost "tendida de brazos sobre la cama" [flat with arms outspread] and then panting "con un brazo oculto en el pliegue de un colchón doblado, se volvió de repente, casi tendida de espaldas sobre la cama" [with one arm hidden inside a folded mattress, suddenly turned over, almost lying back on the bed, 1: 329; 231]. The ferocious domestic chore is used as a euphemistic suggestion of sexual situations. The narrative uses interiors to reveal Fermín's true desires in his relations to Ana, other women, and toward Vetustan society more broadly.

As with Ana, there are events in Fermín's childhood that repeat in his adult life and are framed with interior spaces. In his native village in his mother's tavern his studying space seperates him from the immoral behavior of the drunken miners. As he hides behind "de unas tablas, que dejaban pasar las blasfemias y el ruido del dinero" [a wooden partition which did nothing to exclude the sounds of oaths and coins], Fermín struggles to avoid his mother's corruption, which comes to him via the noises he hears (1: 452; 336). As an adult, on a day when Doña Paula checks the accounts, Fermín can once more hear his mother counting her gold coins. Even though he is again architecturally removed from his mother's business, and refuses to join her in the filthy back room where the money-counting takes place, a room he compares to a cistern of infection, these fraudulent noises reach him: "apagados por la distancia subían por el hueco de la escalera" [softened by distance, floated up the stairs, 1: 460; 342]. The depleted existences he encounters as a child motivate him to take a different path in life, but more importantly this adolescent experience teaches him to hide behind structures and materials that safeguard him from reality but also keep him away from his true self. As an adult, then, Fermín tends to conceal himself with curtains or doors sneaking as he looks onto the world. If in front of the Vegallana palace Fermín listens and looks inside the mansion's salons, hidden inside his house he hears Barinaga's drunken sermons, positioning himself strategically: "entornó las vidrieras hasta no dejar más que un intersticio por donde ver y oír sin ser visto" [closed the windows until only a chink was left through which to watch and listen without being seen, 1: 461; 343]. On the day of Barinaga's funeral Fermín once again is found "detrás de las vidrieras de su despacho" [spying on events from behind his study windows, 1: 675; 525]. Hence his limited possibility of occupying his own interiors and his wish to penetrate those of others is something that still haunts him from his traumatic childhood experiences. In his interior moves he is far more in tune with Vetustan society. Unlike Ana who retreats into her private spaces, Fermín's attempts to withdraw are also disappointments and impossibilities as he is always caught on the threshold with no interior or exterior alternative.

When it comes to Fermín's private interiors, images of physical movement are central to the narrative's development of its emblematic discourse of furnishings and rooms. Clarín's long descriptive digressions and suspensions of time are full of spatial movement, and instead of stagnating the novel's tone, actually move the narrative forward. Interiors in Alas's novel do not simply represent the character in their colors, tones, and historical or cultural references; instead furnishings and objects are more important for the physical interaction that develops between them and the characters. In the case of Ana, this movement consists of a figurative journey through different emotional and spiritual places and times, while De Pas's movements are more physical, sensual, and sexual. Neither protagonist finds a balance in their insides, their rooms, studies, hearts, heads, stomachs or souls. In this respect Fermín and Ana recall Machado's and Eça's protagonists in their dependence, interpretation, and reading of their interior worlds. The representation of character interiority in the novels depends on interior spaces not merely as an extension of the personality. The characters the novels focus on all experience an inner disorder and fragmentation, which ties to their experience with memory and the subconscious. Interior spaces design these inner complexities by creating antithetical forces that pull characters inside and outside and place them in important thresholds where different possibilities emerge. The peripheries of interiors lodge continuities and disjunctions between different pressures and accommodate the interdependence of body and soul, the self and the collective. Interiors are intricately tied to the novel's development of forms of knowing and the limits of understanding; in other words they invent new ontological and epistemological languages for narrating the self and for reading and interpreting reality. In representing interiors and interiorities, showing how imagination works in conjunction with the creation of an interior space and exploration of the inner self, these novels turn interiors and interiority into their main subject of literary and cultural inquiry.

Notes

1. Erich Auerbach, *Mimesis: The Representation of Reality in Western Literature*, trans. Willard R. Trask (Princeton: Princeton University Press, 1953), 470.

2. Ibid., 469.

3. Gérard Genette, *Figures of Literary Discourse*, trans. Alan Sheridan (New York: Columbia University Press, 1982), 135.

4. By major interior spaces, I mean those settings predominantly associated with a protagonist, and by minor interiors, those connected to minor characters.

5. In his introduction to Gregory Rabassa's translation of Machado's novel, David T. Haberly writes "careful readers of *Quincas Borba* come to realize that the novel's third-person omniscient narrator is, like all of the narrators of Machado's greatest novels, utterly unreliable" (xiii).

6. Dona Tonica's care is not limited to her bedroom. She takes great care of her father's household. Siqueira's house clearly reflects the poverty of the family, "Mas o trabalho da filha transparecia em tudo; os móveis reluziam de asseio, a mesa tinha um pano de crivo, feito por ela, o canapé uma almofada" [But the daughter's work showed through everywhere: the furniture glowed with polish, the table had a cloth and a mat of her making, the sofa a pillow, 1: 755; 189].

7. John Gledson, *Deceptive Realism*, 15.

8. Chapters XXIX to XXXII narrate another important scene that takes place in Rubião's sitting-room in Botafogo. It is not a coincidence that the Sunday luncheon Rubião hosts with his two friends Carlos Maria and Freitas sets up another triangular dynamic between the three characters. Freitas and Carlos Maria, as Camacho and Palha, stand opposed to each other and compete for the host's attention, while Rubião's affections, on the other hand, are torn between the two men.

9. Whereas Palha recommends these metals to Rubião, he himself has a "vasta bacia de prata" 'broad silver basin' in his bedroom (1: 763; 203).

10. Peter Brooks, *Realist Vision* (New Haven: Yale University Press), 3.

11. Helen Caldwell, *Machado de Assis: The Brazilian Master and His Novels* (Berkeley: University of California Press, 1970), 132.

12. Brooks, *Realist Vision*, 30.

13. Sigmund Freud, *Introductory Lectures on Psycho-Analysis*, trans. James Strachey (London: Hogarth Press, 1953), 295.

14. Diana Fuss, *Sense of Interior*, 7.

15. Emphasis is mine.

16. See for example Liana F. Piehler's *Spatial Dynamics and Female Development in Victorian Art and Novels*, or Doreen Massey's *Space, Place, and Gender* (Minneapolis: University of Minnesota Press, 1994).

17. Henry James, *Novels*, 1047.

18. Noël Valis, *Reading the Nineteenth-Century*, 25.

19. Nancy Armstrong, *Desire and Domestic Fiction A Political History of the Novel* (New York: Oxford University Press, 1987), 8.

20. Carlos Santos Vargas, "Da Proxémia N'*Os Maias*: Um Caso Exemplar," eds. Elza Miné and Benilde Justo Lacorte Caniato, *150 Anos com Eça de Queirós* (São Paulo: Centro de Estudos Portugueses, Universidade de São Paulo, 1997), 163.

21. Emilio Alarcos Llorach, "Notas a *La Regenta*," *Archivum* 2 (1952), 150.

22. See José Aranguren's "De *La Regenta* a *Ana Ozores*," *Estudios Literarios* (Madrid: Gredos, 1976) for an analysis of Ana's sensuality, Michael Nimetz's "Eros and Ecclesia in Clarín's Vetusta," *MLN* 86 (1971): 242-53, for how religion and sex are positioned on similar plains in the novel, and also Jo Labanyi's study of gender and modernization in *La Regenta*, and Alison Sinclair's "Liminal Anxieties: Nausea and Mud in *La Regenta*," *Bulletin of Hispanic Studies* 74 (1997): 155-176.

23. Noël Valis, "Aspects of an Improper Birth: Clarín's *La Regenta*," eds. Mark I. Millington and Paul Julian Smith, *New Hispanisms: Literature, Culture, Theory* (Ottawa, Canada: Dovehouse, 1994), 97.

24. Gaston Bachelard, *Poetics of Space*, 16.

25. Gonzalo Sobejano, "Introduction," *La Regenta*, 33.

26. Doña Camila often punishes Anita by locking her up in a room. The little girl's silence while trapped inside baffles the cruel governess as she listens and looks through the keyhole. Ana's imprisonment makes her more aware of space and she learns how to create abstract places of retreat. With wide-open eyes Ana as a little girl imagines herself flying over rooftops, and spends "horas y horas recorriendo espacios que ella creaba" [hours and hours wandering through spaces which she herself created, 1: 148; 83]. This traumatic experience teaches Ana to be more sensitive to how her enclosed surroundings transport her to other spaces, time periods, and senses of self.

27. Françoise Bayle and Marina Romero Frías explain that Ana often finds refuge in her bed "para desahogarse o para intentar cancelar la sensación de soledad. Este apego se le debe al hecho de que para la Regenta constituye un retorno, por una parte, a la infancia, casi al vientre materno, y, por otra, al recuerdo de períodos serenos durante una enfermedad de la adolescencia cuando en la cama podía desahogarse con sus fantasías religiosas, y voluptuosas también, soñando un paraíso fuera del mundo y de la realidad" [in order to vent her frustration or to rid herself of her feelings of loneliness. This attachment is due to the fact that for la Regenta it constitutes a return, on the one hand to childhood, almost to the maternal womb, and on the other hand, to a memory of a serene time of an illness during her adolescence when in her bed she could find relief in her religious fantasies, and voluptuous ones as well, dreaming of a paradise beyond the world and reality] (Françoise Bayle and Marina Romero Frías, "Religión y adulterio a través de los objetos en *Madame Bovary* y *La Regenta*," *Realismo y naturalismo en España en al segunda mitad del siglo XIX*, ed. Yvan Lissorgues (Madrid: Anthropos, 1988), 378.

28. Noël Valis, *The Decadent Vision*, 99.

29. María del Carmen Bobes Naves, *Teoría general de la novela: Semiología de* La Regenta (Madrid: Gredos, 1985), 198.

30. If in *Quincas Borba* sight serves as a dominant leitmotif, *La Regenta* privileges the sense of hearing. Characters struggle with the noises of the world, which penetrate their emotions and thoughts. The emphasis on noise to describe a character's important emotional experience suggests that noises are often the expression of someone's feelings. Therefore it is especially curious that different spaces, the church, the casino, and certain rooms and salons, are commonly characterized by silence as if to emphasize the emotional emptiness of their inhabitants, and yet at other moments the noises serve as evidence of society's indecency and adulteration. Hence the repeated divergences between silence and noise compare to the also highly significant antithesis in the novel between light and darkness, both juxtapositions fluctuate between representing both good and evil. The metaphors of light and noises and their contrasts rely on the complex interior constellation that structures the novel.

31. Alison Sinclair, "Liminal Anxieties," 173.

32.   Adolfo Sotelo Vazquez, "Escritura, descripción y relato en *La Regenta*: El salón de Doña Petronila," *Co-textes* 18 (1989), 37.

Part Three: The Discourse of Interiors

Michel Foucault writes in "Of Other Spaces" that while the nineteenth century is obsessed with history and time, the twentieth century "will perhaps be above all the epoch of space."[1] According to Alexander Coleman, the "consciousness of the passing of time, of the 'weight' of the years, is probably the one single distinguishing element that is wholly new in the dense fabric of *The Maias*."[2] Like the Portuguese novel, *Quincas Borba* and *La Regenta* are also highly preoccupied with the development of time and greatly concerned with history. On the other hand, I have shown that spatial dimensions are central for the framing of the main themes and techniques of characterization. Barbacena, Vetusta's cathedral, and Ramalhete are undeniably spatial keepers of a specifically circular progression of time, and clearly the intersection between time and space is what is ultimately at stake in the composition of these novels. In fact one cannot understand these works conceptually only in terms of time and history, since it is the spatial element that makes the chronological component possible. María del Carmen Bobes Naves has already argued this for *La Regenta*; she writes, "Según todos los indicios, *La Regenta* es una novela *espacial* en su primera parte y *temporal* en la última."[3] M. M. Bakhtin names this inseparability of time and space *chronotope* and defines the process as "the intrinsic connectedness of temporal and spatial relationships that are artistically expressed in literature."[4] While focused on weaving time and place in the plot, the authors, nevertheless, privilege the interior space, and indeed Gérard Genette argues that description, associated with the spatial, is more important than the narrative or temporal "perhaps because objects can exist without movement, but not movement without objects."[5] The interior representations in the novels ultimately repeat the important correlation between the temporal and the spatial. The interplay in these novels between spaces and objects, real estate and furnishings, or the

immobile and the mobile, can also be read as a metaphor for the interrelated-
ness of time and space in narrative.

The link between the temporal and the spatial translates in Genette's
terms to the relation between narration and description. Genette calls description an indispensable auxiliary of the narrative and describes it as the "*ancil-
la narrationis*, the ever-necessary, ever-submissive, never-emancipated
slave."[6] Referring to description as the slave of narrative coincidently reflects the thematic concerns the novels frame using interior spaces. I have
tried to show that these works formally explore, with their representation of
interiors, the complex power relations resulting mainly from an interaction
between masters and slaves, and that they question how a colonial history of
violence circumscribes national and individual identities. Interior settings in
these texts are particularly important because the authors blend inside them
the problems upsetting their societies while at the same time articulating their
narrative strategies. Hence the story of homes and furnishings creates what I
call a narrative discourse of interior design: a semiotic language of objects
and objectified things that both communicate different meanings and reflect
on the passage of time. The realist-naturalist fascination with description and
detail, portraying everything from bold wallpaper patterns to a curtain's tex-
ture, is not an inconsequential narrative technique. As Peter Brooks notes in
Realist Vision, scholars are beginning to appreciate once again the wealth of
this "discourse of things" and "eclecticism of styles" that often defines realist
writing.[7] This discourse in fact anticipates twentieth-century concerns with
space, as it begins to make the transition from Foucault's epoch of time to his
epoch of space. It outlines the change from a time obsessed with "themes of
development and of suspension, of crisis and cycle" to one of simultaneity
and juxtaposition, an "epoch of the near and far, of the side-by-side, of the
dispersed."[8] The symbolic importance of the spaces and objects in these
novels relates to problems concerning ideas of progress and to questions of
simultaneity. While I am interested in some economic and social changes
that upset the relationships between characters and objects, I ultimately focus
on rooms, furnishings, and personal belongings for their meta-literary qualities and for the way they help the authors construct and deconstruct their
plots and meanings. As Noël Valis writes, "It is not so much the purchase or
possession of things in themselves but the complex and sometimes unpredict-
able relationship with things that, paradoxically, adds to the human dimensions of nineteenth-century texts and culture."[9]

The settings represented in the novels—Rio de Janeiro, Lisbon, and Oviedo—do indeed experience a significant boom in their import-export economies and industrial progress at this time. Rio de Janeiro experiences along
with this economic development extensive demographic growth as well.
Foreign people and products, or the extraterritorial, to use Deleuze's term,
shape both landscapes and imaginations, and make up a large part of the

period's fashion and taste. The authors are attentive to important developments taking place in interior design and decorate their narrative spaces with the predominant decorative styles of the late nineteenth century, historicism, eclecticism, and exoticism. Their interest in decorative objects and furnishings, however, goes far beyond representing an important cultural fascination or changes in aesthetic taste. These items have human qualities and a narrative life of their own; they evoke significant historical contexts and question the way individuals are connected to power and to other spaces. The interior elements also reenact important encounters between humans and objects and the foreign and the native, which elaborate the creation of a collective identity by looking at how the self interprets his or her circumstances and derives meaning from the world. Furthermore, the interior décor is emblematic of the movement occupying the fixed space, reproducing in this way a creative and imitative process that is also the purpose of art and literature. This interaction is ultimately a meta-literary metaphor, and the authors rely on their discourse of things to transform the possibilities of the narrative genre.

MACHADO'S MINIMALISM AND THE MEANING OF THINGS

The discourse of interior decorating in *Quincas Borba* is inseparable from Machado's "utterly unreliable" narrator, to use David T. Haberly's words. This requires the reader to maintain a certain distance, which as Silviano Santiago explains in "Retórica da verossimilhança" (Rhetoric of verisimilitude), the nature of Machado's writing demands: "a reflexão moral exigida pelo autor requer certa distância dos personagens e/ou do narrador, aliás, a mesma distância que Machado, como autor, guarda deles" [the moral reflection demanded by the author calls for a certain distance from the characters and/or the narrator, in fact, the same distance that Machado, as author, maintains from them].[10] *Quincas Borba*'s narrator relies on interiors to set the tone of the novel, an often ironic and condescending one, usually relying on the link between character and milieu. The narrator takes pleasure in making associations between persons and places and finds it humorous if the description of an interior coincides adequately with the personality of a character. When describing Rubião's last residence, the narrator claims that the interior of the house had a look of abandonment with no regularity of things, but that at the same time, "o transtorno dos móveis da sala exprimia bem o delírio do morador, suas idéias tortas e confusas" [the disorder of the furniture in the parlor expressed quite well the delirium of the one who lived there, his twisted and confused ideas, 1: 798; 260]. The humor made at the expense of Rubião's state of mind is typical of the narrator's indifference, but it also strategically attempts to draw the attention away from the space by making its meaning conclusive. More often than not when the narrator is explicit about what the interior represents, he is actually trying to divert the reader's attention from a space that is highly significant and for reasons other than the ones the narrator underscores. By making the symbolism evident, the narrator succeeds in encouraging the careful reader to take a closer look at the room and its imagery. The significance of Rubião's last home does a lot more than represent his confused state of mind. As I showed earlier, this interior, representing the inner self of Rubião and his dog, acts as a medium through which D. Fernanda achieves a greater level of awareness of her society. A space that either coincides all too perfectly, or is in perfect opposition to the personality of a character is thus likely to be hiding important complexities. Rubião's writing desk is the item that most stands outs in his study and captures the general admiration of all his guests: "era de ébano, um primor de talha, obra severa e forte" [It was made of ebony, a masterpiece of wood carving, a solid, strong piece, 1: 757; 193]. Of course Rubião's character does not represent his desk's qualities nor does he have very much use for it. He seldom sits there, preferring to rest and daydream on comfortable divans and *poufs* in his sitting-room. Hence the narrator is again belittling the protagonist. Still, "primor de talha" [masterpiece of wood carving] recalls the words used to describe one of Rubião's favorite objects, his silver platter, "primor de argentaria" [masterpiece of silver work, 1: 641; 6]. In fact Rubião's desk, his tray, and other decorative pieces, as we shall subsequently see, are crucial because he reinvents himself through these personal acquisitions. They might not coincide with him but they reveal a lot about his character and aesthetic choices. The narrator uses the technique of describing the interior setting to judge the protagonist and divert attention from the semiotic possibilities of the interior settings.

   Furthermore, Machado's narrator deliberately refuses to give generous depictions of interiors and things. Still, the insistence on paying little attention to the setting has the opposite effect, making it central for understanding the narrative. The absence of description increases the significance of the little explained by creating a sense of mystery around the space, and evoking a subdued and repressed meaning. Machado's subtle descriptive discourse surfaces casually through the observation and perspective of other characters. The narrator's indifference toward a room is also evident in the rhetorical, apparently objective, device of listing objects and furnishings. Camacho's office is revealed to the reader through Rubião eyes, who casts his eyes about the room and sees "poucos móveis, alguns autos sôbre um tamborete ao pé do advogado, estante com livros, Lobão, Pereira e Sousa, Dalloz. *Ordenações do Reino*, um retrato na parede, diante da escrivaninha" [Not too much furniture, a few briefs on a stool beside the lawyer, shelves with books, Lobão, Pereira e Sousa, Dalloz, *National Ordinances*, a portrait on the wall facing the desk, 1: 692-693; 88]. Rubião's Botafogo home is also played down by a description provided from Siqueira's perspective. Major Siqueira likes Rubião's new house and "das alfaias, do luxo, de tôdas as minúcias, ouros e bambinelas" [the furnishings, the luxury, all the details, the gold work, the curtains, 1: 709; 114]. The deliberate use of plural nouns is meant to underscore the trivial, general, and abundant yet ambiguous and unimportant characteristics of Rubião's belongings. Palha's interiors illustrate these different narrative tendencies as well. Rubião is the one who often witnesses the improvement in Palha's rooms and homes. The narrator once again emphasizes the insignificance of these details, but Rubião's awareness of Palha's new purchases is extremely important; it functions to underline the irony behind Palha's economic success at Rubião's expense, and to show how the sense of space is a key factor of Rubião's thinking. Palha's increasingly luxuriously interiors are uncovered through Rubião's quick glance: "Rubião lançava os olhos aos móveis, porcelanas, cristais, reposteiros" [Rubião cast his eyes over the furniture, the porcelain, the crystal, the draperies, 1: 740; 166]. When in Palha's office, Rubião observes some servants bringing in something he can not identify and asks Palha what it might be. Palha answers "São uns morins ingleses" [It's some English calico] and Rubião according to the narrator repeats with indifference, "Morins inglêses" [English calico, 1: 713; 121]. It is unclear whether Rubião finds this irrelevant or rather the narrator prefers to show it as inconsequential. The narrative is obviously attentive to pointing out Palha's fascination with décor and details. Unlike Eça's Carlos da Maia or even Rubião, to whom interior decorating becomes a process of invention and reinvention, for Palha his weakness for "adornos de casa, mormente se eram de invenção ou adoção recente" [household furnishings, usually of the latest style or invention, 1: 667; 47], is essentially an economic affair. The narrative uses the subtle acquisition of new homes and furnishings to express Palha's economic cunningness throughout the narrative. The objects are nonchalantly referred to, as in the scene when Sofia sits "na otomana de cetim azul, compra de poucos dias" [on the blue satin ottoman purchased a few days before, 1: 728; 146]. While the narrator tries to be vague, humoristic, and ambiguous in his interior descriptions, he actually attempts to hide the narrative discourse implied in these details and in their relation to the characters and to the narrating of the story.

A closer look at these narrowly decorated interiors is necessary in order to uncover Machado's rhetorical exploration of how the mind develops relationships to the external surroundings. As we have seen the significant opening scene of *Quincas Borba* introduces Rubião, his Botafogo sitting-room, and its most significant content: the newly acquired decorative ornaments and objectified individuals that make up Rubião's new world order ever since he came into his inheritance and moved to Rio de Janeiro. Rubião's latest setting points to an important change in Brazilian interior decorating that occurs in the latter half of the nineteenth century. Economic growth stimulates the upper and middle classes to abandon colonial traditions and reproduce European models in their home furnishings and décor. In Rubião's house, even the Spanish butler and the French cook are European, and he is encouraged by his new friends to dismiss what is considered typically Brazilian. As in *The Maias* and *La Regenta*, characters of *Quincas Borba* inhabit spaces filled with foreign elements that allow them to live a sort of exile within their own nation's territory. As opposed to Clarín's and Eça's characters, however, Rubião is compelled by the influence of others into this interior exile and does not choose it himself. When it comes to furnishing and adorning the Botafogo palace, Palha is a great help to Rubião accompanying him shopping and "guiando-o com o gôsto" [guiding him with his taste, 1: 659; 34]. Rubião must abandon everything that reminds him of home, including hiding his favorite servant (a freed slave) that he brought from Barbacena: "O seu bom pajem, que ele queria pôr na sala, como um pedaço da província, nem o pôde deixar na cozinha, onde reinava um francês, Jean; foi degradado a outros serviços" [His good manservant, whom he wished to keep in the parlor as a touch of the provinces, couldn't even stay in the kitchen, where a Frenchman, Jean, reigned, 1: 641-642; 6]. Rubião also purchases a number of decorative objects, such as the two bronze figures of Mephistopheles and Faust, under pressure from Palha. Without necessarily understanding what these characters imply, Rubião dislikes them. He conforms in order to satisfy the demands of his new friends and the dictates of a society greatly shaped by European fashions but is displaced from a world with which he identifies.

On the other hand there is something very productive about this European influence on both Machado and Rubião. Brazilian interior design makes significant technical progress at this time, and Machado himself notes and is aware of the modernization of the national furniture industry. The predominant method, as was the case in Europe as well, is mainly to reproduce and recreate patterns from past styles. Machado incorporates the developments that are taking place in Brazilian interior decorating into his novel. Rubião and everything from Barbacena, or the Brazilian provinces, such as Rubião's manservant, emerge as representative of the national while at the same time they seem like exotic elements inappropriate for the metropolis. Yet we know that the new furnishings, while inspired by European models, are in fact made in Brazil. The question then is not to distinguish between what is national and what is foreign, but to focus on how an element, be it imported or home grown, is transformed. Machado seems to suggest that originality lies in the process of recreating something. This method of resourceful imitation turns up in the struggle between Rubião and the others who manipulate his aesthetic taste, as it does in the effort of the decorative arts industry to make certain French furnishings Brazilian. Critics who complain about Machado's lack of attention to national matters fail to see that the author is concerned with defining the autochthonous, what is original to Brazil, by focusing on the processes that take place when the national and the foreign intersect. Gilberto Pinheiro Passos has studied the associations in much of Machado's fiction to French history and culture, especially the indirect and direct references made to eighteenth-century enlightened thought, and French eighteenth- and nineteenth-century literature. In *Napoleão de Botafogo* he explains that in *Quincas Borba* "a complexa plasmação do elemento nacional não se faz pelo recurso ao pitoresco exótico e tranqüilizador, como marca distintiva da diferença, mas, ao contrário, pela necessária e conflitante relação entre o nacional e o estrangeiro, característica da sociedade fluminense" [the complex rendering of the national element is not made by resorting to the exotic and reassuring picturesque as a distinctive feature of difference, but, on the contrary, to the necessary and conflicting relation between the national and the foreign, characteristic of Rio de Janeiro society].[11] Thus, Machado renders the contradictory encounter between the national and the imported as the crucial expression for what ultimately transforms and characterizes societies and individuals.

Machado uses this conflict to reveal some of the intricate and creative effects it has on Brazilian society and his characters. The French and European fashions populating Rubião's interior spaces begin to occupy his mind and take over his sense of self. Earlier we explored how Rubião boasts a much more complex imagination than the narrator leads one to believe. The protagonist's fantasies and personal identity are very much influenced by the qualities of his Botafogo home and the illusions these produce: "A casa era ainda um bom repouso ao espírito, com o seu luxo rutilante e os sonhos que vagavam no ar" [His house was still a good place for his spirit to rest in with its glow of luxury and the dreams that floated in the air, 1: 710; 117]. Rubião's own efforts to imitate French decorative styles emerge in his imitation of Napoleon III. He of course understands that the milieu must reflect the person and to complete the simulation he redecorates. In order to become the French emperor he will not only alter his physical appearance but also transform his space. Thus when Rubião's guests find their way into his study one day to admire the well-arranged furniture and the desk another novelty awaits them: "dous bustos de mármore, postos sôbre ela, os dous Napoleões, o primeiro e o terceiro" [two marble busts on it, the two Napoleons, the first and the third, 1: 757; 194]. It is also in this transformed study that Rubião has the French barber give him the same mustache and beard as Napoleon III.

Curiously Rubião's redecorating and hence his reinvention of himself as Napolean III is an imitation of his already complex yet illusory new identity as a capitalist. In order to refurnish his study Rubião uses his living room as a model which as we have seen is characterized by an assortment of complex influences. The two bronze figures reluctantly bought under pressure from Palha transform into the two marble busts on his desk, and the two English engravings become "uma gravura ou litografia representando a *Batalha de*

Solferino, e um retrato da imperatriz Eugênia" [an engraving or lithograph showing the Battle of Solferino and a portrait of the Empress Eugénie] which now adorn the walls of his study (1: 764; 204). The symmetry between the two descriptions is not gratuitous, but rather evidence of Rubião's ability to recreate his interior to reflect his new character. More important than what Mephistopheles and Faust represent is Rubião's semantic talent in replacing the two figures with those of the French emperors. This reveals his ability to interpret and redefine himself and his relation to other characters. Rubião's interior world is a text that he reads and that impacts him the same way the chivalric novels have an effect on Don Quixote. Considering that Napoleon III is himself an inferior copy of his supposed uncle, Rubião, as Brazil, are in reality imitating an imitation. Machado suggests, then, that imitation is both a creative and re-creative process. If Rubião's interior space embodies his reality, then life is in essence a means of invention: a simulation of an illusion. Imitation, recreation, and signification all take place within the interior, turning it into a medium for aesthetic creation. Machado reminds us that the interior world is a reproduction, just as the new Brazilian furnishings, and just as Machado's own novels are. Yet because the interior space is what individuals create and invent in order to give meaning to their lives it also represents reality. Thus, like the narrative genre, the interior is a means for understanding the ways in which reality is intertwined with fiction.

Rubião's interiors undergo important processes and experimentations. This sense of procedure and method is reflected in the way others scrutinize his home, which reminds one of a museum or of a scientific lab filled with curious pieces worthy of inspection. Different characters methodically study Rubião's rooms and possessions. Right after examining Rubião's rose collection in the garden so intensely that it was necessary to pull him away from one rosebed to another, Freitas moves into the house to admire the art work exhibited: "Examinou os bronzes, os quadros, os móveis" [He examined the bronzes, the paintings, the furniture, 1: 661; 38]. The verb "to examine" is repeatedly used to describe Freitas's inspection of Rubião's domestic world. During a luncheon with Rubião and Carlos Maria, Freitas gazes "para um painel da parede" [at a picture on the wall, 1: 663; 41]. Palha finds Doutor Camacho "mirando os quadros" [looking at the pictures] in Rubião's sitting-room (1: 686; 77). This suggests that Rubião is on a number of different levels an object of study. Indeed one could argue that Rubião, as the novel, is an experiment on philosophy, literature, capitalism, and love. Others therefore scrutinize his home for hints on the development and results of the investigation. Throughout his novels and short stories, Machado deals with the question of scientific study, more often than not parodying the obsessive turn toward the empirical. But this compulsive experimentation takes place exclusively indoors. Machado's scientists and narrators are less interested in the natural world and more in studying human nature within its natural habitat, that is, in rooms, salons, and boudoirs.

The narrative experiment is, thus, analogous to the analysis of the private setting. But humans do not exist alone in their interiors, but in conjunction with their things, furnishings, and objects. In Machado's novel objects and people become inseparable from the intimate spaces they inhabit. Human beings begin to resemble things in their function and worth as they are rendered in the novel as a key topic of scientific and artistic inquiry. The narrator describes characters as things and in turn attributes human qualities to material items. In judging Palha's patchy soul, for example, the narrator compares it to a patchwork quilt: "Pode ser; moralmente as colchas inteiriças são tão raras! O principal é que as cores se não desmintam umas às outras,— quando não possam obedecer à simetria e regularidade" [It could well be. Moral quilts made of one piece are so rare! The main thing is for the colors not to contradict each other—when they are unable to follow symmetry and regularity, 1: 687; 79]. The narrator criticizes Palha and other characters by equating them to apparently trivial and domestic things. The material object, however, often has an equal or greater value than the human being. Furthermore, a number of things that Machado describes and reflects on in his fiction connect in very significant ways to the events in the story, which further attests to the author's appreciation of the meaningfulness of objects. The quilt recalls one of Sofia's favorite activities, her knitting and needlework. She seems to be the one marking the passage of time by apparently weaving her husband's soul or quilt. Despite Sofia and Palha's conflictive and often violent relationship, the changes that their minds and souls undergo throughout the narrative are clearly intertwined, as the simile of the quilt seems to suggest. Therefore, the quilt is not just an object independent of the narrative progress but tied to the development of time, characters, and events.

Material things serve more than just as auxiliaries to the narrative; they become aspects and methods of the narration. Critics have repeatedly noted Machado's tendency to give an exaggerated importance to trivialities. In Lúcia Miguel Pereira's words, Machado has a "dom sutil de conferir profundo alcance a pormenores aparentemente banais, de extrair dêles a sua essência" [subtle talent of conferring profound importance to apparently banal details, of extracting from them their essence].[12] This overwhelming significance that the author puts on possessions relates to what she calls Machado's "antropomorfismo" [anthropomorphism] or the lending of human sentiments to objects and animals.[13] *Quincas Borba*'s narrator is quite explicit:

> Quem conhece o solo e o subsolo da vida, sabe muito bem que um trecho de muro, um banco, um tapête, um guarda-chuva, são ricos de idéias ou de sentimentos, quando nós também o somos, e que as reflexões de parceria entre os homens e as cousas compõem um dos mais interessantes fenômenos da terra.

[Anyone who knows the soil and the subsoil of life knows quite well that a
stretch of wall, a bench, a rug, an umbrella are rich with ideas or feelings when
we are, too, and that the reflections of a partnership between men and things
constitute one of the most interesting phenomena on earth, 1: 762; 201]

We find throughout the novel examples of the meaning that trivial things,
which compose our interior domestic environment, are able to impart and
feel. The bench, where Dona Fernanda and Maria Benedita share an intimate
conversation, for example, expresses a sense of relief and happiness once the
women leave and it can once again bask in the sun. When Rubião discovers
Sofia's letter to Carlos Maria and is anxious to open it, he abruptly stops in
the center of his salon. It seems safe for him to open the letter for no one
could see him, "os quadros da parede estavam quietos, indiferentes, o turco
do tapête continuava a fumar e a olhar para o Bósforo" [the pictures on the
wall were silent, indifferent; the Turk on the rug continued smoking and
looking out at the Bosporus, 1: 724; 140]. These minor material elements
unexpectedly become involved in the narrative, and contrary to what the
narrator claims, they are not at all indifferent to the events around them. In
fact they seem to express a deeper understanding of the circumstances than
even some of the human characters. This provokes the reader to inquire into
what might the objects know and reveal. As we shall see specific possessions
of Rubião's—especially his dog, Quincas Borba, his silver platter, silk slippers, and an old chair in the house in Barbacena—tie to important structures
and themes worked throughout the novel: nineteenth-century Brazilian society and politics, slavery, the ideology of patronage, and the social role of the
"agregado."

In *Quincas Borba* while people appear to have more in common with
things, the faithful dog that shares his name with the deceased philosopher
has many human qualities. Chapter XXVIII deals with the dog's intimate
feelings, ideas, pleasures and desires. The following chapter introduces
Rubião's two lunch guests, the young Carlos Maria "que roía as primeiras
aparas dos bens da mãe" [who was nibbling at the first items of his mother's
possessions] and the older Freitas "que já não tinha que roer" [who no longer
had anything to nibble on, 1: 661; 37]. Besides "to nibble" the Portuguese
verb "roer" also means "to gnaw," something dogs commonly do on bones.
While the men chew away at life, we find the dog on the other hand, just a
paragraph before, meditating on existence. Human characters reverse roles
throughout the novel with animals, plants, and things. Quincas Borba leaves
his entire estate to Rubião under the condition that the latter treat his pet as if
he were not a dog but a person. Rubião is aware and even jealous of the
intimacy tying the philosopher to the dog, and therefore, attempts to substitute the philosopher in the dog's life. When the madman departs on his trip to
Rio de Janeiro at the beginning of the novel, Rubião invites the dog into his

own bed in the mornings, as was the philosopher's habit. Rubião also suspects and fears that the soul of his former master has transmigrated to the dog. Still, the animal and the philosopher share little more than their name, while Rubião on the other hand has a significant amount in common with both Quincas Borbas. As Rubião grows in wealth and madness he begins to imitate his late master in act and speech.

Constant references in the novel confound these three intimately connected protagonists, but overall Rubião shares more with the dog than with their master. In his role as Quincas Borba's pupil and servant, Rubião, is very much like the philosopher's trained dog. They have a parallel life and tragic end. They are both loyal and humble servants, and Rubião often identifies himself with the dog's devotion and sacrifice. Even when others beat and insult them, they unconditionally forgive their offenders and return for what seems like more abuse. Quincas Borba, the dog, appears on the scene at very precise moments to remind Rubião of his own subservient role in society and to reflect his owner's subconscious. Rubião goes to the garden to unleash the dog, and this is like "soltar-se a si mesmo" [turning himself loose, 1: 659; 35]. In Machado's short story "Miss Dollar," the dog is described as a "símbolo da fidelidade ou do servilismo" [symbol of fidelity or servility, 2: 28]. The sense of servitude is what bonds Rubião to the two Quincas Borbas. Machado seems to use the relations between the three characters to explore some of the dialectics connecting a master with a slave. Figures of actual slaves are rare in Machado's work and the author seldom deals directly with slavery, which Brazil did not abolish until 1888. [14] But, as Roberto Schwarz and others have argued, slavery's presence is determinant in the form of calculated allusions and emphatic insinuations. Machado uses details and metaphors that implicitly question the human bonds shaped by slavery. It would seem that the complex connection between Rubião and the two Quincas Borbas evokes Hegel's development of the self-consciousness in his *Phenomenology of Spirit*. Just as Hegel explains that the lord's independent consciousness receives an untrue recognition of itself because ultimately the "*truth* of the independent consciousness is accordingly the servile consciousness of the bondsman," in *Quincas Borba*, the borders between lord and bondsman are also unclear. [15] Machado combines in Quincas Borba, the dog, not only the independent and dependent consciousnesses with thinghood, but also suggests, and this would be contrary to Hegel's philosophy, that it is impossible to reach a pure individualized self-consciousness and that perhaps freedom is naturally "still enmeshed in servitude," to use Hegel's own words. [16] The circle linking the three characters also determines their destinies, consciousnesses, and the roles they play in a slave-holding society.

If the slave's existence and self-identity ultimately determine the master's, then one can claim that, similarly, the ideologies promoted by a society that depends on slavery are undermined by the structures that actually control its political and social relations. The system of patronage and clientelism in Brazil undoubtedly grows out of slavery. Brazilian historiographers agree that this system served as the leading ideology shaping relations between the social and the political. Richard Graham's *Patronage and Politics in Nine-teenth-Century Brazil* explores how patronage during the reign of Pedro II (1840-1889) defined social, economic, and political structures that survive well into twentieth-century Brazil. Machado's fiction shows that the ideology of patronage not only served the interests of the elite and conditioned politics, but also connects to slavery and to the human relationships developed out of the experience of servitude. The relations between Rubião and the two Quincas Borbas recall the dynamics of slavery and exemplify the ideology of patronage. In fact almost all personal relationships in the novel are based on power and reflect the way servitude and patronage ultimately structure and implicitly deconstruct the political and social. Egotistical and narcissistic characters in the novel look to subjugate others in order to assure an existence for themselves. Their failure suggests that the system both on the human and state levels is clearly a self-destructive institution that infects everything: places, people, and things.

In *Ao vencedor as Batatas*, Roberto Schwarz points out how already in his early novels Machado confronts the important social problems structuring Brazil, such as paternalism, slavery, and the client system. Machado's fiction explores these complexities through the important role and representation of the figure of the "agregado," a youth, or in many cases an entire family that was wholly dependent, economically and socially, on a wealthier family on whose estate they lived. "Agregadas," often the protagonists of Machado's first novels, illustrate different social and class tensions through the personal relations they develop with the members of the elite family. The later novels, however, do not abandon the role of the "agregado," but its characterization becomes a lot more complex. In Machado's later fiction, the sense of dependence on others is internalized, just like Machado's own instinct of nationality, and even Counselor Aires in the author's last two novels relies heavily on others for his own existence and happiness. All of Machado's characters become to a certain degree dependents. The "agregado" is an existential understanding or state of being that in turn has significant consequences on the literary creation itself since the author himself becomes a dependent of his fiction. Toward the end of his career, Machado internalizes these social roles to the point that they are not only inherent in the relationships between his characters, but also in the relation he maintains with the creation of the text. Thus it would appear that a specific human condition or experience resulting from a very particular combination of economic and historical developments can slowly influence and change an author's narrative form.

This becomes clear through Machado's discourse of interior things in *Quincas Borba*. Rubião oscillates between being an "agregado," a dependent, a servant like figure, and at the same time a powerful member of the elite, a master of others. Rubião's favorite new acquisition is his silver tray. He is personally proud and attached to it and appreciates its symbolism. In the opening Botafogo scene, his Spanish butler serves the morning coffee on the infamous shinny platter, which Rubião surreptitiously and repeatedly admires. Silver and gold are Rubião's favorite metals. If asked to choose among his possessions, "escolhereia a bandeja,—primor de argentaria, execução fina e acabada" [he would choose the tray—a masterpiece of silver work, of delicate and perfect execution, 1: 641; 6]. When Rubião receives Carlos Maria and Freitas in his home a very good moment for him is when his Spanish servant arrives with the "bandeja de prata, vários licores, e cálices" [silver tray holding various liqueurs and some goblets, 1: 661; 38]. This silver tray reminds Rubião that he is no longer a servant but the one who is now waited on. More important, however, is his inability to separate his good manservant from the serving tray. The tray triggers Rubião to think about his former slave from Barbacena whom he wishes were serving him instead of the Spaniard but who unfortunately has been downgraded to inferior duties. This servant would bring him a sense of comfort, and help Rubião feel less alienated in a room filled with European fashions and foreign influences. Rubião unconsciously connects his own experience in Barbacena as Quincas Borba's servant to the nostalgia of his former slave and is evidently powerless to unravel this intricate association from his new reality as a capitalist.

Rubião is not the only character that associates homely comfort and a sense of belonging with a rural slave-holding society. Maria Benedita thinks about her slaves in conjunction with another highly significant intimate object, her slippers. Slippers play an important role in Machado's writing overall and they have a particular effect on Rubião's and Maria Benedita's lives. By focusing on the slipper, Machado highlights the private, sensual, and contemplative side of his characters, while also turning this frivolous and indulgent object into a symbolic narrative tool. The protagonist of Machado's short story "A Chinela Turca" [The Turkish Slipper] considers that the slipper "vinha a ser pura metáfora" [came to be pure metaphor, 2: 300]. Once again a component of the interior and private world helps the narrator tell and invent his story. Slippers can act as mirrors, reminding the characters of their interior selves, and as crystal balls, depicting images from past or future realities that comment on the present moment. D. Conceição in "Missa do Galo" (Midnight Mass) surprises the narrator "arrastando as chinelinhas da alcova" [dragging the little slippers from the alcove] and bringing forth the intimacy of her bedroom to the sitting-room where they meet (2: 607). The female protagonist of "D. Benedita: Um Retrato" (D. Benedita: A Portrait) is irritated upon discovering on her awfully elegant slipper "um roidinho de barata" [a cockroach's nibble, 2: 311]. The blemish exposes an imperfection in her flawlessly ordered domestic world. Important details such as these not only refer to the complex makeup of a character's psychology but also to literary questions, as is the case in *Quincas Borba*.

Maria Benedita reminisces about her slippers when her nostalgic feelings take her back to her native Iguaçu: "Então batia as assas para a varanda da velha casa, onde bebia café, ao pé da mãe; pensava na escravaria, nos móveis antigos, nas bonitas chinelas que lhe mandara o padrinho, um fazendeiro rico de São João d'El-Rei,—e que lá ficaram em casa. Sofia não consentiu que ela as trouxesse" [Then she would fly off to the veranda of the old house where she drank coffee next to her mother. She would think about the slaves, the antique furniture, the pretty slippers sent her by her godfather, a wealthy plantation owner from São João d'El-Rei—and which had been left behind at home there. Sofia wouldn't let her bring them, 1: 699; 99]. Positioned strategically on the threshold of her house Maria Benedita remembers all the different elements that make up her material and emotional interior comfort. Her sense of security is inseparable from her slaves and her domestic setting. Sofia's disapproval of the slippers, as too simple and provincial for the urban and lavish lifestyle of the capital, recalls Palha's censure of Rubião's manservant, both are excluded from the new interiors these characters occupy. These slippers, like the silver tray, reinforce the link between slavery and the memory and consciousness of characters. Rubião is introduced in the novel wearing his exotic Tunisian slippers, which not coincidently are a gift from Palha. The flashback, which follows the opening scene and outlines the submissive relationship between Rubião and Quincas Borba, sets up a very important contrast. In the past Rubião's position required him to help Quincas Borba into his slippers, when Quincas Borba "procurou com os pés as chinelas; Rubião chegou-lhas" [searched for his slippers with his feet. Rubião pushed them over to him, 1: 644; 10]. Now Palha is the one indirectly serving Rubião by making him a metaphoric gift of a pair of slippers. Despite the role reversal, Rubião never fully assumes his new situation as master.

Like the slippers, a simple piece of furniture can tell us a lot about the meaning behind Machado's minimalist interiors. Following the death of Quincas Borba, Rubião can still hear the philosopher's words resonate in the house in Barbacena. He sits in the exact same chair where he first listened to Quincas Borba's speeches and philosophical arguments. The chair appears to embody his relationship to Quincas Borba, and the act of sitting suggests Rubião's conscious or unconscious awareness of his position as pupil and inferior. This is why after pondering over Quincas Borba's famous speech on victors and potatoes, a philosophical diatribe that is meant to be understood as an ironic commentary on positivistic thought, Rubião gets up abruptly and passionately from the chair. Whether Rubião understands the metaphysical claim behind the witty maxim, "Ao vencedor, as batatas!" [To the victor, the potatoes] is far less relevant than his sensitivity to the furnishing and its implications (1: 655; 27). Rubião sits down to reenact this encounter in order to rewrite and reinterpret his inferior position to Quincas Borba. In rising out of the chair, he attempts to assume his new role as master. Rubião is quite aware that space and inanimate objects have the power to transport him to other time periods. As with the two minor characters, Dona Tonica and Teófilo, different spaces or furnishings stir Rubião's memory and under-standing of himself and reality. Rubião's actions here bring to mind what Bachelard calls "topoanalysis," or "the systematic psychological study of the sites of our intimate lives."[17] Bachelard explains that memory is motionless or fixed in space, and found in and through space.[18] After describing this important realization that Rubião experiences, the devious narrator concludes this chapter with a bold statement on perspective that is also a clear reference to slavery: "Tão certo é que a paisagem depende do ponto de vista, e que o melhor modo de apreciar o chicote é ter-lhe o cabo na mão" [It's so true that the landscape depends on the point of view and the best way to appreciate a whip is to have its handle in our hand, 1: 655; 27]. Thus, what Rubião comprehends in this scene seems to have less to do with positivistic thinking, and far more with his understanding of how slavery plagues all relations, including those that provide him with his sense of self and his sense of understanding or misunderstanding of the world around him.

The fact that Rubião never succeeds as a member of the elite in Rio de Janeiro is clearly tied to the fact that he is incapable of being a master of slaves. The first time Rubião meets Palha they are traveling on a train and end up discussing contemporary politics. The narrative refers to the debates that were taking place the years before the controversial 1871 Law of the Free Womb, which would legally free the children of slave mothers. It be-comes clear that Palha and Rubião have contrasting opinions on this deter-mining issue.

Cristiano Palha maldisse o govêrno, que introduzira na fala do trono uma palavra relativa à propriedade servil; mas, com grande espanto seu, Rubião não acudiu à indignação. Era plano dêste vender os escravos que o testador lhe deixara, exceto um pajem; se alguma cousa perdesse, o resto da herança co-briria o desfalque. Demais, a fala do trono, que ele também lera, mandava respeitar a propriedade atual. Que lhe importavam escravos futuros, se os não compraria? O pajem ia ser fôrro, logo que êle entrasse na posse dos bens.

[Cristiano Palha cursed the government, which had inserted remarks concern-ing servile property in the Emperor's annual Speech from the Throne. But, to his great surprise, Rubião didn't leap to indignation. It was Rubião's plan to sell the slaves the testator had left him, except for a houseboy. If he lost anything, the rest of the inheritance would cover it. Besides, the Speech from the Throne, which he'd also read, ordered that current property be respected. What did he care about future slaves, since he wasn't going to buy any? The

houseboy would be freed as soon as he came into possession of his goods, 1:
656; 29.]

Evidently the protagonist has no wish to maintain slaves, and although the
text is not explicit, it does suggest that Rubião's position is closer to those of
the abolitionists. Ironically enough, the philosopher's lessons have taught
Rubião how not to be a winner and a master. Or perhaps they have taught
him too intimately the damages of bondage. A chair, a pair of slippers, and a
silver tray, the detailed objects and things that make up the interior world and
the conscious and subconscious influences on the characters' interiorities,
ultimately reveal how the novel critically deals with the complexity of slavery and other political ideologies, and with the impact these have on individual identities.

Machado once again seems to anticipate the reading and writing of Brazil's social history. Like the author, Brazilian historiographers and sociolo-
gists have tended to study Brazil, and slavery in particular, from the perspective of the private world or domestic space. The general consensus among
historians of nineteenth-century Brazil is that the household, a set of relationships containing both family and servants, is the social foundation operating
as the basic unit of the polity. Nestor Duarte's *A ordem privada e a
organização política nacional* (*The order of privacy and the political national organization*) analyzes the planter household as an institution that historically resists change and the state. Gilberto Freyre uses the metaphor of the
big house and the slave quarters to structure his arguments in *Casa grande e
senzala* (*The masters and the slaves*) and *Sobrados e mucambos* (*The man-
sions and the shanties*). Freyre's writings, albeit controversial, do effectively
disclose the architecture that sustains some of Brazil's social, economic, and
political traditions.[19] Sandra Lauderdale Graham's *House and Street* explores the complexity of domestic circumstances defining the significance of
the lives of female servants and masters in Rio de Janeiro in the second half
of the nineteenth century. She demonstrates how at this time domestic architecture reveals the order and meaning in daily life and in the household by
protecting the home from the public and corrupt affairs of the street. As she
explains breaking social and legal codes "within doors" was more severely
punished than if committed "outside the house."[20] Machado's fiction is highly attentive to the extensive domestic apparatus characterizing the Brazilian
social experience and anticipates this sociological and historical tendency to
investigate Brazil's society and the institution of slavery by focusing on
private life. Within his novels he looks inside minds, homes, and rooms, and
his narrative interiors function as a discourse revealing the conflicting aspects of the national condition.

Thus, the home plays a significant role throughout Machado's fiction not
only because the author's decorative and architectural writing explores im-

portant social and political complexities, but also because for Machado personally a private interior space is home to important emotions and hence forms closer ties between feelings and subjectivity. The death of his wife Carolina in 1904 strengthens the bond that exists for Machado between the home and the writer's interiority. Her parting reminds him of how in a corner or nook of a home, spaces Clarín also esteems, one can sometimes find "um mundo inteiro" [an entire world, 2: 658]. Carolina's death inspires Machado to work with the figure of the house more directly in his fiction, but already in *Quincas Borba* homes and interiors emerge as symbols for love and life. In Machado's work, as in Eça's and Clarín's, the passionate self becomes as important as the conscious and intellectual self. All three novels explore how emotions shape the individual and his or her ontological perspective. This exploration takes different forms in each novel but is ultimately not gender specific. In *Quincas Borba*, both Rubião and Sofia search for an inner more authentic and sensitive self. Their voyage to the inner world is directly related to the way they experience their domestic spaces. The home becomes for Machado a metaphor for this multifaceted interior self that is both male and female, conscious and subconscious. In the prologue to his collection of short stories *Relíquias de Casa Velha* (The Relics of an Old House), Machado writes "Chama-lhe à minha vida uma casa, dá o nome de relíquias aos inéditos e impressos que aqui vão, idéias, histórias, críticas, diálogos, e verás explicados o livro e o título" [Call my life a house, give the name of relics to the unpublished and printed manuscripts that are here, ideas, stories, criticisms, dialogues, and you shall have an explanation for the book and its title, 2: 658]. In this brief preface he asks twice whether the treasures kept inside his home deserve to "sair cá fora" [come out, 2: 658]. The repeated expression of coming out fittingly reinforces the fact that ideas and emotions come from within the interior of the home and the self, and if one understands "valer a pena" literally, which translates exactly to be worthy of the pen then the author's question affirms that interiors represent both the material for and the location of the imagination. What is most intimate, both intellectually and emotionally, resides inside a specific interior, domestic, and protected space.

Quincas Borba draws on analogies between female characters and domestic environments that do not have the effect of engendering space but instead anticipate both Freudian questions concerning the subconscious and feminist readings of the nineteenth-century domestication of the novel. Siqueira encourages Rubião to marry because, in the major's opinion, "a casa de Rubião não tinha alma" [Rubião's house lacked a soul, 1: 709; 115]. A man's soul, such as Palha's, is compared to a quilt, which relates to a craft that depends typically on female work. While a man's inner life or home relies on a woman for the completion of his spirit, a woman's talents include not only fabricating another's essence, but also, according to Siqueira and Machado himself, filling a specific home with eternal life. A soul as immoral as Palha's benefits only from the fact that Sofia, his slave, bears its true consciousness, while a lost individual like Rubião is incomplete, missing his feminine side. For Machado, both the emotional and the intellectual, as both male and female qualities, are necessary in the effort to reach self-consciousness, although these attempts often fail. Sofia is also an unfinished self, and instead of being compared to a home she is associated with an inn. The narrator compares Sofia's eyes to the light coming from a guesthouse "em que não houvesse cômodos para hóspedes" [with no accomodations]. Even if she eventually opens the inn's windows, her eyes, the door "se assim podemos chamar ao coração" [if we can call her heart a door] remains locked tight (1: 667; 48). The text re-conceptualizes Sofia as a domestic space of closed doors and open windows. On a first thought this sounds hopeful; it recalls Virginia Woolf's demands for a woman in *A Room of One's Own*, a personal private working space with open windows and closed doors, and seems to describe a Sofia turning inward, striving for emancipation. Regrettably she is ultimately incapable of reaching a deeper understanding of the life inside and around her. Instead of completing the soul with an internal and eternal life, Sofia, as an inn, offers only a transitory limbo, a space where travelers come and go.

To link female characters with their private environments is typical of the realist genre and suggestive of the social role women were confined to at the time. After Woolf's *A Room of One's Own* and feminist critics' rereading of the nineteenth-century novel's turn toward the private life of women, no one can deny that ultimately this private space has actually allowed for the autonomy of the self and the emancipation of the mind. Woolf writes: "For women have sat indoors all these millions of years, so that by this time the very walls are permeated by their creative force, which has, indeed, so overcharged the capacity of bricks and mortar that it must needs harness itself to pens and brushes and business and politics."[21] The female's interior world has empowered her, and this association between the female and the home becomes an integral part of modernity's thought and discourse. As Nancy Armstrong writes, it "appears that the same figure of the house as a woman's body that contains knowledge came to serve as a model for culture itself at the opening of the modern period."[22] In this respect, Machado seems to prefigure this exploration of the consciousness and its relation to women. Machado is interested in understanding feelings and how emotions affect tensions in the development of his characters. The interior in Machado's fiction provides a refuge to combine the emotional with the reflective. The interior is "female" insofar as it illustrates the significant impact emotions have on the lives of the characters. Taking a closer look at the role that windows and doors play in the novel reveals how they function as perspectives on the construction of a consciousness that is both male and female and reinforces Machado's threshold of in-between spaces.

The window, which serves as a medium to reach inside Sofia, frames a majority of the interior scenes in *Quincas Borba*. Carollo claims that the windows act to fuse the interior with the exterior: "Há ainda que ressaltar a disposição das cenas internas privilegiadas pela descrição de detalhes espaciais, todas elas marcadas pela presença de uma janela aberta, permitindo a fusão do exterior com o interior" [One should also highlight the arrangement of the interior scenes privileged by the description of spatial details, all of them framed by the presence of an open window, allowing for the fusion of the exterior with the interior].[23] On the night at Santa Teresa during Rubião's and Sofia's mutual contemplation, the protagonist stands "ao canto de uma janela, de costas para fora" [by the window with his back to the outside, 1: 667; 48]. When they move out into the garden through "janelas abertas" [the open windows] they can observe the other people in the house (1: 669; 51). The architecture of this scene relies on the window, which more than fusing the interior with the exterior, serves as a point of view, a sort of inquisitive eye that can both reveal and hide events, in the same way characters both look out different openings or close their eyes to see inside themselves. Rubião turns his back toward the window, unconsciously anticipating and hiding from view the intimate scene that takes place in the garden moments later. To a certain degree, it is always through or at a window that Rubião, Carlos Maria, the readers, and even Sofia, see inside the characters. When Rubião sits with Sofia in her sewing room he looks out the window toward the garden, and she is also "sentada no ângulo da janela" [seated at a corner of the window, 1: 760; 199]. Instead of looking at each other they look out the same window. This gives them a deeper perspective into each other's souls, while also underlining the limitations they face in trying to understand one another's inner sides.

An architectural feature, such as the window, gives shape to different forms of meditation, inquiry, and perspective. Numerous characters throughout Machado's fiction reflect when near a window, or when resting on a windowsill. For Sofia and Rubião, abandoning their thoughts is synonymous to pulling themselves away from the window's side. Sofia fantasizes about Carlos Maria and only stops daydreaming about him when she can finally "arrancar-se de todo à janela" [tear herself away from the window, 1: 705; 109]. It is also difficult for Rubião to stop his endless concocting and move away from windows: "Era perto de duas horas quando saiu da janela;" [It was close to two o'clock when he left the window, 1: 722; 137]. The fact that Sofia and Rubião seem to be the two characters that most contemplate by windows is yet another indirect form of communication between them. They attempt to reach inside themselves and one another by an introspective viewpoint that looks simultaneously in and out. The window ironically operates as the most important eye onto the world inside. Machado's spatial architecture is a two way street that gives and takes, and pushes and pulls from various directions.

The window recalls the role mirrors frequently play in Machado's fiction, another important interior fixture. They too facilitate reflection and transition while providing an alternative outlook on events. The short story "Uma senhora" even links the mirror to the window. Beyond acting as frames that fuse the natural world with the interior, windows, like mirrors, serve as spectacles that penetrate into the interior of the character, or what Machado calls one's "alma interior" [interior soul]:

> D. Camila estava ao espelho, a janela aberta, a chácara verde e sonora de cigarras e passarinhos. Ela sentia em si a harmonia que a ligava às cousas externas. Só a beleza intelectual é independente e superior. A beleza física é irmã da paisagem. D. Camila saboreava essa fraternidade íntima, secreta, um sentimento de identidade... Olhava para fora, olhava para o espelho." (2: 426)

> [D. Camila was looking into the mirror, the window was open, and the farm was green and full of the sounds of cicadas and birds. She felt inside herself the harmony that connected her to the external things. Only intellectual beauty is independent and superior. Physical beauty is a sister of the landscape. D. Camila savored this intimate, secretative fraternity, a sentiment of identity... She would look outside, and look to the mirror.]

This rich passage is full of important revelations about Machado's understanding of the interior world and his method of framing it in his fiction. D. Camila's experience in front of the mirror brings to mind *Quincas Borba*'s narrator when he claims that the "paisagem" [landscape] or view depends on one's perspective. Furthermore, the "sentimento de identidade" [sentiment of identity] recalls Machado's "instinto de nacionalidade" [instinct of nationality], which is also tied to interiority and to a dialectic of exterior and interior. While on the one hand D. Camila is looking outside and at herself, fusing her beauty and interiority with the natural or exterior world, she is also looking intensely both inside and outside in search of harmony, the same way Quincas Borba looks into the mirror and says: "Tudo o que está cá fora corresponde ao que sinto cá dentro" [Everything on the outside there corresponds to what I feel inside here, 1: 644; 10]. Machado's windows and mirrors function as points of inquiry and as a narrative view suggesting a desire for harmony between one's interior and exterior soul, which is also exactly what Machado proposes in his essay about one's instinct of nationality. Thus D. Camila's struggle and task is the same as the writer's. Once again we find Machado relying on the experience and figure of the bourgeois woman to give continuity to the narrative genre. Windows and mirrors ought to synchronize the inside and outside worlds, the physical and the psychological, yet this harmony is ultimately unattainable, and these objects and structures composing the interior space can only therefore function as mediums, and the harmony they successfully provide is a literary one.

Critics have paid a significant amount of attention to Machado's fascination with mirrors, a dominant leitmotif in Machado's fiction. He relies on their reflective and distorting qualities to highlight the interiority of his characters, and to ask questions about aesthetic creation and self-identity. Walter Benjamin is particularly interested in the mirror as a symbol for how the interior comes to dominate the exterior in the nineteenth century, and particularly how it represents illusion, since in rooms they merely reflect the outside world and in public places, as in the Paris arcades—Benjamin's larger concept of the domesticated public space—they draw the individual back inside. This illusionary creation, thus, turns a social and collective phenomenon into an individual one. Virginia Woolf in *A Room of One's Own* understands the significance of the mirror from a different perspective. Her possible explanation for what she calls the historic problem inherent in patriarchal societies is that men have traditionally sought humanity's much needed self-confidence by "thinking that other people are inferior."[24] Woolf claims that women have functioned as these inferior beings for men: "Women have served all these centuries as looking-glasses possessing the magic and delicious power of reflecting the figure of man at twice its natural size."[25] These mirrors are as she claims "essential to all violent and heroic action."[26] Woolf reflects on these ideas in her short story "The Lady in the Looking-Glass: A Reflection," and shows the interaction between the mirror and the interior space. In the story the mirror emulates the still and soundless reality surrounding Isabella, the protagonist, while at the same time revealing the emptiness filling her life and not apparent in the changing environment of her old country room. The role mirrors play in Machado's novel curiously both anticipates and confounds Benjamin's and Woolf's social readings and theories of interiority.

Machado's use of the mirror is first and foremost connected to the dynamics between his male and female characters. Palha and Sofia's highly complex and indisputably sadistic relationship is part of the novel's exploration of power and violence. Sofia is very much like Woolf's looking-glass, which reflects a distorted image of her husband so that he can suppose himself superior. Palha often frightens and hurts Sofia physically, and she acts on different occasions as her husband's mirror: "mirando-se no colo da mulher, e circulando depois os olhos pela sala, com uma expressão de posse e domínio" [looking at his wife's bosom, then casting his eyes about the room with a look of possession and domination, 1: 685; 76]. Palha sees his over-confident self reflected on his wife's body and in his room's décor. One evening after much dancing, Sofia lets her hair down and looks into the mirror when Palha alarms her from behind. She trembles and looks at him through the mirror. The reflection here epitomizes the violence that sustains the marital relations and exposes her fears while superimposing the husband

and wife in the same image. As we have seen Sofia's mind and heart move closer to Palha's as the novel progresses and further away from the emotions and thoughts that engage her initially. Alone in her boudoir trying on Rubião's birthday gift of a single diamond pendant, she stops in front of the mirror: "Comprazia-se na contemplação de si mesma" [She enjoyed contemplating herself]. After tightening her corset she "deixou espraiar-se o colo magnífico" [let her magnificent bosom spread out, 1: 738; 162]. Like her husband, Sofia now sees herself on her body. She becomes trapped inside her own room and mirror, and hence inside the reflection or illusion of herself. The mirror tells us about Palha's narcissism and violence but also about how Sofia approaches her husband's selfishness and moves increasingly away from her true self.

The connection between self-absorption, interiors, and reflection also frames the relationship between Maria Benedita and Carlos Maria. Maria Benedita is an imitation of her husband in that her self-annihilating devotion to him compares to his self-devotion. As we have seen, self-love is a dominant theme in the novel, and every character to one degree or another suffers from this sort of destructive egotism. Carlos Maria, who at one point we find reading a study on a famous Narcissus statuette, is the most ostentatiously conceited character in the novel. The narrative parodies his excessive vanity, but also portrays him as one of the darkest and most obscure male figures. He transforms his own self-obsession into a psychological violence that he directs toward his wife and others. Carlos Maria is from the outset of his name also Maria Benedita, the one who adores him. She only exists so far as she is a reflection of his self-adulation. Dona Fernanda, his cousin, informs him of Maria Benedita's unconditional worship of him, and Carlos Maria feels an immense pleasure in imagining this unknown devotee revering him trapped "no aposento, fechada a porta" [in a room, the door closed]. The bedroom that encloses the young woman particularly fascinates him, and he asks himself: "Em que aposento se fechava para rezar, para evocá-lo, chorá-lo e abençoá-lo?" [What room did she shut herself up in to pray, to evoke him, to weep for him, to bless him?, 1: 748; 178]. He stops insisting Dona Fernanda reveal the name, but wants her at least to tell him the room. When Rubião receives a surprise basket full of strawberries for lunch from Sofia, Carlos Maria claims that they "Cheiram a alcova de donzela" [smell of a maiden's chamber, 1: 664; 43]. His obsession with closed spaces, especially those that confine women, suggest he himself is a closeted individual. He loves to be in Dona Fernanda's company, and he claims that being in heaven must be like enjoying conversation in her peaceful and cool sitting-room. Once married, he fantasizes about hiding his wife's pregnancy, hoping to emulate the divine conception: "Viveria de boa mente os últimos tempos no interior de uma casa única, posta no alto de um morro, vedada ao mundo, donde a mulher baixasse um dia com o filho nos braços e a divindade nos olhos" [They would live the final moments with pleasure inside a solitary house on the top of a hill, shut off from the world, and the woman would go down from there one day with her child in her arms and divinity in her eyes, 1: 783; 235]. Despite all the religious undertones in his fantasies, these constant references to barred interiors actually point to a sadistic pleasurable desire on Carlos Maria's part to imprison his wife, and by association himself. Confining her love for him is ironically a form of self-confinement, and these conscious or subconscious wishes and actions reinforce the locking up of his own emotions and desires. His ultimate goal to make her "tôda nada" [all nothing] is thus self-detrimental (1: 750; 182). Machado deals in his fiction with what was the common fate of middle- and upper-class women in nineteenth-century patriarchal societies, which restricted them to enclosed spaces and limited social roles. He does this, however, not by engendering a space, but by revealing how interiors and domestic spaces mirror and open a window to intricate and violent ways of thinking and being in the world. With these disturbing psychological representations of both male and female characters, Machado analyzes and questions traditional gender roles. In the case of Sofia and Carlos Maria, love and self-love seem to metamorphose into violence. The mirror, window, and other inner features central to the composition of an interior act in unison to address the discordant, tense, and unjust relationships that determine the roles women are limited to in society. With a small number of architectural details, furnishings, and decorative objects, *Quincas Borba* develops a sophisticated narrative discourse of the interior as a dwelling place for both psychological and social complexities of the human spirit.

THE NARRATIVE LIFE OF EÇA'S FURNISHINGS

In *The Maias* countless decorative items, objects of art, and furnishings constitute the elaborately described interior spaces and the novel's semiotic universe. In Machado's work objects tend to have an independent existence, while in *The Maias* things are more often important within the context of the space and characters. Unlike in *Quincas Borba*, where a mirror, an uncomfortable chair, or a silver tray tell their own version of the events, the things and places as a whole in *The Maias* convey a collective story. If in *Quincas Borba* a reader is obliged to fill in the blanks left by the absence of details and things, *The Maias* on the other hand is so generous and prolific in depicting the décor that the reader is compelled to paint an image of the interior. Both novels require the reader to conceptualize the inner environment but in different ways: in *Quincas Borba* the reader is curious to know what makes up the world because the novel is strategically minimalist yet very generous with hints, and in *The Maias* the reader is equally inquisitive because the more information on the furnishings, spaces, and details he or she has, the greater the desire to picture the setting and question its meaning.

Eça's descriptive style harks back to Roland Barthes's question in "The Reality Effect" where he considers the significance of the apparently insignificant details in narrative. In Eça's writing, how things are described and their relation to other objects and characters proves to be more important than what furnishings and particulars are depicted. Description in Eça and lack of description in Machado ultimately function in a similar fashion, in that both turn into a discourse of things that points to important transitions and contradictions. *Quincas Borba* uses in-between places and symbolic objects that link different narrative lines as a critical technique of reflection by creating settings for encounters of contradictory elements, while in *The Maias* opposites concealed in the interiors arrange some of the more significant questions that the narrative asks. Eça's highly representative domestic settings hide subtle contrasts in their descriptive details. These fundamental spatial opposites mirror the characters' conflictive emotions and the plot's narrative tensions.

The spatial protagonist in the novel, Ramalhete, best exemplifies some of the important divergences that the novel sets up. Despite its fresh, green name and the joyful bouquet of flowers adorning its façade, Ramalhete is a large, somber house of sober walls with the "aspecto tristonho de residência eclesiástica" [gloomy appearance of an ecclesiastical residence], and the mansion's "gravidade clerical" [clerical gravity] makes it resemble a Jesuit college (5; 1). The religious nuances of the building in ruins link the decadent state of the nobility with that of the Church. The enthusiasm devoted to the remodeling of the sad and disintegrating house would seem to provide a new beginning for Carlos and Afonso, and one would also expect the redecorating to transform the sacred and somber qualities of the Lisbon mansion by making it more secular. Yet the effort to revive and modernize Ramalhete falls short of eradicating the melancholic and religious overtones characterizing the house. Despite the renovations, and the complementing of the old Benfica furnishings with new pieces that Carlos has collected on his travels, important forlorn details remain unaltered. The feudal benches out on the patio are as "solenes como coros de catedral" [solemn as the stalls from a cathedral choir]. The profuse padding in the antechamber muffles all noise and "todo o rumor de passos morria" [any sound of footsteps was instantly muffled]. The Moorish plates are also severe and somber and their whiteness "imaculada" [immaculate, 8; 4], while "antigos quadros devotos" [ancient devotional paintings] fill the hallway. The salon's velvet is "cor de musgo de Outono" [the colour of autumn moss] and the upholstery of the comfortable *fumoir* is a somber scarlet and black (9; 4). Afonso's study assimilates "uma velha câmara de prelado" [a prelate's chamber] with an old family heirloom, a Rubens representing "Cristo na cruz" [Christ on the cross, 9; 5]. The mournful and pious attributes of the house lie not only in these evident analogies, but also in the symbolic value of the recurrent number three. The countess, Afonso's mother-in-law, in Constable's depiction of her wears a tricorn hat, Carlos's sleeping chambers consist of three linked rooms, and three French windows connect the terrace to Afonso's study. Adjectives such as austere, severe, and solemn are plentiful. The modern grandiose décor and luxury do not erase the silence, sadness, and solemnity of the house. The melancholy is not a temporary state of being either, but a transformative form of existence, as the language used to describe the desolation would suggest. In the garden the cypress and the cedar tree are "envelhecendo juntos" [growing old together] like two sad friends, and there are "três pedregulhos" [three large boulders] creating a quaint niche and "melancolizando aquele fundo de quintal" [bringing a touch of melancholy to the far end of the otherwise sunny garden, 10; 5-6]. The use of progressive verbs points to a process of the ongoing sense of sorrow that Ramalhete reflects before and after the renovations.

Nonetheless, the narrator emphasizes the fact that the Maia mansion has been completely redone and explains that after the English architect is done with the redecorating "só restava a fachada tristonha" [all that remained of the old Ramalhete was the grim façada, 8; 4]. Thus Ramalhete, like the novel, should not be judged by its cover; instead one needs to look beyond the surface. The more subdued details of the newly renovated mansion make clear that the only constant in the eclectic décor is its inconsistency. Eça adapts a baroque rhetorical device to compose the interiors with contrasts, as in nearly every room of the house there are elements that contradict each other. The Gothic and dark-wood furniture collides with the strong and bright colors of the upholstery and wallpaper. The patio is now glowing with bright white and red marble but its benches are solemn. The copper and metallic reflexes disagree with the severe tones on the large Moorish plates in the antechamber. The velvet brocades are the color of moss in the rarely used reception room. In her portrait, the countess wears a "vestido escarlate" [scarlet riding habit] but the landscape background is "enevoada" [misty]. The cushioning of the music room furniture adorned with gold and "ramagens brilhantes" [gleaming sprigged silks] differs from the faded Gobelin tapestries on the wall of "tons cinzentos" [various shades of grey, 9; 4]. The contrasts are continuous and rarely obvious. Despite the "paz estudiosa" [studious peace] of Afonso's study, the Rubens paints a "revolto e rubro" [turbulent fiery] sunset (9; 5). Reflected on one of the Moorish plates is a curious girl shivering as she puts her little foot in water. This clearly contrasts with Afonso's audacity and religious love of water explained immediately after the house's description. Jacinto do Prado Coelho calls the differences between Eça's characters in *The Maias* a "jogo de contrastes" [game of contrasts] in his *Ao Contrário de Penélope* and explains that these opposites and paradoxes reflect Eça's larger preoccupation: "O pensamento implícito n'*Os Maias* é problemático, olha o verso e o reverso das coisas; a ironia queirosiana envolve a consciência de que todo o objecto de reflexão é, pelo menos, bifronte, susceptível de ser encarado de duas perspectivas válidas" [The implicit thinking in *The Maias* is problematic, it looks at the reverse of all things; Eça's irony involves the consciousness that all objects of reflection are, at least, two-faced, susceptible to being seen from two valid perspectives].[27] Through the descriptive details, the author creates a physical and emotional interior world that seems to reveal important tensions not only between the inhabitants and the house, but also already between the story that is being told and the discourse. Ramalhete characterizes Carlos and Afonso and their illusions, as it does the novel's own deceptive style and form.

This contest between opposites is an important narrative technique that Ramalhete reveals about Eça's representation of interiors. Another crucial element is how the narrative descriptions relieve words of their obvious meaning and impregnate them with other significations connecting them to different points of the story. The embroidery on Afonso's old armchair reproduces "as armas dos Maias no desmaio da trama de seda" or the "faded silk upholstery still bore the Maia coat of arms' (9; 5). Carlos Reis correctly notes that this sentence already alludes to "o desvanecimento de uma família" [the fading of a family].[28] But details matter within the conjunction of the whole, and this sentence is powerful as a totality and for its parts. The assonant rhyme of this poetic and prophetic line connects the "desmaio," in this case the hem, to its other meaning: fainting. Before and after the renovations there is a tendency throughout the house for elements to faint. The walls are covered in frescos on which the roses on the garlands and on the cheeks of the little cupids "já desmaiavam" [were already fading, 6; 1], and in the music room there are two "desmaiadas" [faded] Gobelin tapestries (9; 4). Furthermore, the coat of arms also relates to how the mansion gets its name. Ramalhete is named after the sunflower bouquet engraved on a panel of tiles on the façade of the house intended for the coat of arms never placed there. Despite the cheerful sunflower bouquet that replaces it, the absence of the coat of arms is present instead in the pervading fading and fainting sense so prevalent in the decoration. The absence of the coat of arms is also the absence of the Maias themselves [grandfather and grandson do not exactly make a family clan]. As Carlos Reis has already claimed, it is difficult to read *The Maias* "estritamente como um romance de família" [strictly as a family novel].[29] The "desmaiar" [fainting] becomes a motif for the house and for the family as the word further linguistically deconstructs the family's name (desmaia). "Trama" is also more than just the fabric; it is also the plot. The novel is then both a writing and an un-writing of the story of the Maias. This sentence is a way of figuring and prefiguring the future tragedy represented by the incestuous love affair. Hence it is no coincidence that the walls in

Toca's master suite are covered in tapestries "onde desmaiavam, na trama de lã, os amores de Vénus e Marte" [whose fading woolen threads depicted the loves of Venus and Mars, 433; 373]. This play on words and descriptive details highlights the significant way interiors write the narrative discourse by hiding in their textures, colors, and crevices their own reading of the events.

The absent heraldic symbol that arms and disarms the family also constructs and deconstructs the novel. *Maias* is Portuguese for a yellow broom in blossom. The family and the novel are also Ramalhete: both the house and the proxy bouquet of flowers. Earlier I suggested that the title of the novel might refer to the pre-Colombian Mayan peoples as an intricate commentary on colonialism. But the title could also be read literally as *flowers*; it would figure this way in the novel's evident language of flowers, and thus relate to Eça's careful naming technique. The author's irony, as Maria Leonor Carvalhão Buescu has already noted in her study of his semantics, establishes "um mundo às avessas ou antes, um *mundo* às avessas do *nome*" [a world of opposites or better yet, a *world* of opposites of the *name*].[30] It is not only the opposite of a name or the reversal of the symbol, but the act of replacing one thing with another that is most striking about the Maias-Ramalhete dialectic. Substituting the flowers for the coat of arms more importantly connects to Afonso's habit of replacing the hearth's fire during the spring and summer months with "braçadas de flores, como um altar doméstico" [armful of flowers, like a domestic altar, 11; 6]. The flowers replace life with death the same way Ramalhete [both mansion and bouquet] serve as symbols of themselves and of their opposites. They both celebrate and announce a new renovated life and the coming death and destruction of the Maia family. Ramalhete's interiors are thus marked by processes of transition and change. The use of progressive verbs, the semantic disruption created in some of the descriptions, and the repeated contrasts cause both continuities and discontinuities; they work to renew and to maintain the interior space the same. Most importantly, these details operate in content and in form, evoking the complexity that ties the family and the house to the narrative.

In all three novels the link between life and death is repeatedly found in the discourse developed within interior spaces. The interiors become a sort of limbo that connects beginnings and ends both of lives and fictions. Ramalhete acts as cradle and tomb for both Carlos and the novel. Carvalhão Buescu skillfully shows in "O regresso ao 'Ramalhete'" (The return to Ramalhete) how Carlos's final homecoming to the Lisbon residence represents a katabatic voyage.[31] The end of the novel narrates his and Ega's last journey through the abandoned family mansion. Buescu traces the mythical qualities and rituals that the two experience on this visit while showing how Carlos's last descent marks a final rupture and a "rompimento definitivo com o passado, marcado pela transgressão" [definitive break with the past marked by transgression].[32] The mansion's role as a catacomb becomes clear from the opening description. The repeated references to Ramalhete's walls and ceilings emphasize the mansion's sense of imprisonment and underpin its function as a burial place. Like Ramalhete, Carlos and Maria Eduarda's love-nest, Toca, which literally means "burrow", also serves to immerse characters under the earth. During the guided tour of the summer retreat, Carlos tells Maria Eduarda how happy it makes him having her "entre estes velhos muros" [between the four walls of that house, 431; 371]. While after meeting with Castro Gomes, Carlos goes to Olivais to confront Maria Eduarda with the truth of her identity, whom he now knows is Madame Mac Gren. Before entering the gate he walks along and very close to the garden wall. The narrator refers frequently to the "escuridão do muro" [darkness of the wall] and describes it as a black wall (494; 426). These walls not only point to Toca's burial qualities for Carlos, but also reinforce the symbolism of the color black, which as I previously argued announces the tragedy in the novel.

The Lisbon mansion, as other immovables or homes, serves this way as a link between history and modernity. Although being renovated by a modern English decorator, Ramalhete still houses the sense of history of two dominating institutions of Portuguese society: the nobility and the Church. While pointing to a new future, the house's renovated interiors also begin to allude to Carlos and the family's demise. Hence the house is a narrative link between the past and the future. This bond works formally within in the novel because, following the mansion's introduction, a flashback sums up the historical background of the former Maia generations, and the reader returns to the story's present by coming back to Ramalhete. The meditation on the connection between past and future—and life and death—in the novel is also taken up in Clarín's narrative, which focuses on the interior space as a place of transition between life and death. In both novels this transition is also the space where fiction and reality meet. Machado's characters are also often in between life and death. Ramalhete ultimately highlights both important transitions and contradictions that continue as the novel progresses. The enigmatic and ambiguous final scene of the novel, which points to both positive and negative elements, and both fatalistic and hopeful ideas, further reinforces Ramalhete's primary role as the novel itself, as a space of tensions and substitutions.

Besides Ramalhete and Toca, other homes also have the quality of burying characters. Referring to the family's Santa Olávia estate, Vilaça warns Afonso that Carlos "não quereria, depois de formado, ir sepultar-se nos penhascos do Douro" [would not want to bury himself among the steep hills of the Douro Valley once he had graduated, 7; 3]. As we have seen the interior space, or the immovables, are inseparable from its components, that is, its lavish furnishings. These movable things not only paralyze characters they submerge them as well. Throughout *The Maias* characters are predominantly found sitting or lounging on comfortable furniture. The novel is particularly overpopulated with couches, armchairs, divans, and sofas that immobilize and render characters powerless. One evening after supper Carlos sits in his armchair, but in Portuguese it is written that he is "enterrado numa poltrona," literally buried in his chair (377).[33] Ega is also repeatedly slumped on sofas and loungers and the narrator describes him as "enterrado no fundo do sofá" (417), or when he is relaxing on the divan at the Gouvarinhos' dinner party he is again "enterrado no divã" (388). In Craft's house, after being kicked out by Cohen from Raquel's birthday party, Ega is once more "enterrado no sofá" distressed and slouched on a dilapidated sofa (286). It is not only when he is defeated and feeling buried by his society that furniture has the power to render Ega immobilized. In the Vila Balzac Ega "enterrando-se de estalo numa poltrona," burying himself abruptly in an armchair, brings to a close his enthusiastic diatribe on interior decorating (149). When the countess drags Carlos, on the pretext that they will check up on her son, Charlie, into a hidden corner of her house, her husband the count and his guest, Sousa, stay behind, helpless, "enterrados num sofá" (401). These constant references do a lot more than just reinforce the "stagnant sameness" that John Gledson claims is vital to the meaning of *The Maias*.[34] These repeated images of characters like Ega, Rubião, or the guests of the Marchioness's yellow salon, lounging about on pillow-stuffed couches, reinforce the idea that dwelling replaces being with a new illusionary and fabricated existence. In other words, in the late nineteenth century finding oneself practically buried on a comfortable divan is a form of existence, not merely a metaphor, but a way of being.

The narrative repeatedly uses the words "móvel" [movable] and "imóvel" [immovable] as adjectives but rarely as nouns, despite the fact that there are countless "móveis" [furnishings] and "imóveis" [real estate] in the novel. The effects that homes and furniture produce on the characters draw on the tension between movement and stagnation. The movables both disable and incite characters to action and have conceptual, physical, and emotional consequences. During her exile in England, Pedro's mother Maria Eduarda spends "semanas imóvel sobre um canapé" [whole weeks reclining on a divan, 19; 14]. Already as a young boy, Eusebiozinho wastes "horas imóvel numa cadeira" [hours motionless in a chair, 69; 57]. Characters often find themselves trapped in a corner of a sofa or caught deep in an armchair and take refuge in these comfortable and passive situations; Dâmaso "atirou-se para o canto do sofá" [plumped himself down on the sofa, 379; 327] and Baptista sees Carlos "atirar-se para uma poltrona" [sink into his armchair, 453; 390]. When Carlos sets his mind to breaking up his affair with Gouvarinho, he finds it difficult nonetheless to "se arrancar aos confortos da sua poltrona" [tear himself away from the comforts of his armchair, 360; 312]. When they meet, Gouvarinho forces him to face his indifference, and all he can think about is how peaceful and contented he was just moments before at home prostrate on his couch. Furnishings render characters motionless reducing them to helpless beings and placing them in vulnerable positions. Characters are shrunk and diminished by the variety of lounging furnishings in the novel. Still, at important moments the characters desire the ease and assurance sofas provide and rely on them. Their consciousness has been reduced to the point where different armchairs are the last and only things left which provide individuals with a sense of protection.

It is thus not surprising to find that the characters' only possibility of defense and expression against their dreadful fates is to react aggressively against their sheltering furnishings: "De repente o Ega deu um murro no sofá, que rangeu lamentavelmente" [Ega gave the sofa a sudden thump, and the sofa uttered a mournful creak, 286; 247]. Dâmaso also takes his anger against Carlos by punching away at innocent couches in the Grémio. When Castro Gomes informs Carlos that Maria Eduarda is his kept woman, the protagonist grips the back of a chair with his hands "tão fortemente que quase lhe esgaçava o estofo" [so hard that he almost tore the fabric, 482; 416], and later when discussing the dreadful news with Ega, Carlos "Atirou uma punhada à mesa" [thumped the desk with his fist, 491; 424]. When Ega tells Vilaça that Maria Eduarda is part of the Maia family, the administrator resists and in his anger hits the table with his fist. When Carlos hears in despair and anger the dreadful news about Maria Eduarda from Ega toward the end of the novel he draws curtains shut with force and grabs chairs violently. On the one hand, furnishings seem to weaken characters and bring them closer to inaction and to death, while on the other hand, they are also clearly the last thing that remains for them to hold on to. This recalls once again Brooks's comment on Balzac's Coralie that "Lack of things is the immediate precursor of death."[35]

Throughout the novel furnishings sustain the characters by providing them comfort, refuge, and obscurity. But, once Ega discovers Maria Eduarda's true identity, some important encounters reveal how the furnishings are no longer stable enough to support the narrative events. The interior scenario and its furnishings begin to ridicule the characters and their situation. Although the climactic events uncover serious and tragic incidents, the furnishings and the enclosed spaces where these meetings take place provide a comic relief that reminds the reader of the important role space and its components play in the narrative as a whole. Toward the end of the novel, readers approach the climax of events and, at the same time, the peak of the significance of the language of furnishings and interiors in the narrative. Just as the characters are left with nothing but their rooms and furnishings, which define and break down their existence as characters, the novel too relies on its representation of interiors for the composition of these climactic closing events. The story of rooms and furnishings functions in the narrative as a meditation on the writing of the novel, a bunch of oak and dusty furniture ultimately represents the story within the story.

The first important scene of these final climactic moments is an encounter between Vilaça and Ega. They meet in Vilaça's office inside a special kind of interior space, a small side room "estreito como um corredor, com um canapé de palhinha, uma mesa onde os livros tinham pó, e um armário ao fundo" [as narrow as a corridor, furnished with a wicker sofa, a desk piled high with dusty books and, at the far end, a cupboard, 631; 549]. This room within a room not only encloses and restricts the actions and thoughts of the two characters, but the real protagonist of the scene, the fragile and brittle wicker sofa begins to overpower the two men. Inside this bolted room, Vilaça falls back onto the rattan chair and Ega also eventually sits down on the wicker sofa to tell Vilaça of Carlos's tragedy. Moments later Vilaça feeling defeated "recaiu no canapé" [fell back again on the sofa] and later he jumps so violently that the sofa bumps against the wall (633; 551). While the suffocating room restrains their actions and confines their options the same way the tragic news they discuss metaphorically kills them, the "canapé" surfaces as the main prop on the stage of the dramatic finish. Among all the great variety of sofas and chairs in the novel, this special seat is one of its more delicate pieces, which further strengthens the irony of the scene. This long chair is made of wicker, a craft highly cultivated in Portugal because of its overseas ties to India. The repeated use of the diminutive further reinforces the paradox. If the fragile and delicate chair attempts to bear the burden of the awful events on the one end, there is no repose on the other side either. Vilaça "foi bufando até ao fundo do cubículo, onde esbarrou com o armário" [strode furiously down to the end of the room, where he collided with the cupboard, 634; 552]. The two men are unable to escape this small rectangular space that reminds one of a coffin, and Vilaça feels crushed, hunched, and defeated. They stumble on all the objects that they commonly depend on for their sense of security. The furnishings literally strike the characters with the devastating realism of the events, as the narrative attempts to deal spatially with its own tragic plot development.

This is especially evident in the significant culminating moment when Carlos finally learns that Maria Eduarda is his half sister. As expected, the narrative centers the interior scene in Carlos's most intimate space. His sleeping quarters are carefully framed with long curtains from where the characters enter the stage periodically interrupting Carlos and Ega's conversation. The curtains indicate the decorator's illusionary touch that hides an apparently dividing line, in this case a door, but that ultimately fails in its function to conceal. When Afonso finally leaves the room with Ega's help "caiu o grande reposteiro, com as armas dos Maias" [The curtain fell in folds behind them, the curtain bearing the Maia coat of arms, 646; 562]. The secret that Carlos and Maria Eduarda are lovers is now known on both sides of the curtain, on stage and off, in fiction and reality. Carlos remains behind buried inside his own defeated consciousness represented by his bedroom. To express Carlos, Ega, and Afonso's anxiety and defeat, the narrative uses repeated images of the characters feeling suffocated, crushed, mute, squeezed, overwhelmed, and annihilated. But the novel also depends significantly on the account of the room and its furnishings. The characters repeatedly fall helplessly, heavily, and desperately onto the chairs in the room. Meanwhile Ega attempts again to escape the situation by hiding in chairs, he moves to a corner of the sofa, shuns making eye contact with Carlos, focusing instead on a rug on the floor or on a decorative object. When Carlos confronts his grandfather with the news, Afonso falls heavily in an armchair by the curtain-covered doors. To dissent is to literally stand up and find release from the furnishings. Carlos's rebellious attitude toward the tragic news is found in his ability to free himself from a sitting position and to revolt against his own room and its contents. He paces about the room with such fury "que abalava o soalho" [that shook the floorboards] and rattled the crystal glasses in the console (646; 563). Ultimately, his attempted uprising against the fittings and fixtures of his room fails, as he finally succumbs with a weary sigh to the comfort of his armchair. This emphasis on the furnishings and the space suggest that the room and its components force Carlos to accept the reality of fatal facts. The narrative of interiors seems to win control over the novelistic account. If earlier, Carlos and Ega attempt to write and invent themselves through interior decorating, toward the end of the novel, the interior concludes the writing of their tragic story for them.

This is the peak of all the tragic-comical incidents in the novel, because despite the fact that this is the most somber moment in the novel; the detail of Vilaça's lost hat turns the tragedy into farce. Óscar Lopes explains that although Eça reproduces formal aspects of classic tragedy, "Os próprios momentos críticos têm sempre um pormenor ridículo que não nos deixa afundar no *pathos* total" [the critical moments are always accompanied with a ridiculous detail that does not allow these moments to sink in total pathos].[36] In this scene, apparently the only thing that the curtains successfully do conceal is the administrator's missing hat. Vilaça's desperate search for his hat obliges him and Baptista to return and interrupt the gravity of the moment between Ega and Carlos. This symbolic loss forces all the characters to scrutinize Carlos's interiors in search for something that is not there. It requires a more profound investigation of the protagonist's bedrooms and private space. Despite his anger, Carlos begins to search for the hat and "Ega procurou também, por trás do sofá, no vão da janela. Carlos, desesperado, para findar, foi ver entre os cortinados da cama. E Vilaça, escarlate, aflito, esquadrinhava até a alcova do banho" [Ega, too, joined in the search, first, behind the sofa, then, in the bay of the window. Carlos, in despair, and in an attempt to bring the matter to a close, went and looked behind the curtains round his bed. Vilaça, scarlet-faced and anxious, even checked the bathroom, 642; 559]. As the characters, the readers ought also to look closely behind and under the curtains, the chairs, and the tables and evermore into the private and sensual world of the characters for answers. However, Carlos looks for the wrong thing in the right place when he tries to find the hat in his bed. The displacement of the object in this scene nevertheless reinforces the centering of the place. By focusing in on Carlos's bed and bathroom, the discourse of the novel centers spatially on the crucial suppressed sexual and sensual account so important for the story.

The narrative does not provide an explanation for the complexity of emotions and events, but with these scrutinized details draws important connections. The aperture of the novel and the sense of tragedy hidden in the hems and textures of Ramalhete's décor resurfaces in the end by the repeated references to the family coat of arms embroidered on Carlos's curtains, bringing to mind the fainting coat of arms on Afonso's armchair and its absence on the house's façade. At the same time, the rain outside progressively worsens, attacks the room's windows, as it did on the night of Pedro's suicide, and brings inside the room the forlorn view of the two epic cedar and cypress trees. If in the opening pages these were "envelhecendo juntos como dois amigos tristes" [growing old together like two sad friends, 10; 5] it is now the two sad friends, Ega and Carlos, who sulk in the melancholy and silence and the room itself "ia entristecendo" [was growing sad, 647; 563]. The narrative technique focuses on the interior space as it stitches one element in the story to another, bringing beginnings and ends, comedy and tragedy, and the outside and the inside together. The interior's narrative discourse functions as an extension of Carlos's emotions, and also shows that other individuals enter and influence his sense of despair. More importantly, however, is the way in which the space and the furnishings take control of the narrative account; both the comic and tragic stories rely on the depiction of the interior space.

This discourse is evident not only within a specific interior, but different private spaces maintain a subtle dialogue with each other throughout the novel as well. As we will see later, continuities and disruptions between different domestic settings are especially significant in *La Regenta*, but important connections surface in the details of the décor, the layout of the furnishings, and in the characters' attitudes toward their inner surroundings in *The Maias* too. The lovers' country home, as Carlos Reis and other critics have noted, is full of significant and abundant "objectos premonitórios da desgraça" [premonitory objects of the misfortune].[37] The fading tapestries of the bedroom suite depict, as noted earlier, the lovers Venus and Mars, creating a link between Toca and the Ramalhete. Maria Eduarda's bedroom in the Toca, like the Lisbon mansion, contains religious overtones; it is compared to a "tabernáculo profanado" [profaned temple] and separating the bedroom from the adjoining sitting-room is an arched doorway typical of a chapel. The room's excessive yellows, which strongly disturb Maria Eduarda, further remind us of "maias" a broom in blossom of yellow flowers. Perhaps the most curious detail of the décor that links the house to the tragedy are the two "negras figuras de núbios, com os olhos rutilantes de cristal" [black Nubian figures with their glittering glass eyes] flanking the famous carved oak fire-place in the dining-room (432; 372). They stand as reminders of the objectifi-cation of the two young Africans that intrigue Carlos at the theater and accompany Maria Eduarda and Castro Gomes to Lisbon. The correlations between Ramalhete, Toca, and the conclusion of the novel reinforce how interiors are involved in the development and thematic concern of the narra-tive to connect the historical context with the personal tragedy.

The renovation of interior spaces and plans of redecorating also associate one domestic realm with another. Maria Eduarda's bedroom in Toca is lined from top to bottom in "um brocado amarelo, cor de botão-de-oiro" [mari-gold-yellow brocade, 434; 374]. Carlos fantasizes about creating a *boudoir* with similar materials. This boudoir or small room, which Carlos wishes to remodel, is where the two lovers share a sort of last supper during Maria Eduarda's visit to Ramalhete: "A mesa fora posta numa saleta que Carlos quisera, em tempo, revestir de colchas de cetim cor de pérola e botão-de-oiro. Mas não estava ainda arranjada; as paredes conservavam o seu papel verde-escuro" [The table had been set in the small room which Carlos had once wanted to hang with pearl and marigold-yellow satins, 470; 405]. Toca's bedroom seems to unconsciously inspire Carlos who will finally realize his imagined plan if albeit on a displaced location. Carlos redecorates the Toca's Japanese pavilion: "Em lugar das esteiras de palha, Carlos revestira-o com as suas formosas colchas da Índia, cor de palha e cor de pérola" [Carlos had replaced the straw mats with his own beautiful yellow and pearl-white Indian bedspreads, 528; 457]. These soft and silky yellow bedspreads have been slowing making their way through the novel and ultimately onto the walls of Carlos's thoughts, emotions, and spaces. The unconscious desire on his part to cover up and protect his love with Maria Eduarda under this illusionary motif parallels the narrative continuity of interior details that hide the tragedy or provide a substitute for what is absent. The content of rooms and the communication that takes place between them is necessary for the reading of interiors in the novel.

Immovables and movables have self-reflective and paradoxical functions in Eça's fiction: they are both tied to action and representation, and they are both symbols and events. The author links the thing or the name to itself and its opposite. In other words, the paradox seems to be paradox itself. The Gouvarinho dinner party provides an excellent example of how Eça's tech-nique focuses not only on communicating but also on experiencing irony. Count Gouvarinho spends the entire evening trying to recall a brilliant but particularly difficult to sustain paradox he heard from the minister Barros. His failure to remember Barros's paradox is not only ironic and humorous but itself a paradox. The inconsistency of not remembering the paradox is reinforced by the dinner's main topic of discussion: slavery and African servants. Slavery then is the subconscious paradox that Portuguese society would seem to prefer to forget or ignore. It is the experience of paradox and not its content that is at the core of Eça's narrative project. The conflictive details that fill the interiors of the novel function to communicate how personal experience is intertwined on different levels with a variety of historical and social contradictions.

The divan serves as a perfect example of an iconic and paradoxical component of Eça's wider interior narrative conception. *The Maias* is full of comfortable furnishings for sitting and lounging, as noted earlier, but divans play an especially important role. The central furniture piece of both Carlos's medical office and laboratory is a divan. In the lab the "divã de crina" [ample horse-hair sofa] is intended for "repouso depois das grandes descobertas" [rest after making some great discovery, 128; 109], while the divan in the consulting room is the center of attention, a worthy item of furniture, "vasto, voluptuoso, fofo" [vast, voluptuous, and soft, 99; 84]. Both the Marquis and Ega believe it is more appropriately made for love. It is already ironical to have divans for the purpose of rest and lovemaking in areas of work, but further satirical when they do not function even for these purposes. These furnishings are in fact quite unnecessary considering that the only ailments the characters suffer from are too much relaxation and too much lovemaking. These two divans serve to prefigure the more important sofa located inside the Japanese gazebo in Olivais, which seems to confound different purposes and succeed in accomplishing what the first two fail at, both in their apparent and real functions. The garden refuge is where Carlos can finally realize his decorative ventures, which proved fruitless in both the places of work he created for himself. Not only does the divan here actually serve its purpose but also the infamous pearl yellow satin that has been on his mind throughout the narrative finally finds a home in the gazebo's walls. Furthermore, the *quiosque* is architecturally the opposite of an interior patio. Instead of a garden within a home, the gazebo provides a home within a garden. As an interior the pavilion is by its very nature contradictory. Maria calls this interior within an exterior space her *pensadoiro* [thinking room, 455; 392]. The shelter is designated as a place for both meditation and the couple's lovemaking. This is where they spend their intimate moments together, but also where Carlos resumes writing on his medical articles. Just as Ega's bed monopolizes Vila Balzac, the gazebo, decorated predominantly in eastern motifs, serves mainly to house its divan: "e todo o ligeiro quiosque parecia ter sido armado só com o fim de abrigar um divã baixo e fofo, de uma languidez de serralho, profundo para todos os sonhos, amplo para todas as preguiças" [and the pavilion seemed to have been constructed solely in order to house a low, soft divan, more suited to the languors of a seraglio—deep enough to accommodate any amount of dreaming and broad enough for every kind of idleness, 455; 392]. The reiteration of "todo," "todos," "todas" further emphasizes the fact that this divan plays the role of all the divans in the novel. Furthermore, it is here that Maria confesses her life story to Carlos. Lastly, while no great discoveries ever take place in the lab that would justify the need for a restful divan, Carlos and Maria surrounded by eastern motifs seem to be recuperating in their love nest from Portugal's centuries long, laborious, sea-faring voyages to the East. The divan and the gazebo is, as Ramalhete, a narrative correlation that connects time periods and hidden criticisms; it is a place where past and present meet and where different details concerning interior décor confound. The plot's progress and its different hidden historical and social narrative levels depend on certain continuities and ruptures between interiors, furnishings, and characters.

The excessive attention that the novel places on the divan also proves that Eça was sensitive to the more recent developments taking place in interior design at the end of the century. The divan's popularity grows and evolves at this time because of the nineteenth century's combined fascination with comfort and Eastern motifs; the word *divan* comes from its Turkish original, defining a low couch usually without armrests or back. Another example that shows Eça's concern with the modernity of spaces emerges in the role that windows, or architectural openings, play in the story. Edith Wharton's turn-of-the-century earlier-quoted treatise on interior decorating, *The Decoration of Houses*, champions a return to the window's classical architectural functions and a renewed appreciation for its own decorative value. The novel heeds Wharton's advice even before she gives it. In the novel a window is crucial for bringing in light, heat, and life into a room, while reflecting its inhabitants' modern sensibilities. Windows evidently bring characters closer to a fuller, freer, more modern lifestyle, and they tend to have a political affiliation, since they are preferred by the more liberal-minded figures in the novel. Large windows leading to the natural world outside characterize Ramalhete and Afonso suggests to Vilaça at the beginning of the novel that all the mansion needs is fresh air and sunlight. It would suffice to "abrir de par em par as janelas e deixar entrar o sol" [fling wide the windows and let in the sun, 7; 3]. Afonso's friends all come over to dine at Ramalhete to celebrate the old man's birthday and in his study "as janelas se conservavam abertas" [the windows stood open, 438; 377], and he very often sits in his study "com as três janelas do escritório abertas" [with the three windows in the study standing open, 186; 161]. He maintains this habit in the city and in the countryside, so that when Vilaça senior arrives at the summer estate in Santa Olávia the "três portas envidraçadas estavam abertas para o terraço" [the French windows stood open, 53; 44]. Carlos inherits his grandfather's sensibilities and when he arrives at Olivais the day he is to receive Maria Eduarda for the first time, the mere act of opening the windows brings him pleasure. Exhausted from their historical tour of Toca's decorative arts and grave furnishings, the couple sits by an open window on a "divã baixo e largo" [long, low divan] covered with cushions and this act is compared to "um fofo recanto de conforto moderno" [a snug corner of modern comfort, 437; 376]. Often characters stand and gather by open windows, as when after lunch Maria Eduarda and Carlos are seated together and the "duas janelas estavam abertas" [two windows stood open, 503; 435]. The three surviving Maias in the story are the figures most receptive to the architectural details that create interiors that ultimately reproduce what was considered at that time a modern quality of life.

Characters with insular and dispirited minds and hearts hide behind closed windows. Papa Monforte's rented home in Lisbon stands in opposition to Afonso's environment. In the Ramalhete wide-open windows and balconies allow nature and the external world to penetrate the private realm. Referring to Monforte's house, the narrator explains that "nunca naquela casa se abria uma janela" [no window ever opened, 24; 18]. At the same time, intolerant ideals and destructive events also force characters and houses to close their windows. After his son's death, Afonso locks himself up in his library with the curtains drawn closing out the "lindo sol de Inverno" [lovely winter sunshine, 52; 43], the same way the Benfica palace is shut up when conservative persecution convinces Afonso to flee with his liberal ideas to England. From that morning on, "as janelas do palacete conservaram-se cerradas" [the windows of the house remained closed, 16; 10]. Besides pointing to a character's genuineness or a period's political openness, the window presents a long horizon, for it unfolds to the future and the past, bringing both hope and despair. After receiving Maria Eduarda's letter requesting he pay them a medical visit, Carlos runs to his private rooms and sits by a windowsill filled with expectation. At the same time, the window and balcony helped Pedro greet death as he contemplated his suicide by its side, and similarly Afonso's limited view of the river Tagus with its traffic and tranquility combines in the same scene both anticipation and hopelessness.

The descriptions of the outside world in *The Maias* make their way inside the interior settings. This is not merely related to the obsession during the nineteenth century with containing, domesticating, and bringing the natural world indoors. The tension between the civilized and natural worlds in Eça, like Machado's own conflict between inner self and society, governs the Portuguese author's reflections on art and being. Throughout his writing, Eça struggles to find a synthesis between the natural and civilized worlds. According to João Camilo dos Santos, Eça probably never convincingly resolved the conflict between the city and the mountains, a polemic that is fully developed in his late novel by the same name. Instead he repeatedly emphasized the natural world in his fiction in order to remind readers and characters of the importance of not losing sight of nature.[38] Yet as the natural world surfaces on tapestries, upholstery, rugs, textiles, and other fabrics, interior qualities help Eça describe and furnish the public and natural settings in the novel as well. With the exception of the occasional wind and rainstorm, the exterior world is often stagnant and mute. A scene of a serene river seen through two open windows introduces Ega's dinner party at the Hotel Central. This landscape view recalls the interior of a room, small clouds are "tocadas de cor-de-rosa" [pink-tinged] and the fields and distant hills begin to disappear beneath "vapor aveludado, do tom de violeta" [velvety, violet mist, 157; 134]. When Carlos and Dâmaso relax on Ramalhete's terrace under an awning on vast Indian bamboo chairs, the spring breeze "aveludava o ar" [turned the air to velvet, 187; 162]. On this quiet spring Sunday, the garden is green and lush and full of color and the same adjectives that are used to describe its beauty and coziness are those used to characterize the house's luxurious interiors. Flowers, skies, rivers, fields, and clouds have textures, tones, and colors just as furnishings, upholsteries, carpets, and wallpaper patterns might have. Carlos looks out the window to see a heavy sky "que pesava como se fosse feito de algodão" [like grubby cotton wool, 252; 218]. Alencar compares Sintra's landscape to a sublime and marvelous painting whose scattered yellow flowers in the foreground are compared to buttons. The dark and light greens of the farmland remind Cruges, who is likewise fascinated by Sintra's natural beauty, of "um pano feito de remendos assim que ele tinha na mesa do seu quarto" [the patchwork cloth covering his desk in his bedroom at home, 239; 206]. Roads are like white ribbons and the natural world evokes the stillness and humble comfort of domestic retreats. At the same time, the tranquility of the exterior world can invade the interiors as well. Carlos laments not being able to receive women in Ramalhete and claims that soon "vinha a nascer a erva pelos tapetes" [grass would begin to grow up through the carpets, 208; 181]. More than the author's critique of the increasing indistinctness between what is natural and artificial, the interior brings together different worlds in its ability to decorate and disguise. The art of interior fabrication is applied to all of reality, making room for a literary and philosophical reflection over how to live in the modern world. In Eça, ideas and emotions, like the "silêncio estofado," which translates literally to the upholstered silence, of the Olivais salon, are crafted, designed, and redecorated (501). The language of interiors that overpowers the characters is ironically the same that empowers the author and gives force to the narrative.

THE DRAMATIC EFFECT OF CLARÍN'S INTERIOR ARCHITECTURE

In *La Regenta* certain architectural details figure in the novel's symbolic universe and contribute to the author's narrative technique. One of the more striking features of the novel is the connection between the various interiors of Vetustan homes and different public meeting places. The similarities among the diverse interiors corroborate Elizabeth Doremus Sánchez's argument that Clarín's novel is an excellent example of Joseph Frank's spatial form, since points of continuity and rupture create meaning in the story line through the narrative representation of space.[39] Sánchez claims that Alas achieves this spatial effect largely through techniques of characterization, further arguing that the spatial form is evidence of Clarín's modernity and ultimately serves as an allegory for his relativistic worldview. Clarín's system of character relationships contributes to the themes of "social interdependence"[40] and "organic interconnectedness"[41] to use Sánchez's words, but characterization is not the only narrative strategy the author employs to explore how individual conscience is tied to Vetusta's social reality. Like Machado and Eça, Alas tells a story with his settings, decorative details, and furnishings. *La Regenta*'s interior spaces establish certain patterns that connect to the diverse discursive levels of the novel.

Lack of light is a particularly widespread quality of Alas's typically hazy, narrow, silent, and dark interior places, leaving characters both metaphorically and literally in the dark. One can barely see Fermín's drawing-room with its green curtains and chairs because "estaba poco menos que a oscuras" [being kept in near darkness, was only half visible, 1: 316; 219]. The casino's game room "permanecía en tinieblas" [never saw the light of day, 1: 198; 124] while its library or reading-room is also left "casi en tinieblas" [in almost complete darkness, 1: 206; 129], and the Marchioness's yellow salon remained "en una discreta oscuridad" [in discreet darkness, 1: 245; 162]. The tall Mesía, the only one that can reach the lamp in Doña Rufina's drawing-room, decides for himself when to turn it on and off, and very appropriately the climactic evening his adulterous affair with Ana begins in the yellow salon, the lights are slowly turned off. Many different atmospheres are excessively shady and silent making it difficult for characters and readers to see clearly, distinguish, and identify the dishonesty and defilement that takes place inside these places. The narrator seems to be disturbed by what these interiors conceal and prefers to subdue and keep them a little murky, and he is not alone in feeling insulted by too much light. When everyone goes to see Calderón's *Life is a Dream*, Ana chooses to stay home alone and favors the moonlight, since in her dining-room the lamp hanging over the table "La ofendía" [offended her, 1: 298; 206]. The contrast between light and darkness is connected to the representation of interior spaces and functions to blur the boundaries between interior and exterior, good and evil, and fiction and reality.

Thus generously lit interior spaces commonly reveal unpleasant incidents, as Fermín learns all too well when he stands outside the Vegallanas's palace in hopes of catching a glimpse of Ana and instead experiences a sort of Platonic crisis. The antithesis between light and shadow troubles the distressed Fermín repeatedly throughout this evening. Outside Páez's front gate, the gaslight "le hizo ver su sombra de cura dibujada fantásticamente" [cast his shadow, the grotesque shadow of a priest] and the fact that the only light he could see when he walks by the Quintanar's house is "la del portal" [the one in the porch] brings him to the brightly lit Vegallana mansion (1: 438; 324). While most interiors are characterized by darkness, the light in the Marquis's salons streams out of its wide-open balconies cutting through the darkness of the streets. This light creates shadows on the wall of the house across the street, which De Pas observes while standing in front of the boudoir windows. Opposite the salon windows "las sombras de la pared eran más pequeñas, pero muchas y confusas; y se movían y mezclaban hasta marear al canónigo" [the shadows on the wall were smaller, but numerous and indistinct, thronging together and making his head swim, 1: 438; 324]. The confusing shadows on the wall suggest Plato's world of sense experience, and hence the light and the interior space from where it shines ought to serve as a source of truth. But this is short-lived and darkness quickly returns innundating the bedroom of the Marchioness's dead daughter, appropriately named Emma. The darkness is compared to a vacuum and stifles and suffocates Fermín's rational reflections, and again the murky interior becomes the site of the unknown and the indefinite. Theatrical metaphors and dramatic effects like this one, which are always associated with interior spaces, abound in *La Regenta*. The interplay between light and darkness is just one technique that the narrative uses to convert the interior into a metaphoric stage. The sun, the moon, and various gaslights often function as spotlights that draw attention to recognitions characters would prefer to hide or to shameful performances in the act of life.

The above scene's complex dialogue between light and darkness, and truth and impression, confuse the reader and Fermín, who looks up at the balcony from below as onto a stage. The kiss he hears above, for example, is compared to Rosina's "en el primer acto del *Barbero*" [in the first act of *The Barber of Seville*, 1: 439; 325]. Fermín panics when he sees the figure of a woman being pressed up against the iron railing, but is ultimately relieved upon seeing that it is Obdulia and not Ana. If in *The Maias* there is an excess of divans and its derivatives, and *Quincas Borba* is full of emblematic mirrors, *La Regenta* is obsessed with balconies. In the case of the balcony to Emma's bedroom the theatrical performance takes place inside, while on other occasions the balcony is like the opera box sheltering the privileged audience while it watches the world perform from above, recalling Walter Benjamin's claim that the individual's living room is "a box in the theater of the world."[42] Part of Vetusta's curiosity and desire to penetrate the intimacy of others is characterized, among other things, in the peeping through key-holes and in the bending over balconies. Visitación's past affair with Álvaro is infamous for the fact that she had apparently jumped from a balcony to meet her lover. She is not the only one who abandons herself in this way; even Fermín imitates Visitación when he spies on Barinaga. The canon "abrió entonces su balcón de par en par y tendió el cuerpo sobre la barandilla, hacia la casa de Barinaga, pretendiendo oír algo" [opened his balcony windows wide and leaned over the handrail towards Barinaga's house, listening, 1: 465; 347]. As Machado creates thresholds with his spatial constructions, Alas too turns the balcony into an indefinite place where it is not always clear on which side truth or the wrong lies, or which part represents the fiction and which the reality. Labanyi argues that the balcony is one of the "ambiguous zones where city and country coincide," indicating the desired and feared fusion of the natural and the social.[43] Sill, it is not the act of adultery, and hence the adulteration of society, alone that is symbolized in this crucial architectural feature. What is most challenging and striking about the balcony is the physical action of the characters and the possible experience of falling, jumping, and squeezing over the balcony. As with Teresa's, Fermín's, and Ana's important body language inside their specific spaces, the corporeal feats that take place in this in-between place are part of the architectural narrative that Alas develops.

The balcony functions in conjunction with what is being performed inside and outside the spaces. Emma's bedchamber, for example, appears to be exclusively available for shameful acts and exploits. Even if the Vegallanas' daughter is dead she nevertheless plays an important role in the novel because her private space is still used whenever necessary, often as a powder-room for the ladies to tidy their clothes and hair. The dead child's bedroom acts then as a backstage area, or a dressing room, where characters can prepare, continue, and reenact their farce. Coincidently Visita keeps in her own house an extra room, separated from the sitting-room by green taffeta curtains, which she uses as a "vestuario de los actores y actrizes de charadas" [dressing-room for the actors and actresses of charades, 1: 252; 167]. Rooms function repeatedly throughout the novel as backstage areas tying interiors to the larger web of the novel's dramatic constructions. Earlier on in the novel, Visitación and Mesía talk on Emma's balcony with their backs towards the interior in order to give Paco and the widow an opportunity to engage in erotic play in the bedroom. By not turning around, Mesía and Visitación protect what takes place inside, and when at this very moment Ana and Petra walk by the Vegallana house, the characters urge her to come inside, or in other words try to entice her to join them in their adulterated and theatrical version of life. Like many of *La Regenta*'s interiors, Emma's room protects the characters' indolent pastimes. This bedroom is particularly emblematic, however, because of the fact that the little girl is dead, and because is it very clearly associated with performance and illusion. In this scene, for example, the setting sun's rays shine into the room, once again like a theatrical light, illuminating the feet of Emma's bed, and "envolvía en una aureola a aquella pareja de aturdidos" [haloing the two scapegraces, 1: 260; 175]. The narrator uses a religious image to emphasize the couple's profanation of little Emma's memory, while at the same time satirizing his own narrative technique of connecting the private realm with memory and with death. As we saw previously Ana's bedroom allows her to relive and invent her childhood while here Obdulia and Paco can also savor their memories. The irony is taken one step further to the level of literary influence because of the clear reference to Flaubert's infamous heroine. In this way equating the characters' adulteration of the bedroom with the author's own revision of the model French novel. Like Machado's and Eça's writing, Clarín's narrative also develops an important meta-literary link between rooms and fiction.

The attempt to lure Ana inside is reversed on All Saints Day when Álvaro gallops on his horse by the Ozores palace and finds the Regenta out on the balcony. In one of her typical depressed moods and disgusted with life, Ana initially places her anguish on external phenomena and carefully examines all the objects on the lunch table interpreting them as ruins of the world. Later she tries to escape these repugnant thoughts by going out to the balcony. As Winfried Menninghaus explains disgust is a mechanism that guards physical integrity by drawing and maintaining the distinction between exterior and interior.[44] Like Machado's Sofia, Ana struggles to preserve this division, first by focusing on the objects on top of the table and subsequently by making her way outside. But the balcony's ambiguous and versatile functions throughout the novel reveal instead that no clear boundary can be constructed between interiors and exteriors of either social or psychological territories. Like Machado's doorsteps and windowsills, Alas's balconies become thresholds that take characters from one level of knowledge or emotional state to another. In escaping herself she goes outside to see Vetusta's citizens on their way to the cemetery, which once again brings her closer to her unconscious thoughts of death. On this occasion Mesía makes an effort to get closer to the balcony by getting as close as he could to her balcony, standing in his stirrups, craning his neck and speaking in a quiet voice forcing Ana thus to "inclinarse sobre la barandilla" [lean over the handrail] in order to hear him (1: 481; 361). Álvaro now strives to draw Ana down from her balcony, and, as Visitación, Fermín and others before her, Ana strains her body over the balcony in order to get closer to different desires and fears. The parade of death and the human stupidity and tedium terrifying her moments earlier are replaced with Mesía's performance of beauty and pleasure. Again a spotlight, a "rayo de sol" [ray of sunlight], shines on the tall horseman as he speaks to her (1: 482; 363). Don Víctor joins Mesía on stage as he arrives on the scene announcing the evening's performance of Zorilla's *Don Juan*, and the narrative takes Ana directly from the balcony of her house to "el palco de los Vegallana" [the Vegallanas' box] in Vetusta's real theater (1: 485; 265).

Hence the balcony is a place where characters act and watch others perform. Much more than representing the dissolution resulting from the impossibility of separating the natural from the social, it shows different characters and the narrator struggling between reality and fiction, between prose and poetry; and for Ana it also stages the conflict between life and death. During Mesía's climactic declaration of love in the Vivero, the threshold functions once again in conjunction with a typical narrow and dark Vetustan interior. This scene brings together many of the recurring images in the narrative that continuously evoke the interior and the discourse between inside and outside as both a metaphysical and aesthetic problem. When Mesía declares his love to Ana in the Vivero "estaban solos apoyados en el antepecho de la galería del primer piso, en una esquina de aquel corredor de cristales que daba vuelta a toda la casa" [Ana and Álvaro were alone, leaning on the handrail in a corner of the glassed gallery which went around the first floor of the house, 1: 807; 632]. The lovers are carefully placed in this enfolded and emblematic location. They are caught between a surprising downpour and storm and the "estrecha galería" [narrow corridor] in whose darkness the others play their childish games (1: 808; 632). After listening to Mesía's words, Ana joins the group inside and later retires to her room, which has a window opening up to the gallery, and at whose sill she and Víctor, very close to their beds, talk for another hour by moonlight with Paco and Mesía. This opening onto the gallery functions as a type of balcony within a balcony, just as many interiors are contained inside other enclosed spaces. Alas, like Machado and Eça, uses interiors and rooms within rooms as a rhetorical equivalent of the framed narrative. Inside with Ana, Víctor is as happy as the night: "Ya todo era silencio en la casa, todos dormían, y sólo en aquel rincón de la galería, junto a aquella ventana abierta había el ruido suave de un cuchicheo" [All was still in the house, everyone else was asleep, and only in that corner of the gallery, by the open window, was there a soft sound of whispering voices]. She is once again reclined with her elbows on the handrail and Mesía casts sidelong glances "con envidia y codicia al interior de la alcoba" [envious and covetous, into the bedroom, 1: 815; 639]. As the narrative advances toward the fulfillment of the adultery, then, Ana begins to give in to her passion, and her physical actions evermore resemble those of the others. She finds herself on one of Alas's obscure corners of the world where the actions of both bodies and minds are crucial for the reading and interpreting of reality and its performance. The interior architecture conveys the sense of being on the brink of a significant change in her life, while also giving form to the multiple interiorities that influence her actions and emotions.

This spatial configuration and interplay between inside and outside as it relates to the development of Ana's attraction to Mesía is prefigured in the first part of the novel at the Vegallana luncheon. As the same juvenile group of adults runs around searching every nook and cranny of the inner rooms of the house and through hallways and up and down staircases, Ana and Mesía stand talking by "una ventana del comedor que daba al patio" [a dining-room window which overlooked the courtyard, 1: 390; 281]. When the couple meets this first time Álvaro is the one who lets his hands rest on the windowsill while Ana observes him from the corner of her eye and looks out at the flagstones in the courtyard. Fermín arrives and sees the couple by the window in a corner of the dining-room and is immediately uncomfortable and jealous. The window seems to look out onto their future adultery, which the canon apparently understands spatially because as the narrator explains "su imaginación estaba fuera" [his imagination was out in the courtyard, 1: 392; 282]. But soon it is Ana and Fermín who speak near a balcony and Don Álvaro who becomes suspicious and bitter. The lunch at the house of the Vegallanas and Álvaro's declaration of love at the Vivero prepare the consummation of their affair. Despite the fact that the affair begins, just as Mesía planned, in Doña Rufina's salons, it is on the balcony left ajar that he finds her one evening and which serves as the emblematic meeting place of the lovers. This architectural figure is a type of turning point, a threshold that the narrative uses to frame the development of the story line, and a place that both imprisons and impels Ana.

The balcony window ties to the larger narrative discourse and plot development. Like interiors in the novel, it is the site of important acts involving both mind and body. The account it tells us is the story of adultery, but Ana's narrative of betrayal is a complex one that is continually framed in paradoxes. Thus the balcony reveals important contradictions and uncertainties. If falling over its ledge suggests seduction and desire so does turning inside and coming away from it. While the balcony can serve as a springboard to other worlds it also protects characters from getting hurt. When Víctor parts with Frígilis at daybreak for his hunting daytrip two hours earlier than planned he stands in the garden below and "miraba al balcón cerrado del tocador de la Regenta" [looking up at the closed balcony-window of his wife's boudoir] is overcome with remorse for having deceived her (1: 141; 78). This scene is cruelly and sarcastically reversed when subsequently Víctor witnesses Mesía descend Ana's balcony and discovers that the betrayal is in fact on her part. The narrator chooses to frame the irony with this architectural detail, which plays a significant role throughout the novel. These complex and paradoxical characteristics turn the balcony, as Eça's divans and Machado's peculiar statuettes, into a real character with its own story to tell, imitate, and reinvent. The narrowness of the balcony and the fact that it represents at least in part a dead-end associates it with the other important interiors such as the tight hallways, naves, and rooms and salons that populate the novel. Entering dark snug spaces and descending into enclosed interiors is typical for Vetustan residences, and for Ana in particular. One would only have to recall the powerful dream she has where she imagines herself being squeezed back in through a tight cavity.

Vetustan floor plans, another important architectural element, also appear to write their own narratives. The preoccupation in the novel with the disbanding of society surfaces in the breakdown of families, which in turn emerges in the peculiar, unsympathetic, almost fantastic interior spaces the characters occupy. Vetustans are also in the habit of dividing their homes into different territories and further widening the gap that already exists among their inhabitants. Vetusta's families, as the town's other institutions, are dysfunctional, fragmented, and unorthodox. This disintegration is evident in the alienation created in different homes. Visitación neglects her husband and children, the Paez have practically let their daughters die, and perhaps, with the exception of Guimarán's family, almost every character represented has either lost someone in their family or grown up with the absence of an important family figure. Like a number of other Vetustans, mother and son divide the house, and the rooms of the powerful Doña Paula are appropriately on top of Fermín's, Doña Paula "habitaba el segundo piso, a sus anchas" [She lived at her ease on the second floor, 1: 327; 229]. Similarly, the Marquis decides to move to the second floor, to the serious part of the house, and furnishes and decorates his own drawing room and study above the Marchioness's notorious yellow salon. The casino's rooms and salons are far away from each other the same way Ana's and Víctor's private quarters are located at opposite ends of their home, and when Fermín and Ana meet in her living-room, Doña Petronila heads to the kitchen, which is "al otro extremo de la casa" [at the opposite end of the house, 1: 720; 560]. As Ian Watt explains, having "a separate fireplace in all the main rooms, so that everyone could be alone whenever they wished," and putting "locks on doors" are but two characteristic features that change urban dwelling and point to the general domestic transformation that begins to define the growing alienation of the modern subject.[45] Alas's homes are especially capable of housing his isolated and alienated characters who amid their loss of communal values fail, nonetheless, to identify themselves with the new private individual. Because, as we will see, even characters like the Marchioness and Don Fortunato, who although quite individualistic thinkers when it comes to their interior décor, never free themselves from society's pressures.

No other dwelling better figures this modern distance between persons than the Ozores palace, and it does this with its floor plan design. Chapter III opens with Ana and closes with Víctor, literally traveling across the couple's mansion to reveal the rift that exists between husband and wife. It begins with Ana's inner world and divided sleeping quarters and ends with the rooms that characterize Don Víctor. Still, more than the house's vast salons, what more effectively portrays the split and remoteness between the couple is once again the movement that takes place within it. Víctor, for example, is very fond of his nocturnal wanderings: "Atravesó un gran salón que se llamaba el estrado; anduvo por pasillos anchos y largos, llegó a una galería de cristales y allí vaciló un momento. Volvió pies atrás, desanduvo todos los pasillos" [He crossed a large room known as the withdrawing-room, walked along broad corridors, came to a windowed gallery, and there hesitated for a moment. He turned back, retraced his steps along all the passages, 1: 136; 76]. Later "emprendió de nuevo su majestuosa marcha por los pasillos" [resumed his majestic progess along the passages, 1: 137; 75]. Sometimes it is Ana who embarks on this long, futile, and ridiculous journey through the dark in search of her husband only to discover him reading aloud and acting out his Golden Age comedies: "qué ridículo viaje por salas y pasillos" [What a preposterous trip through rooms and passages, 1: 693; 538]. Unlike the other Vetustan hallways and rooms, the Quintanar mansion is wide, extensive, and full of empty space while other interiors more often have too little room for its many dwellers. The magnificence of the place impresses readers and Ana in a similar way, rendering the situation ridiculous since clearly the bourgeois couple is badly imitating a noble past. The mansion recalls the many royal palaces one finds across Europe and which are divided into two wings, one for the queen and another for the king. Similarly husband and wife embark on long journeys throughout the plot that seem to guide them nowhere. Víctor travels literally and daily across the city and on hunting trips, and Ana has many mental figurative endless voyages. The floor plan's inappropriateness, nonetheless, ironically suits the ease with which lover and husband can cohabit. The house is large enough for three, and when Mesía becomes Ana's lover, Víctor ironically celebrates Mesía's more intimate relationship with the couple by remodeling the Ozores mansion. He wants to rid the mansion of its melancholic darkness and blackness making it brighter and lighter, whitewashing hallways, scraping the façade, and wallpapering the dining room in a blue and gold checkered pattern.

The narrator's irony when representing Obdulia and Paco savoring their memories in Emma's bedroom repeats itself here with Víctor unknowingly commemorating his wife's betrayal by creating new, fresh, and cheerful interiors. Hence tying a character's mind and spirit to a particular space is a technique the narrator both uses and satirizes. Important ironic designs of this kind surface in the various continuities among Vetustan interiors and create textual links between different spaces. The façade of the Ozores mansion is of blackened stonework just like the casino's portico. One reaches the game room known as the chamber of crime "después de recorrer muchos pasillos oscuros y estrechos" [after traversing many dark, narrow passages, 1: 208; 130]. Similarly Fermín must make his way through comparable and arduous paths before reaching Don Fortunato's bright salon. The casino recalls the ecclesiastical governing offices where the church business is carried out and which has "una mesa en cada esquina" [a table in each corner, 1: 379; 272] the same way the casino's red room has "cuatro mesas en sendas esquinas" [a table in each of the four corners of the room, 1: 199; 125]. Neither does much to differentiate the casino gamblers from the church administrators, as they carry out their corrupt work amidst low conversation, cigar smoke, and silent complacency. These similarities create the spatial continuity that I argue makes Vetusta an architectural whole in the sense that the entire city can be conceptualized as one interior.

Certain particular common points among the different settings develop a spatial discourse on character relationships. Vetusta's bishop, Don Fortunato Camoirán, is perhaps one of the novel's most sympathetic minor figures, and various critics have speculated over just how positive of a character he is. John Rutherford's article "Fortunato y Frígilis en *La Regenta*" argues that Alas does not spare even Fortunato, criticizing and satirizing him as he does the other secondary figures. Rutherford bases his argument primarily on the sarcastic comparisons between Fortunato's bright room, as the room where the bishop receives personal visitors is known, and Doña Rufina's yellow drawing room. There are some important similarities between these two spaces, but Fortunato's rooms also have a significant amount in common with the heroine's bedroom. The first impression of the bishop's palace is decidedly negative, it is described as "un inválido de la arquitectura" [an architectural invalid] and the decoration of the main façade gives the building a grotesque look (1: 355; 252). These initial remarks, combined with the convoluted and dirty pathways Fermín has to surpass before reaching Fortunato, emphasize the contrast between what is left behind and the actual rectangular salon finally encountered. De Pas must pass a cold and empty entrance hall, climb a rotten staircase, cross a narrow and dark corridor, enter an antechamber all covered in cherry red, disappear through a side-door and still traverse "salas y pasadizos" [various other chambers and corridors] before arriving finally in the bishop's salon (1: 357; 253). When he leaves the bishop's room De Pas will again cross "pasillos, galerías y salones" [corridors, galleries and halls] before reaching his designated corner of the ecclesiastical palace (1: 373; 266). The same way Ana is protected in a hard to reach wing of her spacious mansion, Don Fortunato inhabits a secluded and impenetrable space. It could be that Ana and Fortunato selfishly hide in their removed and remote interiors, or that the narrative purposely distances their innocence from the rest of Vetusta's corrupt citizens.

Fortunato's bright room reproduces on the one hand his freedom of expression, inner happiness, and openness of spirit, while on the other hand harboring disturbing elements, which paint instead a space on the verge of the hysterical or insane. The salon's light, cheerful, and colorful atmosphere is unsettling in its contentment. The furnishings laugh hard "a carcajadas, con sus contorsiones de madera retorcida" [with a writhing of contorted wood] and "los pies de las consolas hacían piruetas" [the feet of the console tables made pirouettes, 1: 357; 253]. Meanwhile the bishop's jumping and joyful goldfinches and canaries adorning the balconies "parecían locos" [seemed quite mad, 1: 358; 254]. There are also many feminine qualities about his decoration, and the curious inclusion of four strong but violent biblical heroines seems to reinforce the allegiance between Fortunato and the stories of women. Madness threatens primarily Ana, with the repeated yet unspoken hysterical attacks she experiences, and yet it is the bishop's palace that seems to be pervaded by madness and attentive to these possible plot developments. Still, Fortunato's space is especially interesting because, instead of acting as an extension of his character and personality, the space includes elements symbolizing other figures in the novel. Perhaps this suggests that Fortunato is not as passive and selfish as Rutherford concludes in his essay, but rather that the bishop interiorly and spatially sympathizes with and understands other characters and the imbalances they experience in their inner lives.

Few details and images of the bright salon reveal that this is "la morada de un mitrado" [a bishop's room, 1: 357; 253]. Similarly, Ana's lack of adornment makes Obdulia compare the Regenta's chambers to a student's bedroom. Neither setting paints a traditional picture of its inhabitant, instead they are significant for the way they reflect and comment on important events in the narrative. Furthermore, Ana's room is "grande, de altos artesones, estucada" [large, stuccoed, with a high coffered ceiling, 1: 124; 64] and the bishop's salon is also wide "de techo muy alto cargado de artesones" [with a high ceiling heavy with plateresque coffers, 1: 357; 253]. While this similarity connects the bishop and the heroine, other common points function to comment on Fermín. Out of all the conflicting characteristics of Fortunato's salon the greatest inconsistency is the fact that although the bishop is totally controlled by Doña Paula and Fermín, they have no influence over his decoration: "pero en su salón no había de tocar" [the vicar-general was not to interfere with anything in this room, 1: 358; 254]. The room serves as the bishop's only source of independence and protest against the power they have over him, but ironically it rather identifies with the mother and son's relationship and with Fermín's vulnerability in particular: "Un Cristo crucificado de marfil, sobre una consola, delante de un espejo, que lo retrataba por la espalda, miraba sin quitarle ojo a su Santa Madre de mármol, de doble tamaño que él, colocada sobre la consola de enfrente" [An ivory carving of Christ on the cross stood on a console table before a mirror which reflected the back of the crucifix; Christ gazed across the room at his Holy Mother, twice his size, carved in marble, standing on another console table, 1: 357; 253]. These religious images and their positioning clearly reproduce the power dynamic between Doña Paula and her son. Ana too has one holy image in her bedroom, an ivory crucifix hanging over the headboard, which "inclinándose hacia el lecho parecía mirar a través del tul del pabellón blanco" [as it leaned over the bed, seemed to be looking down through the canopy of white tulle, 1: 124; 64]. This Christ figure represents Fermín who in his room also stands in front of the mirror over his white marble washbasin. Fermín's suffering is often compared to Christ's death on the cross and he frequently feels as if he is being crucified. He also makes an important gift to Ana of a yellow ivory crucifix that she wears around her neck and uses to protect herself against Mesía's charms. As Bayle and Frías explain, the crucifix placed over her heart has the double function of "tentación y de escudo" [temptation and shield, 377]. Specific objects in the bishop's and Ana's most private settings bring together Fermín's inner grief, suggesting the crucial effect these two characters have over De Pas as they stand as constant reminders to him of his inauthentic self. The Christ figure symbolizes, at least in part, Fermín's failed attempts to control Ana and Fortunato, as it also certainly ties to the novel's highly complex web of religious metaphors recurrent throughout the novel.

One significant purpose of Fortunato's salon then is to orchestrate relationships between Vetusta's different inner worlds. The brilliant white walls of the bishop's bright salon reflect "los torrentes de luz que entraban por los balcones abiertos de par en par a toda aquella alegría" [the torrents of light which streamed through the balcony windows, open wide to this joyful scene, 1: 357; 253], evoking the way the sunlight penetrates Doña Rufina's yellow salon also through "los anchos balcones abiertos de par en par" [great balcony windows, opened wide, 1: 388; 279]. The furnishings of both sitting rooms, lined in strong yellows, enjoy themselves tremendously, the narrator claims they are laughing passionately, the same way Vetusta's elite delights in the social life in Doña Rufina's salon. Fortunato's setting recalls some aspects of the Marchioness's salon, just as Rufina's sloth can be read as an extreme version of the bishop's naiveté and passivity. Despite Fortunato's excessive piety he is helpless to commit to any political action thus exonerating the Church's corruption. Similarly, irrespective of her very liberal and tolerant character Rufina's apparently politically progressive beliefs in fact promulgate the upper-bourgeoisie's reactionary ideas and deceitful habits. Her salon is first and foremost a reflection of these contradictions. Doña Rufina intends her interior to mirror her rebellious and untraditional spirit. This is why she ignores everyone's expert advice on interior décor and pays no heed to what she calls official impositions and dogma. The Marchioness insists instead on being on the vanguard of interior decorating and on accommodating her guests with extraordinary comfort, claiming "la moda moderna era lo *confortable* y la libertad" [the modern fashion was all for *comfort* and freedom, 1: 244; 161]. Both Fortunato and Rufina believe in the sovereignty, beauty, and innovation of the inner domains they have created for themselves, but ultimately these interiors hide under the surface significant paradoxes and disturbances.

The narrator and Bedoya and Bermúdez, Vetusta's antiquarians, and others are fairly skeptical of Rufina's taste and describe her décor as anachronistic, shameless, scandalous, chaotic, anarchical, and rebellious. The ironic description of the sitting-room functions less to describe Rufina's spirit and more to allude to the immoral actions that take place comfortably inside it. She does not surpervise her guests' behavior because "todos saben lo que se debe a mi casa" [they are all aware of the regard which is due to this house] and later repeats "Mientras no falten a lo que se debe a esta casa" [So long as they are not found wanting in the respect which they owe to this house, 1: 248; 164]. Paradoxically, the characters do act in accordance with what a house, decorated as such, deserves. The company's conduct, like the room's furnishings and adornments, is a bad imitation and corruption of the Regency period and other periods creating a scandalous hotchpotch. Similarly, her insistence on continually reupholstering and relining her wide collection of couches and pillows suggests an unconscious necessity of the room to accommodate new scandals and remove the traces of old ones. Her various alterations were always on the basis of yellow and she would cover them "con damasco, primero, con seda brochada después, y últimamente con raso basteado, *capitoné* que ella decía" [with damask, then with brocaded silk, and finally with quilted satin, or *capitonné*, as she called it, 1: 244; 160]. These different materials recall Ana's own multiple veils in her bedroom, but the layers in this case cover up and reveal past improprieties and scandals. Rufina's anarchical and comfortable chairs, ottomans, and couches function primarily to recline on, they conspire against action, and tempt guests to stretch themselves out on them. The inhabitants of this space obviously spend most of their time in horizontal positions. The plentiful cozy sofas and armchairs in the Marchioness's sitting-rooms do not only foreshadow the primary adultery in the novel but also the chaos and dissolution that will ensue on the level of the narrative itself.

Another important paradox is that the Marchioness's yellow salon in fact belongs a lot more to Álvaro Mesía than to Rufina. The yellow salon is primarily associated with Vetusta's Don Juan, who dwells in an inn and does not have his own home. He is the one who occupies the salon in all its functions, real and implied, and controls its lighting and noise level. If Fermín inhabits Doña Petronila's salon, whose furnishings remind him of Ana, Mesía makes Doña Rufina's famous yellow salon his own and the site of several of his sexual conquests, Ana Ozores being no exception to the rule. Don Álvaro is profoundly materialistic and his materialism becomes his only sense of faith and self. This surfaces in the tenderness and love he shows, not to his lovers, but instead to the salon's furnishings:

> Aquella Arcadia la veía don Álvaro con ojos acariciadores: en aquella casa tenía el teatro de sus mejores triunfos; cada mueble le contaba una historia en íntimo secreto; en la seriedad de las sillas panzudas y de los sillones solemnes con sus brazos de ídolos orientales, encontraba una garantía del eterno silencio que les recomendaba. Parecía decirle la madera de fino barniz blanco: "No temas; no hablará nadie una palabra." En el salón amarillo veía el galán un libro de memorias.

> [Don Álvaro looked upon this Arcady with loving eyes, for it was the theatre of his greatest triumphs. Each piece of furniture had a secret story to tell him: those plump-bellied chairs and those solemn sofas with arms like the arms of oriental idols had an air of trustworthiness, a guarantee of the eternal silence which was their strongest recommendation. The wood with its fine film of white varnish seemed to declare: Fear not: no one will say a word. In the Yellow Salon the lover could see a whole volume of reminiscences, 1: 249; 165.]

Unlike other characters who use fiction to imagine and write their personal narratives, Álvaro, who usually quotes texts that he has never read or only the first part, uses instead furnishings to relate his self identity to his primary function as seducer and his dramatic role as Don Juan. His relationship to the yellow salon prepares him for his affair with Ana and only when the actual furnishings and things seem ready does Álvaro make his final move. He depends on their assurance and materiality to gain enough confidence. As the novel, the furnishings are restless and threatening to disclose all of their secrets. On the night Álvaro confronts Ana with his desires, the yellow salon is in complete disorder, it looked tired, and resonated dishonesty: "los muebles sin orden, en posturas inusitadas, parecían amotinados, amenazando contar a los sordos lo que sabían y callaban tantos años hacía. El sofá de ancho asiento amarillo, más prudente y con más experiencia que todos, callaba, conservando su puesto" [the disordered furniture, poised in strange positions, seemed to be rebelling and threatening to tell even the deaf what it knew and had kept to itself for so many years, 1: 822; 645]. Álvaro takes his queue from the furnishings, which prepare the narrative for the adultery and motivate Mesía to make his final move. The room and its furnishings communicate with him and he seems especially talented at reading the language of interiors literally. When Mesía goes searching for Ana and enters the Marchioness's boudoir he does not immediately discover her, instead he finds nothing but "sillas y butacas" [chairs, 1: 823; 646]. Ultimately a comfortable furnishing is all he requires to achieve his goals and he can personally relate to these bulky objects far better than he can to his future lover.

The interior décor of the Vegallana palace represents Alas's critique and satire of certain nineteenth-century trends in the fashion of interiors as well. Historicizing and the mixing of past styles led to a chaotic eclecticism and to a huge increase in mass-produced furnishings and decorative objects. There was widespread agreement that these varied fashions and changing economic patterns resulted in a dramatic loss of taste. To a certain degree, Alas sees parallels between changes in interior design and society's dissolution. Developments like the Arts and Crafts and Art Nouveau movements protest exactly this repetition and excess and champion a return to authenticity and restraint. The problem of authenticity is hence an artistic question and a widespread moral concern throughout the novel, which Alas satirizes in a gallery the Marquis keeps with many antiques, and which Bedoya calls the "museo de trampas" [Museum of Forgeries, 1: 250; 165]. Bedoya's efforts to prove that the Marquis's Henry II furniture is fake—he believes Vegallana is victim to a widespread nineteenth-century practice of reproducing inauthentic furnishings, *trucage*—require highly curious proceedings. Whenever anyone doubts his findings, he takes the person aside, locks himself up with them in the gallery and proves the illegitimacy of the furnishings in the following manner:

> Se dirigía a una silla Enrique II, le daba media vuelta, buscaba cierta parte escondida de un pie del mueble; allí había hecho él varios agujeros con un cortaplumas y los había tapado con cera del color de la silla; quitaba la cera con el cortaplumas, raspaba la madera y…¡oh triunfo! esta no se deshacía en polvo; saltaba en astillas muy pequeñas, pero no en polvo.

> [He would…advance upon a Henry II chair, turn it upside-down, and search for a hidden section of the foot where he had made various little holes with a pen-knife and filled them with wax the same colour as the chair; he would remove the wax with his pen-knife, scratch the wood and—this was the moment of triumph!—it did not crumble into powder; it broke up into tiny splinters, but not powder, 1: 250; 166.]

As Valis writes in "Order and Meaning," objects in *La Regenta* "have solidity, then they do not…objects seem to melt away into an earlier, fundamental condition of formlessness."[46] The tension between order and disorder symbolizing the absence, nothingness, and entropy in the novel, is reinforced by the constant effort of the language of interiors to create more interiors. In the scene above Bedoya is not only interested in what makes up our interiors, the furnishings, but also in what constitutes those contents. As we have seen references to the insides of minds, bodies, mountains, rooms, and furnishings are a significant leitmotif throughout the novel. The dust particles inside the wooden chairs, like the furnishings inside the salon, are the broken pieces and disharmonious fragments that make up the whole, the enclosed reality.

They represent what has happened to the world of interior architecture or to our dwelling places and, thus, to our interior world, our inner beings. The novel seems to suggest that the only thing individuals and artists can hope to do is pierce ever more into things, go further inside themselves, in other words, experience more and diverse levels of interiority. It is no coincidence that Bedoya uses a pen-knife to attempt to uncover the authenticity and truth of the piece of furnishing, the same way the author writes his narrative to penetrate into the real meaning of things. Reality and human existence remain inexplicable, but the novel insists on one clear metaphor that serves as an approach to our sense of the world: begin by observing our interior world and attempt to go increasingly further inside. *La Regenta*'s discourse of interior decorating, like Machado's and Eça's, connects characters and events in the novels to material things, rooms, furnishings, and their architectural features. These links write a discourse of interiors, which creates different levels of reading and interpreting the novel for meaning. These interiors and inner things have a responsibility to narrate the novel and to set the stage for the fiction. In their disillusioned existence and weak selves, characters resemble furnishings and objects in their efforts to regain their authenticity and dramatic effect. Similarly, the narrative is very much like one of these interior spaces because it represents the staging of a creative, ambiguous, and conflicting search for a way of being genuine in the world.

Notes

1. Michel Foucault, "Of Other Spaces." *Diacritics* 16 (1986), 22.
2. Alexander Coleman, *Eça de Queirós and European Realism*, 197.
3. María del Carmen Bobes Naves, "Los espacios novelescos en *La Regenta*," *Los Cuadernos del Norte* 23 (1984), 51.
4. M. M. Bakhtin, *The Dialogic Imagination*, ed. Michael Holquist (Austin: University of Texas Press, 1981), 84.
5. Gérard Genette, *Figures of Literary Discourse*, 134.
6. Ibid.
7. Peter Brooks, *Realist Vision*, 20.
8. Michel Foucault, "Of Other Spaces," 22.
9. Noël Valis, *Reading*, 57.
10. Siviano Santiago, *Literatura nos trópicos*, 30.
11. Gilberto Pinheiro Passos, *Napoleão de Botafogo: Presença Francesa em* Quincas Borba *de Machado de Assis* (São Paulo: Annablume, 2000), 80.
12. Lúcia Miguel Pereira, *Prosa de ficção: de 1870 a 1920* (São Paulo: José Olympio, 1950), 56-57.
13. Ibid., 83.
14. In chapter LXVIII of *The Posthumous Memoirs of Brás Cubas* the former slave Prudencio [prudence] punishes his own slaves and seems to have little prudence, despite his name. There are many references to actual slaves in Machado's fiction. I am interested in how slavery infiltrates the interior of characters and societies in Machado's work, and how the author uses the dynamics of slavery as a rhetorical device. A number of character relationships and associations between characters and things or animals in Machado's fiction reproduce the master-slave dialectic.

15. G. W. F. Hegel, *Phenomenology of Spirit*, trans. A. V. Miller (Oxford: Oxford University Press, 1977), 117.

16. Ibid., 119.

17. Gaston Bachelard, *Poetics of Space*, 8.

18. Ibid., 9.

19. The work of Brazilian sociologist and anthropologist Gilberto Freyre has been intensely debated. His theories and concepts, especially his notion of "Lusotropicalism," have been on the one hand greatly influential throughout the Portuguese-speaking world, but they have also created dominant metanarratives and myths about Brazilian society, especially the prevailing conception of Brazil as a benevolent racial democracy.

20. Sandra Lauderdale Graham, *House and Street: The Domestic World of Servants and Masters in Nineteenth-Century Rio de Janeiro* (Cambridge: Cambridge University Press, 1988).

21. Virginia Woolf, *A Room*, 87.

22. Nancy Armstrong, *Desire and Domestic Fiction*, 242.

23. Cassiana Lacerda Carollo, "O espaço e os objetos em *Quincas Borba*," *Letras* 23 (June 1975), 60.

24. Virginia Woolf, *A Room*, 35.

25. Ibid.

26. Ibid., 36.

27. Jacinto do Prado Coelho, "Para a compreensão d'*Os Maias* como um todo orgânico," *Ao Contrário de Penélope* (Lisboa: Bertrand, 1976), 181.

28. Carlos Reis, *História da Literatura Portuguesa: O Realismo e o Naturalismo* (Lisboa: Alfa, 2001), 187.

29. Ibid., 189.

30. Maria Leonor Carvalhão Buescu, "'Para que Precisa Perguntar às Flores?' Aspectos da Semântica das Denominações Espaciais em Eça de Queirós," *Actas do 1º Encontro Internacional de Queirosianos* (Porto: Asa, 1990), 40.

31. Maria Leonor Carvalhão Buescu, "O regresso ao 'Ramalhete'" *Ensaios de Literatura Portuguesa* (Lisboa: Presença, 1985), 104.

32. Ibid., 117.

33. Margaret Jull Costa's version of the novel does not translate literally the Portuguese use of being buried while sitting on furniture. Thus instead of giving the translation here, I point out these incidents from the Portuguese text and provide my own translation within the context of the sentence.

34. John Gledson, "The Meanings of *Os Maias*: The Role of Gambetta," eds. Ann L. Mackenzie and Dorothy S. Severin, *Hispanic Studies in Honor of Geoffrey Ribbans* (Liverpool: Liverpool University Press, 1992), 150.

35. Peter Brooks, *Realist Vision*, 30.

36. Óscar Lopes, *Álbum de Família: Ensaios sobre Autores Portugueses do Século XIX* (Lisboa: Caminho, 1984), 113.

37. Carlos Reis, *História*, 188.

38. Describing Toca, Camilo dos Santos writes, "Nos móveis e tapeçarias dos interiores da casa representa-se o campo, de que se sente uma constante nostalgia e que é bom recordar, que é saudável rever [não perder de vista], mesmo quando, por força das circunstâncias, nos afastamos dele. Deste modo Eça e as suas personagens estão ainda a tentar conciliar os valores do campo e os valores da cidade, a civilização e a natureza, o natural e o artístico" [The countryside is represented on the furniture and tapestries of the interiors of the house. One senses a constant nostalgia of the countryside, a sense that it is good to remember it, it is healthy to see it again and not lose sight of it, even if because of circumstances we distance ourselves from it. In this way Eça and his characters are still trying to reconcile the values of the countryside and the values of the city, civilization and nature, the natural and the artistic, "Ramagens, Arvoredos," 51].

39. German Enlightenment's Gotthold Ephraim Lessing (1729-81) attempts to formulate certain boundaries between the literary and the spatial arts in his groundbreaking essay published in 1766 *Laocoön: An Essay on the Limits of Painting and Poetry* (Baltimore: Johns

Hopkins University Press, 1984). For Lessing, poetry (or literature) is a temporal art form whose true subjects are actions, while painting or sculpture is a spatial artistic mode whose focus are bodies (78). In 1945 Joseph Frank applies Lessing's method to modern literature to emphasize the growing predominance of space in modern writers such as Eliot, Proust, and Joyce, claiming these authors "ideally intend the reader to apprehend their work spatially" (*The Widening Gyre: Crisis and Mastery in Modern Literature* [New Brunswick: Rutgers University Press, 1963], 9). Spaces in *La Regenta*, *The Maias*, and *Quincas Borba* have an aesthetic value of their own, the writers incorporate the spatial arts into their narratives, and hence one could argue that Clarín, Eça, and Machado all already experiment with a type of spatial form.

40.   Elizabeth Doremus Sánchez, "*La Regenta* as Spatial-Form Narrative: A Twentieth-Century Perspective." *MLN* 103.2 (1988), 346.

41.   Ibid., 349.

42.   Walter Benjamin, *Arcades Project*, 9.

43.   Jo Labanyi, "City, Country," 61.

44.   Winfried Menninghaus, *Disgust: Theory and History of a Strong Sensation* (Albany: SUNY Press, 2003), 12.

45.   Ian Watt, *The Rise of the Novel: Studies in Defoe, Richardson and Fielding* (Berkeley: University of California Press, 1957), 188.

46.   Noël Valis, *Reading*, 26.

Epilogue: From Voltaire's Garden to Galdós's Rooms

In Benito Pérez Galdós's most celebrated realist novel *Fortunata and Jacinta* (1886-7) the low-class heroine Fortunata examines the carefully arranged private quarters of her lover and mentor, Feijoo:

> De lo que en la alcoba observó, hubo de sacar el conocimiento de que la casa estaba muy bien puesta. D. Evaristo, que tan práctico quería ser en la vida social, debía de serlo más en la doméstica, y, conforme a sus ideas, lo primero que tiene que hacer el hombre en este valle de inquietudes es buscarse un buen agujero donde morar, y labrar en él un perfecto molde de su carácter.[1]

> [From what she saw in the bedroom, she concluded that the house must be well furnished. Don Evaristo, who aimed at such practicality in social life, was even more practical in his domestic life because, according to his theory of life, the first thing a man must do in this vale of tears is hunt for a good niche to live in that will serve as a perfect mold for his character.][2]

D. Evaristo Feijoo is in some measure an alter ego of Galdós himself. Thus the importance Feijoo attributes to cultivating one's interior can be understood as an autobiographical projection, and the character's theory of life is to a certain extent the writer's as well. The fact that both Fortunata and D. Evaristo comprehend the meaning of a well-appointed room demonstrates how private spaces speak equally to their inhabitants and to observing visitors, a message that crosses class and gender differences. Galdós's novel suggests that the interior has an existential dimension that characters and authors alike rely on in order to make sense of reality. By the late nineteenth century, the novel is in a privileged position to illustrate how the arrangement of our domestic quarters narrates stories that meaningfully shape our understanding of the society we live in and of ourselves. The interior setting has become by this point a crucial way of being in the world, a form of traveling and laboring through our troubles and desires by cultivating our spaces. Cultivation is what links Voltaire to Galdós. Voltaire's eighteenth-century classic, *Candide* (1759), ends laconically with an idea that begins to echo a similar form of existence. Having finally settled down after their long adventures, Candide repeats to Pangloss that all he knows is that "we must cultivate our garden."[3] These last and noteworthy words, famous to the point of having become a truism, bring Voltaire's philosophical and satirical tale to an end. More than a century later, the orchard has changed shape and is now a quiet and refined room. The cultivation of our private shelter has become the individual's only alternative in the face of the reality he or she lives. It is as both Candide and Feijoo claim; nurturing our interior world is all that seems left for the individual to do when confronted with unsolvable social and existential dilemmas. Interacting with our abodes and dwelling within them become prerequisites to founding an identity. The act of refining and creating our interiors emerges, just as Heidegger argued, as a basic primeval human need that is prior to being.

The late-nineteenth-century novel solidifies this shift from Candide's garden to Feijoo's private rooms not only by increasingly elaborating the connection between person and interior, but also by asking what function interior spaces play in narrative. Inhabiting the world is an existential act that takes on a specific socio-economic dimension in the late nineteenth century. The emergence of interior design as a profession, the rise in the mass-production of decorative items and furnishings, and the shifts in social and individual attitudes toward dwelling contribute to the increased significance of interiors and human interiority. The authors I studied here adopt this prevalent theme of interiors to explore the existential question of making the world inhabitable while at the same time giving this philosophical dimension a specific historical signature. Dwelling emerges so intimately tied to the novelistic project in their work that fiction surfaces as a way of inhabiting the world. The narratological parameters of these novels reinforce the primary existential need to make a home in the world. These writers are all exemplary authors that epitomize the peak of nineteenth-century realism of three great literary traditions. The fact that they share these critical approaches and thematic dynamics, I believe, proves the transnational dimension of the trajectory my work analyzes.

Quincas Borba, The Maias, and *La Regenta* are all politically committed novels with a strong historical and social satire that formulate their critique with the interpretation and use of interior space. Through their representations of private architecture these late-realist narratives reflect the disbanding of society and the dissolution of human relationships while posing social and theoretical questions. In Part One: "Furnishing the Novel," I argue that each of the authors create an analogy between on the one hand the furnishing and layout of houses and rooms, and the writing of the narrative on the other. Interiors articulate stories that link the protagonists' vulnerable and complex existences to the experience of slavery, social-class strife, and a culture and political milieu of greed and dominance. "The Threshold: The Ins and Outs of *Quincas Borba*" explores how Machado uses the relocating of houses to ironically comment on the discriminating social structures in place in nineteenth-century Brazilian society. The ongoing upward-downward movement that reverberates to an inside-outside dynamic further develops these social and collective contradictions while revealing the subjective forces at work in power relations between master and slave. These ups and downs surface in the characters' shifts from hilltop to seaside, from standing to sitting positions, and to and fro gardens and sitting-rooms. Located symbolically in between these different places are the verandas, windowsills, and doorsteps. The threshold surfaces in the novel as a point of disruption and is fundamental for understanding Machado's philosophical reflections and narrative constructions. This peripheral location, which is both a beginning and an end, so crucial for Machado's characters, is central for narrative since Homer's Odysseus and Penelope. The liminal is what structures Sofia's and the novel's conceptualization of adultery and slavery. The threshold is also defined in contrast to an impossible center that characters futilely search for in the novel. This strategic configuring of space allows the author to ask questions about cultural dependence between Europe and the Americas, to reflect on the definition of madness, and to construct an intricate link between time and space in his narratives. Ultimately the interior space becomes an aesthetic method for Machado that is closely related to the genesis of his novels.

In "Movables and Immovables: The Legend of *The Maias*" the juxtaposition between mobility and stagnation becomes the most important structuring device in the Portuguese novel. Eça's elaborate representation of homes and furnishings serves to frame this opposition. Historical interconnections between real estate and furniture set the background for how the author develops the intricate relationship between the two terms. Associating immobility and progress is also a metaphor that speaks to the author's own political engagement and disillusionment with Portugal's status quo and future promise. Eça's story of decline ultimately focuses on the country's colonial past, the historical context of slavery, and the representation of the "brasileiro" to organize the breakdown of the Maia family. Three emblematic colors (red, blue, black) are related with interiors and interiorities of characters and linked to a legend in the novel that involves the interior decoration of Ramalhete and the Olivais's collection of antiques. The subtext told through these colors and the crucial figures relies on interior conceptualizations to write a narrative of love and violence that links the characters' tragic fate to colonial history. Homes and furnishings are at the heart of the novel and help the author arrange the tension between movement and fixity while framing the novel's strongest historical and social critique.

In "The Corners of the World: Inside *La Regenta*," I argue that penetrating interiors is the leading narrative technique in the novel. The opening scene with Fermín's metaphorical lifting of Vetusta's various rooftops, Bermúdez's multileveled tour of the cathedral, and the priest's subsequent excursion of the city's homes and rooms set the tone for the narrative as a whole. In his critical writing Clarín expresses his interest in what he calls smoky interiors and this fascination surfaces in the novel's repeated images of tight enclosed spaces and corners. Gaining access to these emblematic spots becomes a crucial and necessary exercise one must undertake in order to more profoundly understand human interiority. The entire narrative turns out to be an ongoing process of interiorization and converges on invading interiors as a form of discovery. Vetusta can be read as one interior with many other inner parts, which the narrator, characters, and readers invade and unlock. The connections drawn between the whole and the fragments, individuals and society, the narrator and the narrative, suggest Clarín conceptualizes the interior on the individual and collective levels. As different characters and the narrator proceed further inside, so too does the novel itself. Hence the function of narrative seems to be to represent and occupy these corners and hazy interior worlds. The competing forces between Fermín and Álvaro are reproduced in a contest of seduction and invasion of interiors. As Eça and Machado, Clarín also connects his narrative architectural framework to a critique of Spain's colonial past. Metaphors of water, drowning, and coal mining are used to describe the interior of rooms, mirror experiences of entrapment, and invoke a specific historical context. Images of the sea and shipwrecks and the figure of the "indiano" relate the interior dissolution of the characters and society to the country's violent political background.

In Part Two: "Interiors and Interiority," I show how the intimate and at times differing associations made between characters and their rooms, houses, and decorative objects relate not only their emotional and psychological complexity, but also express how the novels develop human interiority, memory, and the subconscious. Although the protagonists' inner settings are often more particularized and changing, the private settings of minor characters are likewise significant for understanding the larger purpose interiors have in the novels. We saw in "Inside the Minds and Hearts of Machado's Characters" how the Brazilian author's important minor characters, such as Teófilo and Dona Tonica, conceal important secrets in their private quarters that reflect some of the protagonists' own dilemmas, and more importantly disclose the narrator's own limitations and even his unreliability. By looking closer at a number of Machado's short stories it becomes clear that a woman's interior and feminized experience of interiority help Machado evolve his narrators and wrestle with narrative control. The author uses the inner spaces of the protagonists, Rubião and Sofia, to demonstrate how the two characters identify with their sensuality and sense of existence. The intricate representation of Rubião's sitting-room and the use of the sense of sight as a device to penetrate inner worlds problematizes not only society's influence on the protagonist's unconscious but more importantly gender differences. Sofia's architectural dynamics, which show her evolving romantic relationships, insecurities, desires and recollections, attest to Machado's use of interiors to confound gender specific subjectivities and challenge and anticipate our modern experience of interiority.

As in Machado, the function of the interiors associated with Eça's minor characters similarly connects these figures to the protagonists and to important narrative questions. In "Eça's Interior Decorators," I argue that Carlos's and Ega's faithful pursuit of interior accomplishment, renewal, and innovation supplements their intellectual quests and emotional desires. Their role as decorators reflects the novel's problematizing of the dichotomy between modernity and stagnation. Carlos's relationships with others and his own identity relies greatly on his constant activities involving interior decorating. The analogy drawn in the novel between Carlos's love affair with design culture and his passion for his unknown sister, Maria Eduarda, confirms that homes, furnishings, and interior décor are used to trace the development of their relationship throughout the novel. For Carlos and Ega interiors are the only vehicles available for their epistemological and ontological understanding or misunderstanding of reality and human relationships. Like Machado's rhetoric of interiors, Eça's serves to further contest gender roles. The novel's ubiquitous discourse of interiors dominates the characterization of the male characters, while the female figures, such as Maria Eduarda and Countess Gouvarinho, are able to read and interpret this language of interiors and develop a deeper understanding of Carlos and his motivations. Eça's novel ultimately fuses interiority and interiors by intersecting them much the same way the writing of the narrative interconnects with the spatial discourse. As Balzac frenziedly furnishes his house by writing on the walls, Ega writes frenetically his interiors in his novel. Both rely on an ontology of the interior to realize an aesthetic pursuit.

In "Memory and Movement: Ana's and Fermín's Interiors," I focus on the important private abodes of the two main characters and their significant and subtle interconnections to the other spatial settings in the novel, including those of minor characters. Ana's divided private quarters mirror her fragmented consciousness and associate her traumatic childhood memories to her present life. The importance of Ana's bed resonates in its link to the ferry-boat of her juvenile recollections and its relation to death. Rooms and furnishings frame the different near-death experiences that Ana undergoes throughout the novel. Ana's bed and sense of interior space guide her feelings and frame her search for an inner life that often borders on death. This

personal quest reflects the novel's own pursuit for interiority creating a parallel between her inner experience and the narrative discourse. While also
portraying important relations to other elements in the novel, Fermín's relationship to the interior reveals his particularly physical nature, one desirous
of power and in search of sensual pleasure. De Pas's interior body language
in relation to furnishings, architectural structures, and enclosed spaces show
his sexual desires and feelings of love and frustration toward the heroine.
Interiors are central in structuring memory and movement in the novel and
function not only to problematize the interiority of the two main characters
but also to reinforce the significant narrative function interiors play.

In Part Three: "The Discourse of Interiors," I concentrate on the authors'
design details, decorative objects, and furnishings and analyze how this discourse of interiors transforms itself into a symbolic language of things that
communicates meaning and reflects on the passage of time. The interplay
between homes, furnishings, and ornate things in the novels in fact reproduces the correlation between time and space in narrative, which Bakhtin and
Genette have examined in their critical writings. In "Machado's Minimalism
and the Meaning of Things" I take a closer look at the author's complex and
unreliable narrator and argue that Machado's restrained descriptions of interiors is often made to distract readers from the semiotic possibilities of the
settings. Rubião's choices in interior décor reveal that he is not simply dominated by society's latest tastes or Palha's domineering character but understands that the process of recreating and imitating serves as a tool for interpreting reality and his own identity. Particular possessions of Rubião's, his
dog, silver platter, silk slippers, and an old chair in the house in Barbacena,
become significant markers of how Machado reflects throughout the novel
on the important social and political contexts of nineteenth-century Brazil,
such as slavery, the ideology of patronage, and the consequences of social
dependency. A home thus turns out to be a metaphor for life while being tied
to the construction of a female and sensual consciousness that Machado uses
as an allegory for his fictional writing. Windows and mirrors surface as
crucial inner features central to the composition of an interior and function as
devices for the author to reflect on the discordant and tense relationships
between men and women and individuals and societies.

In "The Narrative Life of Eça's Furnishings," I begin with the renovation
of the interior protagonist of the novel, Ramalhete. The transformations and
consistencies of the family mansion, with the tensions and substitutions that
characterize it and its name, make the house a locus for the encounter of life
and death, and fiction and reality. Specific pieces of furniture are central in
The Maias, especially the many different types of couches, which serve to
bury characters much the same way dwellings do. More importantly, characters rely on couches and furnishings for their sense of existence since these
can act as a defense mechanism against society. The interplay between

movement and stability structured into the novel leaves characters with nothing but their rooms and furnishings, which circumscribe and overwhelm their realities. Although we tend to associate the term "couch potato" with a specific late-twentieth-century sense of reality, in the late nineteenth century the comfort of an armchair was also and often all characters had to fall back on. Thus, the narrative life of furnishings begins to overpower the characters and frame the climactic events bringing tragedy and interior discourse together in the culminating events. The divan is not only particularly symbolic, representative of a modern sensibility as the window, but also draws an important connection to other divans in the text, which indicates that for Eça interior decoration is both an empowering and creative narrative device capable of disguising significant political and historical subtexts.

The last section, "The Dramatic Effect of Clarín's Interior Architecture," centers on the importance of spatial structures that turn interiors into dramatic representations staging the thematic complexities of the novel. The lack of light in many of Vetusta's smoky and narrow interiors and the juxtaposition of light and darkness establish the ambiguous boundaries between interiors and exteriors. The balcony is one of the novel's most significant architectural features in terms of its imagery, the emblematic body language it inspires in characters, and primarily the role it plays throughout the story. As other design traits that we analyzed in Machado's and in Eça's novels, the balcony operates for Clarín as a formal tool that tells its own version of the plot. The uncertainty of the balcony is like the impossibility of separating existence from demise, and aesthetics from reality. It frames the affair between Mesía and Ana by prefiguring the adultery at the Vegallana luncheon, structuring its culminating moment at the Vivero, and revealing the marital betrayal at the Ozores palace. Emma's bedroom and its balcony not only reinforce the dramatic effect of Clarín's interiors since it serves as a dressing room, but also articulates the use of the interior to reflect on death, memory, and fiction. The floor plans of Vetusta's residences are central for showing the alienation of the characters and Vetustan society. The Ozores palace and the figurative interior voyages the couple take inside its salons and rooms reveal the rift between husband and wife while also drawing consequential spatial connections in the novel. Many interior settings have important points in common, Fortunato's private rooms and Rufina's yellow salon suggest that their interiors are not independent spaces but bring together the problems characters face. These spatial associations reinforce the idea that interiors are collective in nature and that the stories they chronicle are part of the narrative discourse.

Description of interior decoration and architectural details in these literary traditions, far from interrupting the flow of the plot, are significant in developing the story line. In fact rooms, furnishings, and ornamental objects drive the novels forward. They do not merely constitute some index of character or atmosphere but are a central part of the novel's semiotic structure and have a narrative life of their own. In these cultivated interiors, authors can stage the contradictions and questions that most preoccupied them. The interior is a center with shifting boundaries where the authors, while attentive to modernity and progress, can also hold on to certain of their traditions. It becomes clear that the interior cannot exist without an exchange with an exterior; that these framed inner structures are also the uncovering of life's and the inner self's irresolvable complexities. Thus the interior turns into a threshold, a peripheral center, an impossible interior, but one the individual and the artist must continue to invade, unlock, embellish, and reinvent. The authors place themselves and their characters on this dynamic threshold where they can find a medium between the civilized and the natural worlds, and combine their emotional with their rational forms of thinking.

Although Machado, Eça, and Clarín are very different writers in tone and style, they all turn to the interior in order to articulate and interpret their country's late-nineteenth-century society. The interior setting lies at the center of both the content and form of the novels, mediating and assisting authors, readers, characters, and narrators in making sense of the different semantics narrated within these spaces. The rhetoric of interior space that these authors develop is drawing on the discourse of interior decorating, the new art form gaining momentum at the turn of the century. Like interior architects, the authors seek structure, harmony, a sense of openness, and an ongoing continuation with the past, a more sensual, intimate, and personal experience. The narrative discourse of interior constructions anticipates an understanding or misunderstanding of both national and individual identities. Furnishings and rooms become languages that translate desires, fears, and doubts into a narrative of decline and transformation. The novels are determined to remain open, discontinuous, nonfinite, and to create an inventory of the forces imposed by modernization and historical circumstances.

Spatial configurations of the interior characterize late realism's narrative worlds. Whether they express and characterize individual problems or whether they link these to the construction of nations and their societies: it is the space that mediates and figures these novels' contributions to an understanding of their time. The pessimistic portrait of decay is not only alleviated by moments of comic relief, but also by the fact that these authors search for alternative epistemologies. Whereas traditionally interior spaces are perceived as a dimension of female submission, my analysis of these works has shown how in the tradition of the novel, the subjective search for an inner life associated with modernist writing originates in the private interior as a space of retreat for both female and male characters. In this interior world, attention and weight is given to the seemingly insignificant details that communicate an existential need and historical density. This intensified contemplation of interiors and interiority influences the development of narrative by overpowering characters and empowering narratives. The unfolding and building of a meaningful private universe manifests a desire to understand an irreconcilable world. Inhabiting interiors thus offers us a narrative language to elaborate and furnish this world.

Notes

1. Benito Pérez Galdós, *Fortunata y Jacinta*, ed. Francisco Caudet (Madrid: Cátedra, 1999), 2: 119.
2. Agnes Moncy Gullón, *Fortunata and Jacinta* (London: Penguin Books, 1988), 506.
3. Voltaire, *Candide or Optimism*, trans. Theo Cuffe (London: Penguin, 2005), 94.

Works Cited

Alas, Leopoldo (Clarín). *Obras completas*. 11 vols to date. Oviedo: Nobel, 2002-.

Amann, Elizabeth. "A Marriage *Sans-Culotte*? Revolution, Repetition and the Adultery Novel." *Bulletin of Hispanic Studies* 78 (2001): 319-338.

——. *Importing* Madame Bovary: *The Politics of Adultery*. New York: Palgrave, 2006.

Aranguren, José Luis L. "De *La Regenta* a *Ana Ozores*." In *Estudios Literarios*. Madrid: Gredos, 1976.

Aristotle. *The Politics of Aristotle*. Translated by Ernest Barker. London: Oxford University Press, 1958.

Armstrong, Nancy. *Desire and Domestic Fiction: A Political History of the Novel*. New York: Oxford University Press, 1987.

Assis, Joaquim Maria Machado de. *Obras Completas*. 3 vols. Rio de Janeiro: Aguilar, 1962.

Auerbach, Erich. *Mimesis: The Representation of Reality in Western Literature*. Translated by Willard R. Trask. Princeton: Princeton University Press, 1953.

Azorín. "Oviedo. En la biblioteca de "Clarín." In *Leopoldo Alas "Clarín."* Edited by José María Martínez Cachero. Madrid: Taurus, 1978.

Bachelard, Gaston. *The Poetics of Space*. Translated by Maria Jolas. Boston: Beacon Press, 1994.

Bakhtin, M. M. *The Dialogic Imagination*. Edited by Michael Holquist. Austin: University of Texas Press, 1981.

Balzac, Honoré de. *The Human Comedy: Introductions and Appendix*. Edited by Jim Manis. Hazleton, PA: Pennsylvania State University *Electronics Classics Series*, 2002.

Banham, Joanna, ed. *Encyclopedia of Interior Design*. 2 vols. London: Fitzroy Dearborn, 1997.

Barthes, Roland. "The Reality Effect." In *French Literary Theory Today*. Edited by Tzvetan Todorov. Cambridge: Cambridge University Press, 1982.

Bayle, Françoise and Marina Romero Frías. "Religión y adulterio a través de los objetos en *Madame Bovary* y *La Regenta*." In *Realismo y naturalismo en España en la segunda mitad del siglo XIX*. Edited by Yvan Lissorgues. Madrid: Anthropos, 1988, 368-383.

Belgum, Kirsten. *Interior Meaning: Design of the Bourgeois Home in the Realist Novel*. New York: Peter Lang, 1991.

Benjamin, Walter. *The Arcades Project*. Translated by Howard Eiland and Kevin McLaughlin. Cambridge, MA: Belknap Press of Harvard University Press, 1999.

Bernstein, Susan. *Housing Problems: Writing and Architecture in Goethe, Walpole, Freud, and Heidegger*. Stanford: Stanford University Press, 2008.

Berrini, Beatriz. "A Casa: Uma em Machado, Outra em Eça." In *Recortes Machadianos*. Edited by Mariano, Ana Salles and Maria Rosa Duarte de Oliveira. São Paulo: EDUC, 2003, 277-295.

———. "A Polémica Recepção de Eça de Queiroz no Brasil: Considerações em Torno da Acolhida Feita por Machado de Assis e Outros." In *Recortes Machadianos*. Edited by Ana Salles Mariano and Maria Rosa Duarte de Oliveira. São Paulo: EDUC, 2003, 299-316.

———. *Eça de Queiroz: Palavra e Imagem*. Lisboa: Inapa, 1989.

———. *Portugal de Eça de Queiroz*. Lisboa: Imprensa Nacional-Casa da Moeda, 1984.

Beser, Sergio. "Espacio y objetos en *La Regenta*." In La Regenta *de Leopoldo Alas*. Edited by Frank Durand. Madrid: Taurus, 1988, 47-68.

Bobes Naves, María del Carmen. "Los espacios novelescos en *La Regenta*." *Los Cuadernos del Norte* 23 (1984): 51-57.

———. *Teoría general de la novela*: Semiología de La Regenta. Madrid: Gredos, 1985.

Booth, Wayne. *The Rhetoric of Fiction*. Chicago: University of Chicago Press, 1983.

Brooks, Peter. *Body Work: Objects of Desire in Modern Narrative*. Cambridge, MA: Harvard University Press, 1993.

———. *Realist Vision*. New Haven: Yale University Press, 2005.

Buescu, Maria Leonor Carvalhão. "'Para que Precisa Perguntar às Flores?' Aspectos da Semântica das Denominações Espaciais em Eça de Queirós." In *Actas do 1º Encontro Internacional de Queirosianos*. Porto: Asa, 1990, 39-46.

———. "O Regresso ao 'Ramalhete.'" *Ensaios de Literatura Portuguesa*. Lisboa: Presença, 1985.

Cabezas, Juan Antonio. *"Clarín" El provinciano universal*. Madrid: Espasa-Calpe, 1962.

Cachero, José María Martínez, ed. *La Regenta*. Leopoldo Alas (Clarín). *Obras completas*. Oviedo: Nobel, 2003.

Caldwell, Helen. *Machado de Assis: The Brazilian Master and his Novels*. Berkeley: University of California Press, 1970.

Cândido, António. *Formação da Literatura Brasileira*. 5ª ed. 2 vols. São Paulo: Universidade de São Paulo; Belo Horizonte: Itatiaia, 1975.

———. *Vários Escritos*. 3ª ed. São Paulo: Duas Cidades, 1995.

Carollo, Cassiana Lacerda. "O Espaço e os Objetos em *Quincas Borba*." *Letras* 23 (June 1975): 53-69.

Castilho, Guilherme de. *Eça de Queirós: Correspondência*. 2 vols. Lisboa: Imprensa Nacional-Casa da Moeda, 1983.

Cervantes Saavedra, Miguel de. *El ingenioso hidalgo Don Quijote de la Mancha*. 2 vols. Madrid: Castalia, 1978.

Chandler, Marilyn. *Dwelling in the Text: Houses in American Fiction*. Berkeley: University of California Press, 1991.

Coelho, Jacinto do Prado. "Para a Compreensão d'*Os Maias* como um Todo Orgânico." In *Ao Contrário de Penélope*. Lisboa: Bertrand, 1976, 167-193.

Coleman, Alexander. *Eça de Queirós and European Realism*. New York: New York University Press, 1980.

———. "Uma Reflexão a Respeito de Eça de Queirós e Machado de Assis." In *Eça e Os Maias: Actas do 1º Encontro Internacional de Queirosianos*. Porto: Asa, 1990, 67-72.

Cordeiro, Francisca de Basto. *Machado de Assis na Intimidade*. Rio de Janeiro: Pongetti, 1965.

Costa, Emília Viotti da. *The Brazilian Empire: Myths and Histories*. Chapel Hill: University of North Carolina Press, 1985.

Costa, Margaret Jull, trans. *The Maias*. By José Maria de Eça de Queirós. New York: New Directions, 2007.

De Fortuny a Picasso: Trente ans de peinture espagnole, 1874-1906. Paris: Réunion des musées nationaux, 1994.

Deleuze, Gilles and Félix Guattari. *A Thousand Plateaus: Capitalism and Schizophrenia*. Translated by Brian Massumi. Minneapolis: University of Minnesota Press, 1987.

Dias, Marina Tavares. *A Lisboa de Eça de Queiroz*. Lisboa: Quimera, 2001.

Duarte, Nestor. *A Ordem Privada e a Organização Nacional (Contribuição à Sociologia Política Brasileira)*. São Paulo: Companhia Editora Nacional, 1939.

Durand, Frank. "Structural Unity in Leopoldo Alas' *La Regenta*." *Hispanic Review* 31.4 (1963): 324-335.

Eliot, George. *The Mill on the Floss*. London: Penguin, 1994.

Favaretto, Celso. Afterword. "The Misadventures of Unity." In *Quincas Borba*. By Joaquim Maria Machado de Assis. Translated by Gregory Rabassa. New York: Oxford University Press, 1998, 273-289.

Fernández, James D. "America Is in Spain: A Reading of Clarín's 'Boroña.'" In *Bridging the Atlantic: Toward a Reassessment of Iberian and Latin American Cultural Ties*. Albany: SUNY Press, 1996, 31-43.

Fitz, Earl E. "The *Memórias Póstumas de Brás Cubas* as (Proto)type of the Modernist Novel: A Problem in Literary History and Interpretation." *Latin American Literary Review* 18:36 (1990): 7-25.

Flaubert, Gustave. *A Sentimental Education*. Translated by Douglas Parmée. Oxford: Oxford University Press, 1989.

Foucault, Michel. "Of Other Spaces." *Diacritics* 16 (1986): 22-27.

Frank, Joseph. *The Widening Gyre: Crisis and Mastery in Modern Literature*. New Brunswick: Rutgers University Press, 1963.

Freeland, Alan. "Evolution and Dissolution: Imagery and Social Darwinism in Eça de Queirós and Leopoldo Alas." *Journal of the Institute of Romance Studies* 2 (1993): 323-36.

Freud, Sigmund. *Introductory Lectures on Psycho-Analysis*. Translated by James Strachey. London: Hogarth Press, 1953.

Freyre, Gilberto. *Casa-Grande & Senzala: Formação da Família Brasileira sob o Regime da Economia Patriarcal*. Rio de Janeiro: Livraria José Olympio, 1980.

——. *Sobrados e Mucambos: Decadência do Patriarcado Rural e Desenvolvimento do Urbano*. Rio de Janeiro: Livraria José Olympio, 1977.

Fuss, Diana. *The Sense of an Interior: Four Writers and the Rooms That Shaped Them*. New York: Routledge, 2004.

Galdós, Benito Pérez. *Fortunata y Jacinta*. Edited by Francisco Caudet. Madrid: Cátedra, 1999.

Genette, Gérard. *Figures of Literary Discourse*. Translated by Alan Sheridan. New York: Columbia University Press, 1982.

Gledson, John. *The Deceptive Realism of Machado de Assis*. Liverpool: Francis Cairns, 1984.

——. "The Meanings of *Os Maias*: The Role of Gambetta." In *Hispanic Studies in Honor of Geoffrey Ribbans*. Edited by Ann L. Mackenzie and Dorothy S. Severin. Liverpool: Liverpool University Press, 1992, 147-154.

Gómez-Santos, Marino. *Leopoldo Alas "Clarín," ensayo bio-bibliográfico*. Oviedo: C. S. I. C., 1952.

Gonzalo, Gerardo, ed. *Leopoldo Alas Clarín*. Madrid: Eneida, 2005.

Graham, Richard. *Patronage and Politics in Nineteenth-Century Brazil*. Stanford: Stanford University Press, 1990.

Graham, Sandra Lauderdale. *House and Street: The Domestic World of Servants and Masters in Nineteenth-Century Rio de Janeiro*. Cambridge: Cambridge University Press, 1988.

Guevara, Luís Vélez de. *El diablo cojuelo*. Edited by Enrique Rodríguez Cepeda. Madrid: Cátedra, 1984.

Gullón, Agnes Moncy, trans. *Fortunata and Jacinta*. By Benito Pérez Galdós. London: Penguin Books, 1988.

Haberly, David T. Introduction. In *Quincas Borba*. By Joaquim Maria Machado de Assis. Translated by Gregory Rabassa. New York: Oxford University Press, 1998, xi-xxvi.

——. *Three Sad Races: Racial Identity and National Consciousness in Brazilian Literature*. Cambridge: Cambridge University Press, 1983.

Habermas, Jürgen. *The Structural Transformation of the Public Sphere: An Inquiry into a Category of Bourgeois Society*. Translated by Thomas Burger. Cambridge, MA: MIT Press, 1989.

Hegel, G. W. F. *Phenomenology of Spirit*. Translated by A. V. Miller. Oxford: Oxford University Press, 1977.

Heidegger, Martin. *Poetry, Language, Thought*. Translated by Albert Hofstadter. New York: Harper Collins, 1971.

James, Henry. *Novels 1881-1886: Washington Square, The Portrait of a Lady, The Bostonians*. New York: Literary Classics of the US, 1997.

——. *The Spoils of Poynton*. Edited by David Lodge. Middlesex, UK: Penguin Books, 1987.

Jones, Peter. Introduction. In *The Odyssey*. By Homer. London: Penguin, 1991, xi-xlv.
Labanyi, Jo. "City, Country and Adultery in *La Regenta*." *Bulletin of Hispanic Studies* 63 (1986): 53-66.
——. *Gender and Modernization in the Spanish Realist Novel*. Oxford: Oxford University Press, 2000.
Lansing, Amy Kurtz. *Historical Fictions: Edward Lamson Henry's Paintings of Past and Present*. New Haven: Yale University Art Gallery, 2005.
Lessing, Gotthold Ephraim. *Laocoön: An Essay on the Limits of Painting and Poetry*. Baltimore: Johns Hopkins University Press, 1984.
Lima, Isabel Pires de. *As Máscaras do Desengano: Para uma Abordagem Sociológica de Os Maias de Eça de Queirós*. Lisboa: Caminho, 1987.
——. "Eça e *Os Maias* Pensar-se Pensando Portugal." *Colóquio/Letras* 103 (1988): 19-27.
Lisboa, Maria Manuel. *Teu Amor Fez de mim um Lago Triste: Ensaios sobre Os Maias*. Porto: Campo das Letras, 2000.
Llorach, Emilio Alarcos. "Notas a *La Regenta*." *Archivum* 2 (1952): 141-160.
Lopes, Óscar. *Álbum de Família: Ensaios sobre Autores Portugueses do Século XIX*. Lisboa: Caminho, 1984.
Löve, Katharina Hansen. *The Evolution of Space in Russian Literature: A Spatial Reading of 19th and 20th Century Narrative Literature*. Amsterdam: Rodopi, 1994.
Magalhães, José Calvet de. *Eça de Queirós: A Vida Privada*. Lisboa: Bizâncio, 2000.
Magalhães, Luís de. *O Brasileiro Soares*. Lisboa: Círculo de Leitores, 1991.
Malnar, Joy Monice and Frank Vodvarka. *The Interior Dimension: A Theoretical Approach to Enclosed Space*. New York: Van Nostrand Reinhold, 1992.
Mariano, Ana Salles and Maria Rosa Duarte de Oliveira, eds. *Recortes Machadianos*. São Paulo: EDUC, 2003.
Márquez, Gabriel García. *Cien años de soledad*. Madrid: Cátedra. 1967.
Martins, António Coimbra. "O Incesto d'*Os Maias*." *Ensaios Queirosianos*. Lisboa: Europa-América, 1967. 267-287.
Martins, Odete R. G. de Barros. "Para um Estudo da Descrição em *Os Maias*: Leitura de Algumas Descrições de Interiores." *Broteria: Cultura e Informação* 127.6 (1988): 511-523.
Massa, Jean-Michel. *A Juventude de Machado de Assis (1839-1870)*. Translated by Marco Aurélio de Moura Matos. Rio de Janeiro: Civilização Brasileira, 1971.
Massey, Doreen. *Space, Place, and Gender*. Minneapolis: University of Minnesota Press, 1994.
Matos, A. Campos. *Eça de Queiroz-Emília de Castro: Correspondência Epistolar*. Porto: Lello & Irmão, 1995.
——. *Imagens do Portugal Queirosiano*. Lisboa: Imprensa Nacional-Casa da Moeda, 1987.
——. *Viagem no Portugal de Eça de Queiroz: Roteiro*. Amarante: Fundação Eça de Queiroz, 2000.
Medina, João. "O Pessimismo Nacional de Eça de Queirós: Estudo Sobre *Os Maias*." *Seara Nova* 1514 (1971): 21-30.
——. *Reler Eça de Queiroz: Das Farpas aos Maias*. Lisboa: Livros Horizonte, 2000.
Memmi, Albert. *The Colonizer and the Colonized*. Boston: Beacon Press, 1965.
Menninghaus, Winfried. *Disgust: Theory and History of a Strong Sensation*. Albany: SUNY Press, 2003.
Moisés, Massaud. *Machado de Assis: Ficção e Utopia*. São Paulo: Cultrix, 2001.
Montello, Josué. *O Presidente Machado de Assis*. Rio de Janeiro: José Olympio, 1986.
Morant, Guadalupe Gómez-Ferrer. "El indiano en la novela realista." *Nueva Revista de Filología Hispánica* 466 (1989): 25-49.
Moura, José de Almeida. "*Os Maias*, Ensaio Alegórico Sobre a Decadência da Nação." *Cadernos de Literatura* 14 (1983): 46-56.
Nanfito, Jacqueline C. "Topographies of the Self: The Mapping of Narrative Space in *La Regenta*." *Quaderni Ibero-Americani* 87-88 (2000): 5-19.
Nimetz, Michael. "Eros and Ecclesia in Clarín's Vetusta." *MLN* 86 (1971): 242-53.
Nunes, Maria Luisa. *The Craft of an Absolute Winner: Characterization and Narratology in the Novels of Machado de Assis*. Westport, CT: Greenwood, 1983.

Oleza, Juan. *La novela del XIX: Del parto a la crisis de una ideología*. Valencia: Editorial Bello, 1976.

Ortega, Soledad, presentación. *Cartas a Galdós*. Madrid: Revista de Occidente, 1964.

Paleólogo, Constantino. *Eça de Queirós e Machado de Assis*. Rio de Janeiro: Tempo Brasileiro, 1979.

Passos, Gilberto Pinheiro. *Napoleão de Botafogo: Presença Francesa em* Quincas Borba *de Machado de Assis*. São Paulo: Annablume, 2000.

Pereira, Lúcia Miguel. *Machado de Assis: Estudo Crítico e Biográfico*. 5ª ed. Rio de Janeiro: José Olympio, 1955.

——. *Prosa de Ficção: de 1870 a 1920*. São Paulo: José Olympio, 1950.

Pérez de Mendiola, Marina, ed. *Bridging the Atlantic: Toward a Reassessment of Iberian and Latin American Cultural Ties*. Albany: SUNY Press, 1996.

Piehler, Liana F. *Spatial Dynamics and Female Development in Victorian Art and Novels: Creating a Woman's Space*. New York: Peter Lang, 2003.

Pimentel, Luz Aurora. *El espacio en la ficción*. México D. F.: Siglo veintiuno, 2001.

Poe, Edgar Allan. "The Philosophy of Furniture." In *The Unabridged Edgar Allan Poe*. Philadelphia: Running Press, 1983, 641-646.

Posada, Adolfo. *Leopoldo Alas: Clarín*. Oviedo: La Cruz, 1946.

Pratt, Dale J. "Mapping, Realist Narrative and Cartographic Imagination in *La Regenta*." *Revista de Estudios Hispánicos* 35 (2001): 91-110.

Queirós, José Maria de Eça de. *A Cidade e as Serras*. Lisboa: Livros do Brasil, 2002.

——. *A Ilustre Casa de Ramires*. Lisboa: Livros do Brasil, 2003.

——. *O Crime do Padre Amaro*. Lisboa: Livros do Brasil, 2004.

——. *O Primo Bazilio*. Lisboa: Livros do Brasil, 2001.

——. *Os Maias*. Lisboa: Livros do Brasil, 2001.

——. *Prosas Esquecidas II*. Lisboa: Presença, 1965.

Rabassa, Gregory, trans. *The Posthumous Memoirs of Brás Cubas*. By Joaquim Maria Machado de Assis. New York: Oxford University Press, 1997.

——, trans. *Quincas Borba*. By Joaquim Maria Machado de Assis. New York: Oxford University Press, 1998.

Ranum, Orest. "The Refuges of Intimacy." In *A History of Private Life, Volume III, Passions of the Renaissance*. Cambridge, MA: Belknap Press of Harvard University Press, 1989, 207-263.

Rego, Enylton de Sá. "The Epic, the Comic and the Tragic: Tradition and Innovation in Three Late Novels of Machado de Assis." *Latin American Literary Review* 14:27 (1986): 19-34.

Reis, Beatriz Cinatti Batalha. *Eça de Queiroz e Jaime Batalha Reis: Cartas e Recordações do Seu Convívio*. Porto: Lello & Irmão, 1966.

Reis, Carlos. *Estudos Queirosianos: Ensaios Sobre Eça de Queirós e a Sua Obra*. Lisboa: Presença, 1999.

——. Direcção. *História da Literatura Portuguesa: O Realismo e o Naturalismo*. Vol. 5. Lisboa: Alfa, 2001.

——. *Introdução à Leitura d'*Os Maias. Coimbra: Almedina, 1986.

——. Coordenador. *Leituras d'*Os Maias. Coimbra: Minerva, 1990.

Reis, Jaime Batalha. Introduction. "Na Primeira Fase da Vida Literária de Eça de Queiroz." *Prosas Bárbaras*. Lisboa: Livros do Brasil, 2001.

Romines, Ann. *The Home Plot: Women, Writing, and Domestic Ritual*. Massachusetts: The University of Massachusetts Press, 1992.

Rosa, Alberto Machado da. *Eça, Discípulo de Machado? Formação de Eça de Queirós*. Lisboa: Presença, 1965.

Rua Cosme Velho, 18: Relato de Restauro do Mobiliário de Machado de Assis. Rio de Janeiro: Academia Brasileira de Letras, 1998.

Rutherford, John. Introduction. *La Regenta*. By Leopoldo Alas (Clarín). Athens: University of Georgia Press, 1984.

——. "Fortunato y Frígilis en *La Regenta*." *Clarín y su obra: En el centenario de* La Regenta. Barcelona: Universidad de Barcelona, 1984.

——. *Leopoldo Alas*: La Regenta. London: Grant & Cutler, 1974.

Salvador, Nélida and Elisa Rey, eds. *Los espacios de la literatura*. Buenos Aires: Academia del Sur, 2001.
Sánchez, Elizabeth Doremus. *"La Regenta* as Spatial-Form Narrative: A Twentieth-Century Perspective." *MLN* 103.2 (1988): 335-349.
Sanchez, Justo García. *Leopoldo Alas Universitario*. Oviedo: Universidad de Oviedo, 1990.
Santiago, Silviano. *Uma Literatura nos Trópicos: Ensaios sobre Dependência Cultural*. Rio de Janeiro: Rocco, 2000.
Santos, João Camilo dos. "Ramagens, Arvoredos, Folhagens…Breves Reflexões sobre o Campo Semântico do 'Ramalhete' em *Os Maias*, de Eça de Queirós." *Queirosiana: Estudos sobre Eça de Queirós e a sua Geração* (2º semestre 1999): 39-53.
Schwarz, Roberto. *Ao Vencedor as Batatas*. São Paulo: Duas Cidades, 1977.
——. "Duas Notas sobre Machado de Assis." *Que Horas São? Ensaios*. São Paulo: Companhia das Letras, 1987.
——. *Um Mestre na Periferia do Capitalismo: Machado de Assis*. São Paulo: Duas Cidades, 1990.
Sena, Jorge de. *Estudos de Cultura e Literatura Brasileira*. Lisboa: Edições 70, 1988.
Sennett, Richard. *The Fall of Public Man*. New York: Norton, 1974.
Sinclair, Alison. "Liminal Anxieties: Nausea and Mud in *La Regenta*." *Bulletin of Hispanic Studies* 74 (1997): 155-176.
Sobejano, Gonzalo. Introduction. *La Regenta*. By Leopoldo Alas (Clarín). Madrid: Castalia, 1981.
Stifter, Adalbert. *Indian Summer*. Translated by Wendell Frye. Bern: Peter Lang, 2006.
Stilgoe, John. R. Foreword. In *The Poetics of Space*. By Gaston Bachelard. Translated by Maria Jolas. Boston: Beacon Press, 1969, vii-x.
Tanner, Tony. *Adultery in the Novel: Contract and Transgression*. Baltimore: Johns Hopkins University Press, 1979.
Tomasi di Lampedusa, Giuseppe. *The Leopard*. Translated by Archibald Colquhoun. New York: Pantheon, 1960.
Trigo, Luciano. *Viajante Imóvel: Machado de Assis e o Rio de Janeiro de Seu Tempo*. Rio de Janeiro: Record, 2001.
Turner, Harriet. "Vetusta: espacio-fuerza en *La Regenta*." *Clarín y su obra: en el centenario de La Regenta*. Edited by Antonio Vilanova. Barcelona: Universidad de Barcelona, 1985.
Un siglo con Clarín: Exposición bibliográfica en el centenario de su muerte. Oviedo: Universidad de Oviedo, 2001.
Utt, Roger L. *Textos y con-textos de Clarín*. Madrid: Istmo, 1988.
Valis, Noël Maureen. "Aspects of an Improper Birth: Clarín's *La Regenta*." In *New Hispanisms: Literature, Culture, Theory*. Edited by Mark I. Millington and Paul Julian Smith. Ottawa, Canada: Dovehouse, 1994, 94-126.
——. *The Decadent Vision in Leopoldo Alas: A Study of* La Regenta *and* Su único hijo. Baton Rouge: Louisiana State University Press, 1981.
——. *Reading the Nineteenth-Century Spanish Novel: Selected Essays*. Newark, DE: Juan de la Cuesta, 2005.
Vargas, Carlos Santos. "Da Proxémia N'*Os Maias*: Um Caso Exemplar." In *150 Anos com Eça de Queirós*. Edited by Elza Miné and Benilde Justo Lacorte Caniato. São Paulo: Centro de Estudos Portugueses, Universidade de São Paulo, 1997.
Vázquez, Adolfo Sotelo. "Escritura, descripción y relato en *La Regenta*: El salón de doña Petronila." *Leopoldo Alas, Clarín*: La Regenta. *Co-textes* 18 (1989): 23-42.
Viana Filho, Luís. *A Vida de Machado de Assis*. Rio de Janeiro: José Olympio, 1989.
Villaverde, Cirilo. *Cecilia Valdés o La Loma del Ángel*. Madrid: Cátedra, 1992.
Voltaire. *Candide or Optimism*. Translated by Theo Cuffe. London: Penguin, 2005.
Watt, Ian. *The Rise of the Novel: Studies in Defoe, Richardson and Fielding*. Berkeley: University of California Press, 1957.
Weiner, Hadassah Ruth. "Integralismo de Clarín: Los 'interiores ahumados.'" *Los Cuadernos del Norte* 2:7 (May-June 1981): 84-93.
Wellek, René. *Concepts of Criticism*. New Haven: Yale University Press, 1963.

Wharton, Edith and Ogden Codman, Jr. *The Decoration of Houses*. New York: W. W. Norton, 1997.

Woolf, Virginia. *A Room of One's Own*. San Diego: Harvest, 1981.

Yeazell, Ruth Bernard. *Art of the Everyday: Dutch Painting and the Realist Novel*. Princeton: Princeton University Press, 2008.

Zubiaurre, María Teresa. *El espacio en la novela realista: Paisajes, miniaturas, perspectivas*. México, D. F.: Fondo de cultura económica, 2000.

Index

235

About the Author

Estela Vieira is assistant professor in the Department of Spanish and Portuguese at Indiana University Bloomington. Her publications include articles and book chapters on Portuguese, Brazilian, and Hispanic literature, culture, and film.

www.ingramcontent.com/pod-product-compliance
Lightning Source LLC
Chambersburg PA
CBHW071510110726
47908CB00003B/794